PREACH
WHAT YOU
BELIEVE

PREACH WHAT YOU BELIEVE

Timeless Homilies for Deacons

LITURGICAL CYCLE B

Deacon Michael E. Bulson

PAULIST PRESS
New York/Mahwah, NJ

Imprimatur:
+Most Reverend George Niederauer
Bishop of Salt Lake City
11 May 2005

The imprimatur is an official declaration that a book or a pamphlet is free of doctrinal or moral error. No implication is contained therein that the one who has granted the imprimatur agrees with the content, opinions, or statements expressed.

Cover Art: Saint Stephen's sermon outside the walls of Jerusalem [detail of townscape], by Vittore Carpaccio (1455–1525), c. 1511. Louvre, Paris, France. Photo credit: Erich Lessing of Art Resource, NY. Used by permission.

"The Rabbi's Gift," as it appears in M. Scott Peck's Prologue from *The Different Drum: Community Making and Peace* (New York: Simon and Schuster, 1987). Used with permission.

"We are Three, You are Three" from *The Song of the Bird* by Anthony de Mello (New York: Image Books, 1982, 1984). Copyright © 1982 by Anthony de Mello, SJ. Reprinted with permission of Gujarat Sahitya Prakash.

"To Live with the Spirit" from *The Selected Poetry of Jessica Powers,* published by ICS Publications, Washington, DC. Copyright © 1999 by the Carmelite Monastery, Pewaukee, WI. Used with permission.

Extracts from the documents of the Second Vatican Council are from Walter M. Abbott, ed., *The Documents of Vatican II* (New York: The America Press, 1966). Used by permission. All rights reserved.

The Scripture quotations contained herein are from the New Revised Standard Version of the Bible, Catholic Edition, copyright © 1989 and 1993 by the Division of Christian Education of the National Council of the Churches of Christ in the United States of America. Used by permission. All rights reserved.

Cover design by Cynthia Dunne
Book design by Lynn Else

Library of Congress Cataloging-in-Publication Data

Bulson, Michael E.
        Preach what you believe : timeless homilies for deacons—liturgical cycle B / Michael Bulson
        p.   cm.
        Includes bibliographical references.
        ISBN 0-8091-4342-9 (alk. paper)
        1. Church year sermons.   2. Catholic Church—Sermons.   3. Sermons, American—21st century.
4. Catholic Church. Lectionary for Mass (U.S.). Year B.   I. Title.
BX1756.B827P74 2005
252'.02—dc22

                                                                                        2005012200

Published by Paulist Press
997 Macarthur Boulevard
Mahwah, New Jersey 07430

www.paulistpress.com

Printed and bound in the United States of America

CONTENTS

DEDICATION

To family and friends,
with love and gratitude,
and for all who preach what they believe

ACKNOWLEDGMENTS

It is impossible to acknowledge all those who have somehow contributed to this series of homilies but I do wish to express my gratitude to a few, including Father Colin Bircumshaw, who was pastor of St. Joseph Parish, Ogden, Utah during the first years of my ministry as a deacon. Father Colin's depth of knowledge in theology, liturgy, and homiletics was a great inspiration to me; his patient support of my work as a deacon is greatly appreciated. I wish to thank as well my wife, Mary Lou, for her patience and her critical eye in reading the manuscript. Finally, I am grateful for the encouragement and skills of my editor at Paulist Press, Kevin Carrizo di Camillo.

INTRODUCTION

In the week preceding ordination to the diaconate on November 30, 1997, each member of my class was asked by a representative of our diocesan newspaper, *The Intermountain Catholic*, what the goal for his ministry would be. I responded, using a slight variation on the words spoken during the presentation of the Book of the Gospels in the ordination rite, that my goal was "to believe what I read in Scripture, preach what I believe, and put into practice what I preach."[1] When I spoke those words, I had only a dawning awareness of the significance preaching would have for me as a deacon. Since then I have come to regard preaching as one of the greatest joys of diaconal ministry. To proclaim the word of God, to break it open for those assembled, and to craft a message that is faithful to the gospel and yet relevant to our times is a great challenge—and a great blessing. This series of homilies is the fruit of that effort.

One of the things I believe comes from the Gospel of Matthew where Jesus, after giving his disciples a long series of parables, asks, "Have you understood all this?" (Matt 13:51). The disciples answer, "Yes." And then our Lord says, "Therefore every scribe who has been trained for the kingdom of heaven is like the master of a household who brings out of his treasure what is new and what is old" (Matt 13:52). In these homilies I have tried to emulate that master of the household Jesus had in mind, by bringing out both what is old and what is new. For example, in Homily No. 2, "What Would John the Baptist Say?" the message of John the Baptist is old: Repent! Reform your lives! But the words are new: they could refer to the scandal surrounding the 2002 Winter Olympics in my home state of Utah. And, of course, if you choose to use some of the ideas and images in these homilies, which I encourage you to do, the message of the gospel will be the same; only *your* words, *your* images, the particular *local* event that concerns you, will be new.

I believe the image that the homilist is like the master of the household who brings out both the old and the new is particularly appropriate for deacons who preach. A deacon is essentially a servant. A critical part of that service has to be connecting the liberating message of the gospel with our own mission to serve others. As Deacon William Ditewig says in his book *101 Questions & Answers on Deacons,*[2] "the character of the deacon's preaching should reflect the uniqueness of diaconal ministry. The deacon should bring to his homilies a prophetic sense of the service to which all are called." I have tried to be faithful to those words in these homilies—including, for example, Homily No. 27, "We're All Deacons Now"—by showing how Christ's example of washing the feet of his disciples at the Last Supper tells us unequivocally that "if you want to be important, then be a servant of all." Similarly, in Homily No. 22, "Fundamental Things Apply," I try to show how the powerful forces at work in the Mass first draw us in to communion and then send us out in service to all.

The task of being a good householder, a good steward, a good deacon, is not an easy one. Essential to that task is being a good listener. It means listening to what is going on around you in the parish, in the wider community and in the world. But it has to be a kind of "contemplative listening," a listening, as Deacon Owen Cummings says in *Mystical Women, Mystical Body*, "across the centuries for the accent of truth and, having found it, to blend that accent with our own speech."[3] I have tried in these homilies to engage in that kind of listening, to let the accents of truth found in ancient voices be heard and not obscured by my own speech. My hope is that these homilies will be a starting point for you to add your own speech in a way that will make the ancient accent of truth heard even more clearly in our own times.

As you will see, I like to use a story or image in these homilies as a kind of catalyst for the ideas developed in the homily. I do this because I believe appropriate stories, lines of poetry, even cartoons and news articles, can be important tools for the householder who strives to bring out both the old and the new. As one source puts it, "Whoever can give his people better stories than the ones they live in is like the priest in whose hands common bread and wine become capable of feeding the very soul."[4] When I preached Homily No. 54, "The Messiah is One of You," and made the suggestion that we look on the person sitting next to us as possibly being the Messiah, there were many smiles and good-natured comments about who might—or might not—be the Messiah among us.

If there is one image I would leave with you as you read and use these homilies, it would be the image of a great feast, a gourmet dinner, such as the one captured in the movie, *Babette's Feast*. I try to approach a homily in the same way a dinner is prepared for dear friends: searching for the very best ingredients, using what is fresh, and laboring to make it appealing in every way. I offer these homilies in that same spirit. *Bon appétit!*

PART ONE

Advent

HOMILIES 1–4

It is a time of darkness, of faith,
We shall not see Christ's radiance in our lives yet;
it is still hidden in our darkness; nevertheless, we must believe
that he is growing in our lives; we must believe it so firmly
that we cannot help relating everything, literally everything,
to this most incredible reality.

Carol Houselander, *The Reed of God*[1]

1

AN ADVENT GAME OF HIDE AND SEEK
First Sunday of Advent (B)

- Isaiah 63:16b–17, 19b; 64:2b–7
- 1 Corinthians 1:3–9
- Mark 13:33–37

I was thinking this morning about a bumper sticker I saw once. It read: "Jesus is coming soon. Look busy!"

Look busy! Now, that would be an easy lesson to preach. Looking busy would certainly be one way of describing many of us at the start of Advent. We *are* busy. And we will likely get busier as Christmas day approaches—busy with shopping, card-writing, parties—all that goes into preparing for Christmas. But it is not busyness that the prophet Isaiah had in mind when, in the first reading he says of God, "You meet those who gladly do right, those who remember you in your ways" (Isaiah 64:5). Isaiah gives us a clue to how we should be acting during Advent and, indeed, throughout the entire liturgical year that begins today—doing right, remembering God and God's ways.

Being awake and aware is what Mark emphasizes in his gospel today. He says, "Beware, keep alert" and "Keep awake" (Mark 13:33, 37). It is easy to picture ourselves standing at the door, peering toward the horizon, anticipating the return of the Lord of the house. But if we are mindful of God in all our ways, we will remember that God comes to us at Advent and Christmas in the form of a little child! Is it not logical, then, to think of God from the perspective of a child?

Here's what I mean. When we hear Mark saying "the master of the house will come" (Mark 13:35), we naturally think of the adult Christ, coming in glory and in judgment. Another bumper sticker I once saw read: "Jesus is coming soon. And boy is he upset!" But think for a moment outside the box this morning, outside the Advent Box, if you will. Think of the master of the house as a playful child, already *in* your house, but hiding, hiding the way small children do when playing an Advent game of hide-and-seek.

I base this suggestion on sound theology. Hans Urs von Balthasar in his book *Man in History* meditates on the different stages of Christ's life.[2] He says each stage of Christ's life is relevant for our spiritual well-being, including the first stage—Jesus' life as a child.

3

Since we anticipate during Advent the birth of a child, we might ask: What do children like to do? One author commenting on Balthasar's meditations notes:

> Another dimension of childhood is playfulness. Adult life is regulated by rules. Children invent their games with creativity and feel free to change the rules to suit their fancy. So in the spiritual life one cannot bind Christ to our rules. We must allow him the seeming caprice of choosing according to his pleasure.[3]

Advent, then, is a time to play games with the Christ-Child. But, as the author warns, this Child may play by his own rules!

One game all children play is hide-and-seek If the master of the house is among us as a child, might he not be enjoying a game of hide-and-seek? I think so. Remember the hide-and-seek story from the Hasidic tradition:

> Rabbi Barukh's grandson Yehiel was once playing hide-and-seek with another boy. He hid himself well and waited for his playmate to find him. When he had waited for a long time, he came out of his hiding place, but the other was nowhere to be seen. Now Yehiel realized that he had not looked for him from the very beginning. This made him cry, and crying he ran to his grandfather and complained of his faithless friend. Then tears brimmed in Rabbi Barukh's eyes and he said, "God says the same thing: 'I hide, but no one wants to seek me.'"[4]

If we want to avoid disappointing the hiding master of the house, we have to ask: how do we find him? The best suggestion during Advent, and throughout the liturgical year, is simple: listen! If we are silent for awhile, with ourselves, with Scripture, with our prayer, then it is likely we will detect a giveaway sound that tells us where the Child is hiding. It is tempting to rush off in search of the Child without first doing the listening. And perhaps that is what we are doing for much of Advent—rummaging about, expecting to find him in our often overworked lives, in shopping malls, at parties. He can be found there, but it is more difficult; those are not his favorite hiding places.

If you listen deeply, you will likely hear a stirring of the Child in more simple places. One of the simplest places where he likes to hide is in the family gathered to share something exquisitely simple: human affection. Affection is a form of love that takes time to develop. We cannot expect to love everyone the way we love a spouse or a close family member but we can nurture affection. The family gathering may not always be ideal, but we can experience real affection, if we are mindful.

Where else might the master of the house be hiding? We know that one characteristic of the child is playfulness. Look for him in the places where you are at play. Such places are hard to find sometimes, because play is hard for adults. That is why we have to be mindful of God's ways during Advent. If we enter mindfully into the chaos of crowded shopping, the choosing of a meaningful gift, gathering with friends, we may very well find God at play there. But to experience the play of God, to find the master of the house, you have to be like a child and make up your own rules. Forget the conventional rules that compel us to seek out the most expensive gift, the hottest item on the market. Play by the rules that you know should apply: creative and simple expressions of caring. Be less mindful of the growing rivalry of Christmas decorations and more mindful of your neighbor's true self, which you may encounter if you are really listening. Most importantly, be more attentive to the real needs of the poor this Advent than to the apparent needs of those who are already quite well off. If you can adjust to such rules, and be confident they are God's rules, you will find the one you are seeking—the Christ, the master of the house.

But what if you come to the end of Advent and still haven't found him? Well, think some more about the ways of children. Children like to sleep. Maybe the master of the house who is already with you is asleep! If so, how to awaken him? One suggestion: enter actively into Advent worship. Sing as loud and as well as you can! There is nothing that awakens this sleeping Child more than Catholics who enter into the liturgy with full hearts and minds. Go Christmas caroling. Find a good radio station with classic Christmas songs. Put on Handel's Messiah. Sing along joyfully and from the depths of your heart. And while you are singing, see if, maybe, just perhaps, you hear a tiny voice harmonizing with your own. That's the master of the house you have awakened.

But, finally, if all this does not work, I have one further suggestion. Give up. Surrender! Say to the Child of the house, "I cannot find you. You will have to find me." And here is the paradox of Advent: while we are preparing to receive him, he is doing the same. While we are seeking him, he is seeking us. While we are watching for him to return, he is watching to see if we will return. Return where? To our hearts, of course, for that is where he has been all along. And so, in the end, it is just a matter of saying as children do: The game is over! Here I am!

Questions for Further Discussion

1. Have you ever thought of Advent as a game of hide-and-seek with the Christ Child? Where might you look for him in your life?

2. What does it mean to simply "surrender"?

2

WHAT WOULD JOHN THE BAPTIST SAY?
Second Sunday of Advent (B)

> • Isaiah 40:1–5, 9–11
> • 2 Peter 3:8–14
> • Mark 1:1–8

In 2002 the biggest story in Utah was the Winter Olympics; the second biggest story was the Olympic bid scandal.

Over the course of several months, the embarrassing truth trickled out: millions of dollars had been handed out to members of the International Olympic Committee in the form of gifts, tuition payments, and outright cash, all in an effort to have Salt Lake City named as the site of the 2002 Winter Olympics. As preparations for the event were nearing completion, leaders of the Salt Lake Olympic Committee were indicted on bribery charges which, on December 5, 2003, were dismissed by a federal court judge. In dismissing the case and thereby bringing the scandal episode to an end, the judge remarked that the attempt to prosecute those who headed the Olympic committee "offended his sense of justice." The jurors indicated they were not persuaded that anything wrong had occurred. State officials and Olympic supporters expressed relief that the court proceeding was over and that the whole "unseemly" matter was now "old history."

Advent was just beginning as I read the post-mortems on this sad episode which now belongs to the Utah history books. I could not help asking: What would John the Baptist say? What would the voice of one crying out in the Utah desert sound like today?

From what I know of Old Testament prophets—and John was of that line—he would have been outraged! He would have raged and roared; he would have chastised and scolded. But in the end he would have offered hope and compassion.

The best authority on the prophets I know of is Rabbi Abraham J. Heschel, who says:

> Indeed, the sort of crimes and even the amount of delinquency that fill the prophets of Israel with dismay do not go beyond that which we regard as normal, as typical ingredients of social dynamics. To us a single act of injustice—cheating in business, exploitation of the poor—is slight; to the prophets, a disaster. To us injustice is injurious to the welfare of the people; to the prophets it is a deathblow to existence; to us an episode; to them, a catastrophe, a threat to the world.[5]

John the Baptist was the last of the Old Testament prophets, a transitional figure between the covenant God made with Israel and the covenant established by Christ. In his calling, his lifestyle, and his message, John the Baptist stood in that great line of Hebrew prophets that included Elijah and Elisha. We get a clear sense of that in today's gospel from Mark where the words of Isaiah are invoked: "See, I am sending my messenger ahead of you, who will prepare your way; the voice of one crying out in the wilderness: 'Prepare the way of the Lord, make his paths straight'" (Mark 1:2). John the Baptist, like the Old Testament prophets, came as a messenger of God, expressing that message in "notes one octave too high for our ears...using words that begin to burn where conscience ends."[6]

John would have railed against our moral laxity, of which the Olympic bribery scandal is but a locally grown example. But he would have done so for a purpose. As a prophet, his ultimate concern would have been to bring back to God those who would listen. Rabbi Heschel says of the prophet that "behind his austerity is love and compassion for mankind."[7] John would use strong language to condemn the scandal, but his motivation would be love. John knew what every prophet knew: that a person cannot have an inordinate desire for anything other than God—whether it be something good, like the dazzling beauty of Olympic events, or the wealth, power and prestige that are now as closely associated with the Olympics as the famous symbols—and at the same time be open to God. From a prophet's standpoint, that is the *real* scandal of the 2002 Olympics: something other than God became so attractive that decent men and women would do in the darkness what they would be ashamed to do in the light.

The Olympics and the ethical compromises they caused are a good point of departure for us on this Second Sunday of Advent. Most of us live daily with the temptation to desire something more than God. Our sins of moral compromise, our ethical equivocation, is probably not of Olympian proportions, but it is there all the same. It is against such tendencies that John the Baptist preached. And he preaches to us today as well. He is given center stage during Advent to give us a full blast of righteous indignation in hopes that we will turn back to God with the same kind of passion and perseverance that the Salt Lake Olympic Committee showed in pursuing the Winter Olympics.

Unlike Olympic Committee members, God cannot be bribed. If we make our gifts of praise to God, our sacrifices, our good works, thinking that God will have to reward us, we will be disappointed. But if we simply surrender, if we empty our hearts and minds of all else, we will find, quite unexpectedly, that God is there waiting for us. Meister Eckhardt, the great fourteenth century Dominican preacher, knew this very well. One source summarizes Meister Eckhardt as saying that "God must act and pour himself into us *when we are ready*, that is, when we are totally empty of self and creatures....God's very nature compels him to 'pour great goodness into you whenever he finds you so empty and so bare.'"[8]

That is the hope in the message of John the Baptist: if we prepare ourselves well, if we empty out all other desire, God has no choice but to fill us with goodness. That is a prize worth pursuing this Advent.

Questions for Further Discussion:

1. Can you think of other things in our society that John the Baptist might rage about?

2. What does it mean that behind the prophet's austerity there is love and compassion?

3

THE ADVENT WOLF
Third Sunday of Advent [Gaudete Sunday] (B)

- Isaiah 61:1–2a, 10–11
- 1 Thessalonians 5:16–24
- John 1:6–8, 19–28

It is the third Sunday of Advent, the Sunday traditionally known as Gaudete Sunday, a Latin word which directs us to *rejoice*. But you may ask, "*Why* should we rejoice? What reason can you give us for rejoicing?" To answer your objection, I will turn to nature. I will tell you the story of the Advent Wolf.

But before I tell you the story, let me review the authority for turning to nature to find cause for rejoicing. I turn to nature, because in nature we can discover the ways of God.

Consider the first reading from Isaiah. Isaiah proclaims: "For as the earth brings forth its shoots, and as a garden causes what is sown in it to spring up, so the Lord God will cause righteousness and praise to spring up before all the nations" (Isaiah 61:11). Is not Isaiah positing a clear connection between the ways of nature and the ways of God?

Jesus himself knew that God's ways could be discovered in nature, for he used many such examples from nature in his teaching. Remember how he spoke of a grain of wheat falling into the ground as a way of showing us how we must die to self, if we are to enter the kingdom? Remember how he used fig trees, birds of the field, foxes, sparrows and camels, ordinary things from nature, to reveal God's ways to us? Jesus did this because we can find in nature not just analogies to God's ways, but processes and patterns which have a close affinity with God's saving action in our world.

And so, on this third Sunday of Advent, I turn to nature and the story of the Advent Wolf to show you why we have good cause for rejoicing.

Shortly before the start of Advent, a young male wolf was captured in the mountains to the east of us, north of Morgan, Utah. As the story unfolded, we learned that he came all the way from Yellowstone Park, where he was known as Wolf No. 253 . But because of his significance for my story, I call him the Advent Wolf.

The Advent Wolf came from the Druid pack and had a noticeable limp, probably from an earlier injury. Despite his handicap, he was known as a highly capable wolf who did all things well in protecting and caring for the pack. Several months ago the Advent Wolf left the safety and security of his pack and traveled south all the way to Utah. It is believed that along the way he found friends, companions, perhaps even a lover, someone who might become his mate for life. But freedom came to an end in Utah when a local trapper caught the Advent Wolf. Then he was drugged, put in a cage, and returned to Yellowstone.

The Advent Wolf came to Utah as a sort of nature prophet. He came with this message: nature will not be denied. If given a chance, nature will reclaim what has been lost. Nature will spread into every niche where life can be supported. Nature will regenerate, repopulate, reenliven our wild places—if we humans let her. The Advent Wolf came bearing this clear message.

The Advent Wolf reveals God's ways as well. The message is this: God will not be denied. Given half a chance, God will restore what has been lost through our own sinfulness. God will fill every niche of our world with God's life. God waited patiently through the long centuries of human history until, in the fullness of time, God entered the world to reclaim, restore, and yes, redeem the world. And not just the world in general but our hearts in particular. Anywhere an inviting heart waits for God, God will appear; God will establish a home there; God will be born there; God will bring forth new life there. That is what nature teaches us about the ways of God.

Two thousand years ago John the Baptist appeared on the banks of the Jordan as unexpectedly as the Advent Wolf. People were so confused by his appearance that they thought he must be Elijah or the Prophet. But he was neither. He was simply a voice in the wilderness, a lone wolf, if you will, announcing the advent of new light and life. He was announcing that the source of all light and life was coming to restore, to renew, to redeem the world. We learn about nature from the Advent Wolf; we learn about God from John the Baptist.

But we know that nature does not easily restore the earth. We humans impede and frustrate the constant effort of nature to regenerate and renew the earth. So too we impede God's efforts to renew our world. We treat God much the way the Advent Wolf was treated. We try to capture him, take away his wildness. We drug him with the many addictions of our society. We lock him up in a cage of commercialism and we try our best to send him back to where he came from. We would prefer him to be domesticated and not roaming freely in the wilderness of our lives.

Like nature, God needs our help and cooperation. We must create an environment in our hearts where God is welcome. You see, God is like a shy, vulnerable, wild creature who will not intrude. God can only be enticed to appear when hearts are open and receptive. And so we spend our Advent creating in our hearts the kind of wilderness in which God, like the wild things of nature, will appear.

It is said by those who know about wolves that the Advent Wolf will likely return to Utah. Tracks were spotted that indicated he had friends with him, perhaps a mate. He knows the way to Utah and he has good reason to return.

We, too, live with the certain hope that God will return to us. We are the friends, the companions, the lovers of Christ. And he knows the way. On this Gaudete Sunday we rejoice in knowing that, when our hearts are ready, when our hearts become a welcoming wilderness, Christ returns to us. We rejoice in knowing that God will not be denied. God will come to us again and again.

Let us *rejoice*!

Questions for Further Discussion:

1. What signs do you see that God is restoring our world?
2. In what do you rejoice this Gaudete Sunday?

4
GOD FINDS A HOME IN THE HUMAN HEART
Fourth Sunday of Advent (B)

- 2 Samuel 7:1–5, 8b–12, 14a, 16
- Romans 16:25–27
- Luke 1:26–38

King David lived in a royal palace. King David lived in a fine house of cedar. King David loved God and proposed to build for God a house finer than his own. But King David soon learned that *no* house he could build with his hands, using the finest materials available, would ever be suitable for God. And so for all his days David was left with the question: What *is* a suitable house for God?

The angels in heaven soon took up the question: What is a suitable house for God? For a while, some thought Solomon's Temple might be the answer. But in 587 BC the great temple was destroyed and it never was a suitable house for God.

Some of the angels said, "God is a God of great power. Perhaps the house of Alexander the Great, the Greek general who in the third century conquered all the known world and who, when he reached the banks of the Indus river, stood weeping because there were no more nations to conquer—perhaps the war tents of Alexander would be a suitable house for God?"

But Alexander came and went. And still God was silent.

Some of the angels suggested, "God is a God of beauty. Perhaps the palace of Helen of Troy, a woman so beautiful her face launched a thousand ships and brought down the pillars of Troy—perhaps the palace of Helen of Troy would be a suitable house for God?"

But Helen of Troy came and went. And still God was silent.

Then some of the angels offered, "God is a God of wisdom. Perhaps the great halls of Athens where Plato and Socrates teach people their wisdom—perhaps the halls of Athens would be a suitable house for God?"

But Plato and Socrates came and went. And still God was silent.

Then there came a moment in time when a great stir went through heaven. A rumor spread—and rumors spread very quickly among angels—a rumor that at long last God was going to give an answer to King David's question. The angels' excitement reached its highest pitch when the angel Gabriel was seen descending to earth— to Palestine, to Galilee, to Nazareth. And suddenly the angels heard the long-awaited answer: The only suitable house for God is in human nature. Not in the camps of the powerful, not in the palaces of the beautiful, not in the halls of the wise, but in the open and receptive heart of a teenage Jewish girl from the lowest class. God found a home in the heart of Mary.

St. Gregory of Nyssa says that the angels were "entranced" to learn that God would find a home in human nature. He says that until they learned this the angels knew only God's simple wisdom; now they knew God's diversified wisdom: that God who is transcendent would become imminent; that God who is all powerful would become vulnerable; that God who is perfect, beautiful, and wise would see fit to find a home in human nature. Gregory dares to say that the Bride (the Church) showed to the Bridegroom's friends (the angels) what before was invisible and incomprehensible to all beings.

The angels were overjoyed that an answer had been given to King David's question. But now the angels ask another question. They ask: Given the reality that God has found a suitable house in human nature, why are humans so often lacking in joy?

What answer do we give? Is it because of our human condition? Is it because our need to attend to our human necessities blocks out the clear truth that rang out so clearly from tiny Nazareth 2000 years ago? We have legitimate needs and we have a responsibility to attend to them. But too often, perhaps, we miss out on the joy of the incarnation because we have not really heard, or don't fully believe, that a full and complete answer has been given to King David's question. God truly does prefer human company. God prefers the humble comforts of a loving human heart more than any place in the universe. That's simply the way God is.

Perhaps we are still laboring under the illusion that, if we build a fine house of cedar, God will come. And so we try to build a house according to the designs of our own egos, our own material wants—a house so busy and preoccupied that God is not even noticed there. Meister Eckhardt says that God is always at home in our hearts; we are the ones who have gone out for a walk. We live with the reality that God has taken permanent possession of our nature; God has pitched a tent among us. And God is *not* leaving. God has secured an eternal lease on the house that is the human heart.

On this final Sunday of Advent, why not hear and believe the answer given to King David's question? There is still time to prepare a suitable house for God. Offer to God in these final days of Advent the only house God wants: the house that is the human heart. If God is not at home in our hearts, it matters little that, after a thousand years of suspense, God found a home in the heart of Mary.

What answer will you give this morning to the angels' question?

Questions for Further Discussion:

1. What does Eckhardt mean when he says that God is always at home in our hearts, but we have gone out for a walk?

2. What are you doing to prepare your heart to be a suitable home for God this Advent?

Part Two

Christmas Season

HOMILIES 5–12

And now God says to us what he has already said to the world as a whole through his grace-filled birth: "I am there. I am with you. I am your life. I am the gloom of your daily routine. Why will you not bear it? I weep your tears—pour out yours to me, my child. I am your joy. Do not be afraid to be happy, for ever since I wept, joy is the standard of living that is really more suitable than the anxiety and grief of those who think they have no hope....This reality—incomprehensible wonder of my almighty love—I have sheltered safely in the cold stable of your world. I am there. I no longer go away from this world, even if you do not see me now. I am there. It is Christmas. Light the candles. They have more right to exist than all the darkness. It is Christmas. Christmas that lasts forever."

John Shea, *Starlight*
(quote attributed to Karl Rahner)[1]

5
WRITING STRAIGHT WITH CROOKED LINES
Christmas Vigil (B)

- Isaiah 62:1–5
- Acts 13:16–17, 22–25
- Matthew 1:1-25

You have heard the saying, "God writes straight with crooked lines." Nowhere is that truth more evident than in the long genealogy we just heard from Matthew's gospel. When you first hear it, you may think that Matthew has traced a straight line of descent from Abraham to Jesus. In fact, however, the lines are quite crooked.

Matthew claims that there are fourteen generations from Abraham to David. In fact, there are only *thirteen*. The second set of names from David to the Babylonian exile does contain fourteen generations but, scholars tell us, Matthew omitted four historical generations and six kings.[2] The third section is also flawed, since it contains only thirteen generations.

Then there is the matter of the four women mentioned—Tamar, Rahab, Ruth and Uriah's wife (Bathsheba). Why does the otherwise straight line deviate in four places to mention these Old Testament women? The best scholarly conclusion is that Matthew intended to highlight these women because each of them took the initiative in some way to continue David's line of descent, even though a certain scandal surrounded them. Tamar tricked Judah into conceiving a son; Rahab was a prostitute; a certain irregularity existed in Ruth's relationship with Boaz; Uriah's wife, Bathsheba, had an adulterous relationship with David. In spite of these irregularities, their unions were regarded as the work of the Holy Spirit and as "examples of how God uses the unexpected to triumph over human obstacles...."[3] To Jewish ears, then, the mention of these four women helped prepare them for understanding how Mary could conceive the Son of God in an equally irregular fashion. The hearers of Matthew's gospel did not see scandal in Mary's mysterious conception of Jesus; they saw, instead, another example of how God could intervene to insure the birth of the Son of David. They would have known implicitly what we mean when we say, "God writes straight with crooked lines."

And if God could do such things in the genealogy from Abraham to Jesus, is it not also likely that God continues in our own day to write straight with crooked lines? How many of us looking back over our own lives see only straight lines? If you are like me, the crooked lines stand out quite prominently. But those crooked lines have led to where we are tonight—waiting in vigil for the birth of the Christ Child. It is not the inconsistencies in our personal and family histories that matter, not the irregularities and even scandal that matter. What matters is that we are here waiting in anticipation of the great miracle of Christmas.

What Matthew does not say, but which we can rightly infer, is that the incarnation trumps any errors and irregularities that might have existed in the family tree of Jesus. It did not matter that the numbers did not add up or that generations were skipped. What mattered is that God had been faithful, God had vindicated those who had hoped for a Messiah. God had been revealed as the God of hope.

The incarnation trumps any flaws in our own genealogy, for in this great mystery which we await tonight we are transformed. Our human nature has been touched by the divine. And we cannot be the same again.

We are a new people: the people of God.

And so the final word I would leave with you as we vigil together toward Christmas morning is to stop focusing on the crooked lines in your life. If you want to take it up again later, that's fine. But for now, on this night, see the clear, bright straight line of God's grace that has brought you to this moment in time! Leave the crooked lines for others to puzzle over. God has shown through irrefutable evidence from Abraham to Jesus, from Jesus to this very parish, that God is not bothered by apparently crooked lines. God sees only where the lines lead— to the incarnation, to our adoption into the life of the Trinity.

Questions for Further Discussion:

1. Do you believe God writes straight with crooked lines? In what way?

2. Are you able to keep your focus on the clear, straight line of God's grace that brought you here? If so, how?

6
REMEMBER AND REJOICE
Christmas Midnight (B)

- Isaiah 9:1–6
- Titus 2:11–14
- Luke 2:1–14

It was Christmas Eve on a great battlefield. On one side, in a maze of trenches, young British and French soldiers huddled together against the cold. On the other side, across a no-man's-land about the length of a football field, young German soldiers braved the same numbing cold of the trenches.

The soldiers on both sides waited in the darkness, waited like the people Isaiah had in mind when he proclaimed, "The people who walked in darkness have seen a great light" (Isaiah 9:2).

And see a great light they did!

The British and French soldiers crouching in their trenches began seeing points of light appearing in the fir trees on the German side. And then came the sound of voices singing, *"O Tannenbaum, O Tannenbaum, wie treu sind deine Blätter."* Soon the trees were dotted with candles.

The French then responded with a Christmas carol, *"Angels We Have Heard on High."* Candles began to fill the trees on both sides. Light slowly overcame the darkness, illuminating the desolate strip of land that separated the two armies.

Next the British took up the singing, *"Silent night. Holy night. All is calm. All is bright...."*

And from the German side came the words, *"Stille nacht! Heilige Nacht!"*

Suddenly a young German soldier scrambled up the side of the trench and, clutching a violin in half-frozen fingers, began to play. The cold night air was pierced by the strains of Handel's Messiah.

Against the orders of their commanders, soldiers from both sides came up out of the trenches and into the no-man's-land. They greeted each other, embraced, exchanged gifts. A young British officer gave a German officer his silk scarf. The German gave him a picture of his sister living in Liverpool. And throughout the night and next day there was not a sound of war; only the sound of *"Silent Night,*

Holy Night...Stille Nacht, Heilige Nacht." It was Christmas,1914, on a great battlefield of World War I.

What happened that night? How do you explain this brief interlude of peace in a war that would produce 10 million casualties?

What happened, I believe, is this: For a brief time, and imperfectly, a few men, Germans, French, British, remembered their *true* identity. There was unity, there was joy, there was well-wishing among these men, for they had briefly abandoned their false identities symbolized by uniforms, flags, and national anthems. And they remembered their true identity as children of God, made in the image and likeness of God. Truth overcame illusion; the partial and incomplete was subsumed in the Absolute.

Christmas is a time to remember and rejoice.

The joy you experience tonight comes from remembering. Not just the memories of Christmases past but something more. Something much deeper. The source of your joy is a faint memory, a memory as thin as gossamer, a memory of a time when our race walked in harmony with a loving, all-provident God in paradise. It was a time when our race knew its true identity. We knew who we were. We knew we were made in the image and likeness of God. We knew we were made for joy and contemplation in God. And that was enough.

But, of course, something happened to disturb that happy state. Original sin might be described as the Great Forgetting. We forgot who we were. We began to construct new identities for ourselves apart from God. The identity of being one in God was not enough. We began to think of ourselves as individuals, separated from God and from one another. Through long centuries of struggle and suffering, we as a race wrapped ourselves in an identity of our own making. And from that false identity came all the wars, all the anguish, all the destruction and suffering that history records.

But through it all, the memory of our true identity never completely faded from our consciousness. Holy men and women remembered it. Psalmists sang of it. Prophets proclaimed it—proclaimed there would come a time when God would restore to the human race its true identity.

And so it happened. In Bethlehem, when Caesar Augustus ruled and Quirinius was governor of Syria, in a small stable surrounded by shepherds and angels, God came among us. Not in a cameo appearance, but forever. God took on our nature, not just some corner of it: All of it. The incarnation restored us to our true identity. Now we are no more Jew or Greek, male or female; now, no more German or French, American or Iraqi. The incarnation transformed who we are. From that moment on, we could be a part of Christ, and through the Holy Spirit, sharers in the life of the Trinity. That is our true identity. That is what we celebrate tonight.

Christmas is a time to remember and rejoice. It is also a time to exchange gifts.

The God who comes to you this night in the form of a small child wants a gift from you. Not gold, not frankincense, not myrrh, but this gift: He wants you to give him, for a brief time, any partial and limited identity you have brought with you tonight. If you think your identity is American, or Mexican, or Colombian, give it to him. If you think your identity is your style of clothing, your personality, your money, your position, the car you drive, give it to him. Give him all the provisional, tentative, self-created identities you have collected over a lifetime.

If you can do this, something miraculous will happen: The Christ Child will give you back your true identity. And what's more, he will give you back all the identity-gifts you have given him, only now you will see them from a different perspective. Then you will see yourself in a new light—the light of the incarnation! Then you will realize your true identity. And what you see will give you joy!

Remember and rejoice tonight in knowing who you are!

Remember and rejoice in knowing that our true identity has been permanently restored to us!

Remember and rejoice in the great mystery of the incarnation!

Questions for Further Discussion:

1. What do you think made it possible for two warring armies to pause from fighting on Christmas Eve? Why do you think they started again?

2. What does it mean that our true identity has been restored to us?

7

THE SEEDS OF EVANGELIZATION
Christmas Dawn (B)

- Isaiah 62:11–12
- Titus 3:4–7
- Luke 2:15–20

In today's gospel we discover the seeds of evangelization. They are seeds which, as Jesus will later describe in parable, sometimes fall on good ground, sprout, grow and bear fruit. Or they may never take root, never achieve the full potential God intended.

I speak of evangelization on this Christmas dawn, because of something Pope Paul VI said in his message *On Evangelization in the Modern World* (1975). In their 1992 document entitled, *Go and Make Disciples: A National Plan and Strategy for Catholic Evangelization in the United States,* the United States Catholic bishops rephrased Pope Paul VI's message to describe evangelization in this way:

> [E]vangelizing means bringing the Good News of Jesus into every human situation and seeking to convert individuals and society by the divine power of the Gospel itself. At its essence are the proclamation of salvation in Jesus Christ and the response of a person in faith, which are both works of the Spirit of God.[4]

We see examples of evangelization in today's gospel reading from Luke. Both the shepherds and Mary have been given the seeds of evangelization—the good news of Jesus. The shepherds do what Pope Paul VI described: they carried the good news into the human situation in which they found themselves. The gospel says of the shepherds: "they made known what had been told them about this child..." (Luke 2:17). We do not know whether the shepherds converted anyone. The text says only that those who heard them "were amazed." All we know is that the seeds of evangelization had fallen in the shepherds' hearts and they responded in some fashion by carrying the Good News into their human situation.

Although perhaps limited in their capacity to evangelize, the shepherds are our first models for action on this Christmas day. If you are here because you believe the good news, then the seeds of evangelization have been planted in your heart as well. The next question—and it is the most important question you can ask yourself this morning—is: What will I *do* with that good news? Will the seeds sprout in your imagination and your will? Will the seeds be watered by your love for those who see this day as no more than a secular holiday? Will a seed grow into a fruitful vine which will nourish those who know you in your family, in the community of your parish, at work? These are the important questions that must be asked on the dawn of this great day.

We can increase the likelihood that the seeds of evangelization will flourish by listening further to what the U.S. bishops said on this subject. In their document the bishops identify two equally important aspects of evangelization. They write:

> Evangelization...has both an inward and an outward direction. *Inwardly,* it calls for our continued receiving of the Gospel of Jesus Christ, our ongoing conversion both individually and as Church. It nurtures us, makes us grow, and renews us in holiness as God's people. *Outwardly,* evangelization addresses those who have not heard the Gospel or who, having heard it, have stopped practicing their faith....It calls us to work for full communion among all who confess Jesus but do not yet realize the unity for which Christ prayed.[5]

There is only one person in today's gospel whose life and holiness matches this description of evangelization. That person, of course, is Mary. Unlike the shepherd-evangelists, about whom we know very little, we know from the gospels that Mary became the evangelist *par excellence.* Mary, not the shepherds, is our perfect model for becoming true evangelists. Mary received the seeds of evangelization—the good news of Christ—and she nurtured them through a life of prayer. The gospel, after relating how the shepherds arrived at the manger bearing the message the angels had given them about her child, says simply, "But Mary treasured all these words and pondered them in her heart" (Luke 2:19). Mary would become the perfect evangelist because she pondered the Good News throughout her life, despite the many strange and agonizing demands it would make on her. For Mary, the inward direction of evangelization would make possible the outward direction. And it would bring about the conversion of individuals and whole societies. Even today, we are the beneficiaries of Mary's evangelization. We reap the fruits of the good seeds of evangelization that she received that first Christmas dawn.

Then, of course, the focus must shift back to us. How do we internalize what the bishops are saying about evangelization? One bishop with a good suggestion is my own Bishop George Niederauer in Salt Lake City who, in his book, *Precious as Silver: Imagining Your Life With God,*[6] tells "A Tale of Two Benches." The two benches are a bus bench and a park bench. On the former, we sit pragmatically, restless in anticipation, waiting for the bus to arrive. But not on a park bench. Says Bishop Niederauer:

> [I] go to the park bench for its own sake. I may sit in silence, with birds singing, children playing, and the sun shining through the leaves of the trees. Nothing is produced. Nothing gets done.[7]

The seeds of evangelization that fall so easily on the good soil of our hearts this Christmas dawn will not grow well if we never sit on a park bench. We cannot avoid the bus bench entirely, but we can consciously choose to sit where Mary would likely be found: on a park bench, pondering the good news in our hearts.

Questions for Further Discussion:

1. What will you do today to nourish the seeds of evangelization that have fallen into your heart?
2. Do you find time to sit on a park bench? How do you do it?

8
THE JOY OF HIGH THEOLOGY
Christmas Day (B)

- Isaiah 52:7–10
- Hebrews 1:1–6
- John 1:1–18

Today we celebrate one of the great mysteries of our Catholic Christian tradition—the incarnation. At the Christmas Masses that preceded this one, we heard again the wonderful stories from Matthew and Luke of how Jesus was born. They are very down-to-earth stories, humble accounts of this great mystery. You cannot get much earthier than a cow stable. If you use your imagination you can almost smell the cows, the hay, the unwashed shepherds. From those stories comes a clear understanding that this Jesus we call Christ was one of us. This is theology from below.

But John's gospel gives us another type of theology: theology from *above*. If you go to John's gospel today during your meditation time, you will not find there the earthy accounts of Jesus' birth. You will encounter, instead, a high theology that emphasizes the divinity of Christ. You get your first taste of that in the gospel we just heard: "In the beginning was the Word, and the Word was with God, and the Word was God" (John 1:1). That is one of the richest theological statements in all the New Testament. It means that this Jesus we see in the crib this day was *more* than just the son of Joseph and Mary born in Bethlehem: his origins are in God. And he comes from God to us in order that we might have life and light.

While John's account lacks the humble, earthy manger scene so well portrayed in Luke, there is, nevertheless, humility to be found in this gospel as well. But it is a divine humility. It is the humility of Christ who, as St. Paul hymns so beautifully in Philippians, emptied himself of divinity and took the form of a slave. And why? The ancient fathers of the Church summed it up in this phrase: "God became human so that we might become divine." God took on our human nature in order to elevate us to our true dignity as participants in the life of the Trinity. And all we need do is accept it.

The incarnation, the investing of our nature with the divine, is pure gift. And perhaps that is why our world still finds it so hard to accept. Much of our world approaches life not on the basis of a theology from above, or even a theology from below, but on the basis of what might be called Promethean theology.

Prometheus was one of the tragic figures of Greek mythology. Greek mythology contains delightful fictional stories involving superhumans and gods through which the Greeks sought to offer explanations for why things are the way they are. Although they are fictional, they contain important kernels of truth about human nature. One of the most poignant myths concerns Prometheus, the Titan who stole fire from the gods on Mount Olympus and gave it to humans so they might be happy. In Greek mythology, Prometheus suffered the cruel fate of being chained to a mountain where an eagle preyed on his liver which was restored as quickly as it was devoured.

The personal stories of many people in our own times are a retelling of the myth of Prometheus. Like Prometheus, many do not accept the fiery gift of life in Christ, but still try to steal it from the gods. There are those who live as though the fire of life must be taken forcibly from the gods, not accepted as gift. Lives of conspicuous consumption are a way of stealing the fire of immortality as if flagrant materialism might give a happiness unknown to other mortals.

Myth can also refer to "an unproved collective belief that is accepted uncritically and used to justify a social institution."[8] The unproved collective belief that happiness is to be found in health and power is a common myth in our world but it is a myth contradicted by the words of John's gospel. The gospel reveals truth that refutes myth. Happiness cannot be stolen from the gods through wealth, or violence, or any other force. Happiness is freely given; all we must do is accept it. Accept the God who has come among us this day, the God who is love. The theologian von Balthasar teaches there is a close connection between love and truth. The more we love, the more we are able to recognize truth. The way into the truth of the gospel is through love and all that it entails.

In Greek mythology there is a counterpart to Prometheus. It is Pandora, the first woman. We have all heard of "Pandora's Box." One version of the myth is that Jupiter gave to Pandora a box in which were contained all the blessings that could be bestowed upon humankind. But Pandora incautiously opened the box and all the blessings escaped. Only one blessing remained—hope. Despite all the sufferings humans might suffer, there remained hope.

Our hope is in Jesus Christ who came to us this day to restore all the blessings that are our heritage. In claiming the truth of the gospel over myth we bring those blessings upon ourselves and upon all the world.

Questions for Further Discussion:

1. How would you describe the humility to be found in the reading from John's Gospel?

2. Can you think of examples of Promethean theology?

9
NUNC DIMITTIS
Holy Family

- Sirach 3:2–6, 12–14
- Hebrews 11:8, 11–12, 17–19
- Luke 2:22–40

If you are ever looking for a phrase to use to sum up your feelings at the end of a significant period of your life—say, for example, retirement, or even at the approach of death—today's gospel from Luke provides it. The phrase, in Latin, is *nunc dimittis*. It is the opening phrase of Simeon's canticle which we translate as, "Master, now you are dismissing your servant in peace" (Luke 2:29). Since it reflects the desired state of mind of every person approaching death, including the small death that is symbolized every time we close our eyes and fall asleep, it is recited during night prayer, Compline, in the Liturgy of the Hours. In fact, it has been part of the Liturgy of the Hours since the fifth century.[9]

Simeon's canticle is evocative of strong emotions because it captures the feeling of a holy and devoted person who has waited patiently and dutifully for the arrival of a particular moment in time. It has the sentiment of a watchman who is joyful that his watch has ended combined with the emotion of a dying person's last words.[10] Thus there are twin themes of joy and peace. For the followers of Jesus, the canticle—spoken in the context of Jesus being presented in the Temple—would have carried the reminder of Jesus' own words: "For I tell you that many prophets and kings desired to see what you see, but did not see it, and to hear what you hear, but did not hear it" (Luke 10:24). Simeon is one of the favored prophets who, in the approaching shadows of death, has been privileged to see "a light for revelation to the Gentiles and for glory to your people Israel" (Luke 2:32). For the early Christians of Luke's community, who at the time were probably experiencing persecution and expulsion from the synagogues themselves, Simeon's canticle must have been comforting.

The peace and the joy associated with the *nunc dimittis* are not confined to the experience of an aging prophet or a persecuted band of Christians; it has been recited down through the centuries in our prayer life because it says something to *us* as well. Every generation of Christians hears the *nunc dimittis* spoken for the first time. The key to this understanding is the first Latin word, *nunc,* meaning "now." The light to be revealed to the Gentiles which Simeon delighted in comes to us *now,* in every moment of every day, if we, like Simeon, know how to wait for it. We are especially attentive to this happening *now* during the Christmas season when we celebrate the coming of the Light of Christ into the world. And if we are aware of this continual Simeon-event happening in our lives, then we should be continually responding, "*Nunc dimittis*–Master, now you are dismissing your servant in peace." We have seen the light of Christ, have felt the joy and peace that it brings, and now there is nothing more in this moment to expect. *Nunc dimittis.*

But the lectionary has not placed this rich Scripture passage in isolation. Rather, it has given it to us as the centerpiece of the feast of the Holy Family. That being the case, it must have a relationship to the other readings, all of which have to do with family life. I will look at just one of the many possibilities given us, the reading from Sirach. The reading describes the kind of life which, if lived faithfully, would merit the blessing of *nunc dimittis.* I mean that one who honors his father and mother in the way described in the passage from Sirach would through such actions have seen the light of Christ, for Christ is revealed in the living out of the commandments. Let's consider the story of one man who lived out the fourth commandment.

The famous Jewish psychiatrist Victor Frankel recalls how, at the start of World War II, he had the chance to escape the impending disaster that everyone knew the Nazis would bring. Frankel was living in Vienna, Austria at the time and was already on his way to a brilliant medical career. But he was not alone. He lived with his elderly parents. And when he obtained the precious visa to America, Frankel knew he was facing a momentous decision. He walked around the neighborhood for a long time seeking some sign to tell him whether he should go to America or whether he should stay with his parents.

When he finally returned home, he met his father. His father was holding a tiny piece of tile. When asked about it, his father explained that he had picked it up at the synagogue which had been destroyed by the Nazis. He said the tile contained a Hebrew character which could only be from one of the commandments. Frankel asked his father which commandment the tiny Hebrew character was from. His father replied, "The fourth commandment: Honor your father and your mother, so that your days may be long in the land that the Lord your God is giving you" (Exod 20:12). Frankel had his sign. He would stay in Vienna until he and his parents were taken to a concentration camp.

There he would care for his parents until they died. At an early age, Frankel had learned the meaning of the fourth commandment.

The challenge for each of us on this feast of the Holy Family is to care for our families in such a way that when the end of our days approaches we may have the joy and peace that comes from knowing we have lived the commandments faithfully, especially the honoring of father and mother. When we do so, we will be blessed with the light of Christ and be able to say, *"Nunc dimittis."*

Questions for Further Discussion:

1. Has there been a time in your life when you could say *"Nunc dimittis?"*

2. What are some ways of living faithfully the fourth commandment?

10
A STABLE MEDITATION
Solemnity of Mary, the Mother of God (B)

- Numbers 6:22–27
- Galatians 4:4–7
- Luke 2:16–21

"But Mary treasured all these words and pondered them in her heart" (Luke 2:19).

If you were to consult a good book on meditation, or consult a good spiritual director on how to meditate, you probably would not be advised to seek out a barn, heated only by the warmth of cattle and donkeys. You probably would not be told to seek out a busy place, filled with shepherds and flocks of sheep coming and going—let alone magi with rare and expensive gifts. Most likely you would be told to seek out a place of quiet where you could reflect peacefully and fairly comfortably.

And yet on this feast of the Solemnity of Mary, the Mother of God, we find Mary who, on the basis of this text, some have referred to as the first Christian theologian, meditating in what had to have been the busiest stable in Palestine. What is the meaning of this strange scene?

It is safe to say that the account Luke gives us is not intended to teach us about meditation techniques. If one wants to grow in spiritual knowledge, it is wise to seek out a quiet place for prayer and meditation. Rather, this scene may suggest to us that if the meaning of the Christmas miracle is to be prolonged, it has to happen in the everyday circumstances of our lives.

Had one of us been consulted to create the setting for the birth of God's son, we likely would have done things quite differently. We might have created a quiet, peaceful setting, a warm comfortable place with just the right lighting and smells. But Luke is telling us that God comes into our lives, is born in our hearts, in the midst of our busy, sometimes confused, lives. Our hearts are often like crowded stables—works in progress—but it is *there* that God chooses to be born, day after day after day. And, what is most important: we can find God there, if we try.

The great feast of Christmas we just celebrated a few days ago gave us an ideal opportunity to reflect on the mystery of Jesus coming to us as a baby. With our excellent music, our well-proclaimed readings, our beautiful liturgy that every year draws crowds to this church, we created a few moments of time that were extraordinary. But soon we move into Ordinary Time. It is in the ordinary flow of our lives, filled with the smells and noises, the deadlines and demands, that crowd the stables of our hearts, like the Bethlehem cattle and donkeys, that we must discover and prolong the meaning of Christmas. It is in the daily extending of hospitality to all the unexpected shepherds that show up in our lives that the mystery of the incarnation is lived and understood a little better; all the good things and the bad, the things that make us sad and the things that cause us to glorify and praise God; all the unexpected, unwashed shepherds of life that we, like Mary, can reflect upon; all of these can be a means to realize the truth that God is truly with us.

And what did Mary reflect on in that busy stable? Our imagination suggests many things: the message of the shepherds, the ordinariness of her circumstances, the dazzling visit of angels. But we remember that Mary was a deeply religious woman steeped in the Hebrew scriptures. Perhaps what Mary pondered was the blessing we heard in the first reading. Perhaps she saw that the words God spoke to the people of Israel through Moses were now spoken to all people:

> The Lord bless you and keep you;
> The Lord make his face to shine upon you,
>   and be gracious to you;
> The Lord lift up his countenance upon you,
>   and give you peace. (Num 6:24–26)

Perhaps, in this tiny child lying in the manger, Mary saw *all* of that. For is that not what we see? In the tiny face of this vulnerable infant, the face of God shines upon each of us. Through the eyes of this child God looks kindly upon each of us, and we experience true peace.

Mary's pondering did not end that day in the crowded stable at Bethlehem. Like any good mother, thoughts of her son must have pre-occupied her mind all her life. The Scriptures tell us that she pondered the meaning of her son's words when, after three days missing, he was found in the Temple. She reflected on his words, she struggled to understand his public ministry and she anguished at the cross, pondering the mystery of his death.

The Church tells us that Mary's work as a mother goes on, for now she reflects on her son present in his Church on earth. Mary continues to pray for Christ's Church, to intercede that the blessing pronounced by Moses might be more fully realized and lived. Mary shares with us the fruits of her own reflection. Every time we hear the sound of rosary beads, or words from a familiar hymn—Ave Maria, Hail Holy Queen—or pray with a favorite Marian icon, we are reminded that Mary, the Mother of God, is with us in the Church. She reminds us throughout history that her son is the source of our blessing. In the busy, crowded stables of our lives, Mary continues to reflect with us on the great blessing God has given us this Christmas season.

Questions for Further Discussion:

1. What role has Mary played in your life?
2. How has the blessing of Moses touched you?

11
VISITORS FROM THE EAST
Epiphany of the Lord (B)

- Isaiah 60:1-6
- Ephesians 3:2-3a, 5-6
- Matthew 2:1-12

Have you ever wondered what ever became of the magi, those mysterious visitors from the East who followed a star to Bethlehem to pay homage to the newborn Son of God? They are mentioned only in

Matthew's gospel. Luke has shepherds; John and Mark have no infancy narrative at all.

What happened to them? Did they simply return to their homes by another way and disappear into history?

This morning I have the answer to that burning question. One ancient writer tells us that the three magi, known to us as Balthasar, Melchior, and Gaspar, converted to Christianity and in AD 54 at Sebaste in Armenia, a few days after the celebration of the Christmas Mass, they died.[11] Their relics can now be venerated in Cologne, Germany in "a magnificently enameled shrine."[12]

How we got from the brief account in Matthew's gospel to what I have just told you is what one Catholic biblical scholar calls a type of "Christian midrash."[13] Midrash, which we normally associate with Jewish biblical study, is the name given to a process by which Scripture stories are imaginatively reflected upon and become over time the basis for popular devotion. As "Christian midrash," such accounts have enriched our Catholic tradition, giving meaning to the gospel truths and expanding the possibilities for catechesis, worship, and practice.

The tale of the three mysterious visitors from the East—who start out as magi and end up as saints—is based on the historically plausible account in Matthew's gospel. Astronomers tell us it is possible that the star that led the visitors to Bethlehem was a supernova, or a rare conjunction of planets, possibly even Halley's comet. Whatever the phenomenon that occurred, the thought of travelers from the East following a star to pay tribute to a great ruler would not have struck the early hearers of Matthew's gospel as preposterous. There were accounts of similar events circulating in the culture of the Middle East at that time.

But what made the story of the magi dear to early Christians, what gave it legs to travel as far as it has, is Jesus Christ. The author of Matthew's gospel took a fragment of historical memory and used it to say to his followers: "Look! Even though you have been rejected by the Jewish authorities, just as Jesus was, remember that he was recognized by those *outside* the Jewish tradition." Matthew was saying to people with some of the same doubts we sometimes have: "Not everyone accepted and believed in Jesus Christ as the one sent from God. But these magi *did*. They came, they saw, they believed, and they paid him homage."

With that as its starting point, the magi story took on a life of its own. Three visitors who began as magi, or astrologers, grew in the minds of Christian faithful to become kings of the Orient. Thus, we sing, "We three kings of Orient are," not "We three magi." The number of kings also evolved over time. Because Matthew mentions three gifts, it was logical to assume three kings. But other religious depictions have as few as two kings or as many as twelve. The names and places of origin have also changed. In the Western Christian world, we have gradually settled on Balthasar, Melchior and Gaspar.

So how did the three magi-kings make it all the way to Cologne, Germany? According to tradition, the Emperor Zeno brought the relics from Persia to Constantinople in 490. Later they found their way to Milan. From there the relics, which were said to include the incorruptible bodies of the three, were taken by Emperor Frederick Barbarossa back to Germany in 1162 as spoils of war.[14] Hence, the following obituary notice in the calendar of saints at Cologne:

> Having undergone many trials and fatigues for the Gospel, the three wise men met at Sewa (Sebaste in Armenia) in AD 54 to celebrate the feast of Christmas. Thereupon, after the celebration of Mass, they died: St. Melchior on January 1st, aged 116; St. Balthasar on January 6th, aged 112; and St. Gaspar on January 11th, aged 109.[15]

What, then, is the significance of the magi for us *today*? Is the story no more than a naïve, though charming, account which we recall at Christmas? No. The story of the magi has a potentially far greater significance for us today. We, the Christian descendants of Matthew, still receive visitors from the East. They come, not as magi or kings, but as Muslims, Hindus, Buddhists. Sometimes they come in a hostile manner as happened on September 11th. They often come attracted to our way of life with its freedoms and material comforts.

But the question we might ask ourselves on this feast of the Epiphany is: Do visitors from the East *still* seek Christ, the Son of God, in the one place he must be found today—in the hearts of his twenty-first century followers? Do they recognize Christ in us? Do the modern day magi, the contemporary kings of the Orient, still find Christ, not in a stable in Bethlehem, but in you and me?

We profess to be Christians, which means we hold ourselves out as being close imitations of the Son of God himself. If visitors from the East do not see Christ in us, then we have to ask: Where have *we* gone wrong? And if visitors from the East do not find Christ in us, where will they find him? Will they realize the richness of Christ by their encounter with us, or will they simply return to their country by another way?

Questions for Further Discussion:

1. What is an "epiphany?" What is the significance of the magi for your faith life?

2. Do you think visitors from the East are able to find Christ in us? Why or why not?

12
BAPTISM IS LIKE A ROSE
Baptism of the Lord (B)

- Isaiah 42:1–4, 6–7
- 1 John 5:1–9
- Mark 1:7–11

For those who love roses, I have a story that might interest you. I recently heard about a rose, long thought to have vanished from North America, that has been rediscovered. It is called the musk rose and it blooms late in the fall, even in early winter. It was brought to this country from England during colonial times and was thought to have died out. But a group of rose lovers began a search for it in old cemeteries and abandoned home sites, until eventually they found a lone specimen growing not far from Thomas Jefferson's Monticello. Now it is being protected and cuttings are being made, in hopes that it will be further propagated.

I tell you this story because it reminds us of our baptism. Our baptism is like a beautiful rose planted in the good soil of our lives, usually when we are infants; then it is usually forgotten, while it continues to grow secretly, with a kind of veiled beauty. At certain times in our lives it is rediscovered and celebrated, bringing us new grace like the splendor of a rose in full bloom.

By reflecting on the baptism of Jesus, we can better appreciate the hidden rose which is our own baptism. From my own reflection, there are two words I would give you regarding the baptism of our Lord. They are: *assurance* and *mission.* Jesus' baptism was a moment of assurance and a moment of mission.

First, assurance. It may seem strange at first to think that Jesus needed assurance, that he needed affirmation and acceptance. That thought seems strange only if we forget that Jesus was human. Jesus, like us, experienced self-doubt and indecision, especially at this point in his life.

Indeed, the gospel accounts of Jesus' baptism reflect that uncertainty. Part of the uncertainty had to be the paradox of a man without sin accepting a baptism that was proclaimed to be for the remission of sin. John the Baptist shares in that uncertainty, for he tries to discourage Jesus from being baptized. St. Jerome in one of his early writings quotes fragments from an apocryphal work that suggest that it was Mary and the family of Jesus who urged him to be baptized by John. The fragment from the *Gospel According to the Hebrews* that St. Jerome quotes has Jesus saying: "Wherein have I sinned, that I should go and be baptized by him? Unless perhaps this very thing that I have said is a sin of ignorance." Jesus lived with uncertainty.

It is comforting for us to know that Jesus experienced uncertainty, that he came slowly to realize who he was and what he was called to be. We too live with uncertainty. We spend our lives struggling to accept as real the great truths about ourselves: that we are made in the image of God, loved unconditionally by God and destined for an unimaginable life in union with God. We need assurance—just as Jesus did—if we are to claim the dignity of who we are.

Jesus needed assurance at this critical juncture of his life. And he received it. His baptism was a moment of assurance. It was that moment when the voice of God resounded in the depths of his heart, giving him assurance that he was God's beloved Son. From that assurance came the courage to enter fully into the saving life he was called to live.

We receive that same assurance, that same affirmation and acceptance, at the moment of our baptism. It is then that the voice of God is heard in the depths of our being: "You are my beloved child. I accept you into the love of the Trinity."

I have never seen a sad face at a baptism. The reason for that is clear: at the moment of baptism, the voice of God giving assurance that a new member of Christ's body has been received by God is heard mysteriously by those present. And if we listen deeply, we can still hear those same words of assurance echoing softly in our own lives, day after day, moment by moment. The words of assurance are like a hymn, sometimes whispered softly, and at moments rising to a great crescendo.

His baptism was not only a moment of assurance for Jesus, it was also a moment of *mission*. Perhaps that, too, accounts for some of the uncertainty. With the assurance of God came the clear realization that he was being commissioned by God for something no human had ever before undertaken: the redemption of our race. The sinless one had accepted baptism and with it accepted the sins of all humankind. In the words of Isaiah, Jesus was being sent to "bring forth justice to the nations." Jesus must have known at that moment of mission that he was being sent as "a covenant to the people, a light to the nations, to open the eyes that are blind, to bring out the prisoners from the dungeon, from the prison those who sit in darkness" (Isaiah 42:6-7).

Perhaps the reason the rose which is our baptism remains hidden, perhaps the reason we do not tend to it, is because our baptism sets us as well on a mission. We are not baptized to be rugged individualists, we are baptized into a community. We are baptized to be partners with Christ in fulfilling his mission of bringing light to the nations, of opening the eyes of the blind, of freeing prisoners from confinement. The implications of this mission we undertake at baptism are immense. At baptism we receive an indelible mark on our souls. From that moment on everything we do is to be equally marked with a sign of God's love and favor.

The mission we accept at baptism is *not* a painless journey. The rose of baptism blooms surrounded by thorns. Real growth is *always* painful. But from the pain and suffering of our mission comes increased awareness that we are truly accepted and chosen by God. The clarity that comes from living faithfully the life begun at baptism enables us to experience at a deeper and deeper level the love God has for us and all of creation. What began as a moment of assurance gradually becomes a life of assurance, blossoming out into eternity.

Today is a day to stop and smell the roses. Stop and appreciate what was begun in us, and which often remains hidden. Spring is not far away. Soon the roses which now are hidden will break forth again in blossom. Attend to those roses. Attend as well to the rose of your baptism.

Questions for Further Discussion:

1. Describe what your baptism means to you. Has it remained hidden like a forgotten rose?

2. Do you experience both assurance and mission in your baptism?

PART THREE
Ordinary Time
HOMILIES 13–19

The term "Ordinary Time" may be misleading. In the context of the liturgical year the term "ordinary" does not mean "usual or average." Ordinary time here means "not seasonal." Ordinary time is that part of the Liturgical Year that lies outside the seasons of Lent-Easter and Advent-Christmas. In Ordinary Time, the Church celebrates the mystery of Christ not in one specific aspect but in all its aspects. The readings during the liturgies of Ordinary Time help to instruct us on how to live out our Christian faith in our daily lives.

The Liturgical Year: An In-depth Look[1]

13
COME AND SEE
Second Sunday in Ordinary Time (B)

- 1 Samuel 3:3b–10, 19
- 1 Corinthians 6:13c–15a, 17–20
- John 1:35–42

In today's Gospel, Jesus asks the perennial question that, in some form, we hear repeated again and again in our own lives: "What are you looking for?" It is an intriguing question with broad theological implications. Jesus probably was not concerned that the two disciples might be stalking him; he was more concerned with what they were really seeking in their lives.

But notice that the two disciples, like ourselves, perhaps, as we struggle to discern the meaning of our own lives, do not give an answer. They respond, instead, with another question: "Rabbi, where are you staying?" (John 1:38). This evasive response is an equally provocative question. Does it mean a physical place or is it a shy way of seeking for a deeper spiritual answer? The Greek word *menein*, translated as "staying," can mean "to lodge." It can also have theological content, suggesting a desire to dwell or abide with God.[2]

Were the mystery of God-among-us simply a philosophical matter, Jesus might have answered with an abstract dissertation on the ramifications of his question and the equally pregnant question posed by the disciples. But the mystery of the incarnation is not imparted to us through abstract theses. It is not something that can be solved in the mind. Rather, it is best approached through the ordinary. And so, Jesus says, "Come and see" (John 1:39).

And how do you picture the two disciples passing the time with Jesus on that day, at "about four o'clock in the afternoon," when they came to see the place where Jesus was staying? Do you picture him describing what it was like when, as we heard last Sunday, the Spirit descended like a dove upon him? Do you see Jesus laying out for them an explanation of what it meant when John said in today's gospel, "Look, here is the Lamb of God"? Do you imagine Jesus making a kind of PowerPoint presentation on the mystery of the incarnation? What it meant to be the Christ? Probably not.

Here is how I picture that first encounter: They sat around, talked, shared food and drink. They talked about fishing, about the harvest, local politics. In short, they hung out together. It was most likely small talk with huge implications. Rather than filling up their minds, Jesus lifted up their hearts. They liked him—the way he smiled, the way he moved, the look in his eyes, his changing expressions—everything about him pleased and attracted them. They liked the way he embraced them, the way he smelled, the way he touched them, the way he listened, his silences, his keen observations, his laughter, his humor, his stories, the way he understood, accepted and acknowledged their deepest needs. And before they left, they had fallen in love with him. Perhaps during the course of this first encounter Jesus may have quoted the Old Testament, may have given some tentative hints of what his ministry would be and, perhaps, how it would differ from that of John the Baptist, whom these two disciples had been following. But my bet is that, for the most part, they just enjoyed each other's company.

I base my own imaginative reflection on what I have observed of how contemporary disciples come to follow Jesus. If you were ever present for the RCIA rite of acceptance for catechumens and candidates, you've heard the presider ask this question: "What do you ask of God's Church?" Which is another way of saying, "What are you looking for?"

The candidates answer in a strong voice that echoes our own deepest desire: "Faith."

The candidates are then asked, "What does faith offer you?"

Their simple response: "Eternal life."

When the rite of acceptance is finished and we move to the Liturgy of the Word, what gospel is suggested? *Today's* gospel! Today's gospel, with its thought-provoking questions and its directive, "Come and see."

There is a clear connection between the candidate's response of faith that offers eternal life and the disciples hanging out with Jesus at four o'clock in the afternoon. In John's gospel, eternal life is promised to those who come to Jesus, to those who look on him, and to those who believe in him.[3] The candidates who enter the Church during the rite of acceptance embody each of these three ways: they are coming to Jesus, they want to see him, and they want to believe in him. But, of course, faith cannot be handed to them, it cannot be given to them as a neatly packaged theological gift on an ecclesiological platter, it cannot be given them through even the best of instruction. It comes to them the same way it came to the two disciples—by hanging out with Jesus, by seeing Jesus, by experiencing his hospitality, his touch, his ordinariness. And where do they find these qualities? Where do they see Jesus? You know the answer to that. It is in *us* that they must meet *Jesus*. If they don't meet him there, it is unlikely they will find him in anything else we have to offer as Church.

During the RCIA process the candidates will learn much about "the faith." But that is not what brings them into a loving relationship with the Lord through the Church. It is their recognition of Jesus in each person they meet in the parish: the RCIA team, the pastor, and most importantly, each one of you as individual members of this congregation. This is the way they come to faith. Your hospitality is now the hospitality of Jesus. Your smiles, your stories, your reaching out to others through a friendly word after Mass, your very body language now mirrors what the first two disciples saw in Jesus during that Galilean four-o'clock-in-the-afternoon rite of acceptance.

That is how the mystery of the incarnation is revealed. That is how we come to see Jesus.

Questions for Further Discussion:

1. What do you picture the first disciples doing during that four-o'clock-in-the-afternoon meeting with Jesus?

2. How do you think people come to faith in Jesus?

14
THE UNIVERSE IS MADE OF STORIES, NOT ATOMS
Third Sunday in Ordinary Time (B)

> • Jonah 3:1–5, 10
> • 1 Corinthians 7:29–31
> • Mark 1:14–20

If you think back to last Sunday's gospel, you will remember that it was very similar to the gospel we just heard. Both the Gospel of John, heard last Sunday, and Mark's gospel today describe the call of the first disciples. One difference is that Mark tells us the first four disciples—Simon, Andrew, James, and John—were fishermen. Simon and Andrew were casting their nets when the call to discipleship came; James and John were mending their nets.

I remember that in his homily a priest I know posed the intriguing question: "What did they talk about that afternoon, when the disciples left what they were doing and followed Jesus?"

Today, I have the answer. Jesus and the four disciples told stories.

How do I know they told stories? Because a wise person once said, "The universe is made of stories, not atoms." (That wise person was Muriel Rukeyser, the poet.)[4]

What kind of stories did they tell? They told fish stories.

How do I know they told fish stories? Simple. All four of the first disciples were fishermen. When you are with fishermen, you tell fish stories.

So, you might be asking, "What kind of fish story did Jesus tell?"

He probably told the greatest fish story in the entire Bible—the story of Jonah. How do I know *that*? Because the Church has placed a short excerpt from that story in the Sunday lectionary as today's first reading. Moreover, the story of Jonah has much to say about discipleship.

If you knew only today's short excerpt from Jonah you might think Jonah was a perfect disciple. After all, the reading describes the prophet as a great success: Jonah heard God's call, walked only one day through the city when everyone there converted and believed in God, proclaimed a fast, "and everyone, great and small, put on sackcloth" in repentance (Jonah 3:5). Even God's mind was changed, for the Ninevites were not destroyed as God had threatened. Some accomplishment! Some disciple!

But it is the *rest* of the story of Jonah that really teaches us about discipleship. It is the part of the Jonah story you did not hear today that tells us the most about being a disciple, whether you are Simon, Andrew, James, John, or one of us sitting here this morning.

Jonah was, in truth, a very reluctant disciple—a disobedient disciple, a whiner, a complainer. At the start of the story, God calls Jonah to preach to the Ninevites, Israel's worst enemy. And what does Jonah do? He immediately jumps on a ship—heading in the *opposite* direction. A violent storm comes up and the ship is in danger of sinking. The sailors somehow know that Jonah is the cause of their peril because he is fleeing from the Lord. They confront Jonah.

And then we catch a hint of why Jesus might have told this fish story to his new disciples. Despite all his many weaknesses, Jonah offers himself to save the stricken ship. Jonah is a type of redeemer figure. He says to the sailors, "Pick me up and throw me into the sea;

then the sea will quiet down for you" (Jonah 1:12). And the sailors did just that. And suddenly calm spread over the sea. All was well.

And what happened to Jonah? Now you come to the part that convinces me that the author of Jonah has to be the patron saint of people who tell fish stories. You know this part. A fish—a really big fish—a fish bigger than the one that got away—swallows up poor Jonah.

And how long did Jonah remain in the belly of the whale? I think Jesus might have paused here to let this imagery sink in. *Three* days. Matthew tells us that later, when the Pharisees were pressing him to work some sign, that Jesus would say: "No sign will be given to [this generation] except the sign of the prophet Jonah" (Matt 12:39–41).

The story goes on. The great fish miraculously spits Jonah out on the dry land so that Jonah could travel to Nineveh, the very place God had called him to. And as today's reading tells us, his preaching was a great success.

But the story does not end there. After Nineveh is converted, Jonah begins to sulk, he grows angry and complains that God has been merciful to the Ninevites. God causes a gourd plant to grow up and give Jonah some shelter but then, just as suddenly, it withers. Jonah was so depressed by now that he asks for death. God concludes:

> You are concerned about the bush, for which you did not labor and which you did not grow; it came into being in a night and perished in a night. And should I not be concerned about Nineveh, that great city, in which there are more than a hundred and twenty thousand persons who do not know their right hand from their left, and also many animals? (Jonah 4:10–11)

If they were paying attention, the first disciples might have drawn some important lessons about discipleship from this story of Jonah. We might, too. The first lesson is that sometimes we hear God's call but we go in the opposite direction. We say to Jesus that we will follow him, but then the memory of that resolution fades and we go back to our nets. And yet, in spite of that tendency, God still brings about good through us, just as God did through Jonah.

That was certainly the case with Peter and the other disciples. Simon left his nets, swearing to follow Jesus wherever he might lead, only to turn and run in the opposite direction from Calvary. And where did Jesus find him? Back with his nets. But the story did not end there: Peter left his nets again and followed Christ, even to his own martyrdom. It is the same with us: We turn back again and again to our nets, only to encounter Christ again, to hear the call again and to follow him.

The second lesson the disciples might have drawn from the story of Jonah is that God's mercy cannot be limited. Jonah, and the Israelite people for whom it was written, could not conceive of God being merciful to a people as wicked as the Ninevites. The story of Jonah strikes directly at this viewpoint. The story prepares the way for the gospel of Jesus with its message of redemption for all, both Jew and Gentile. All four of the disciples in today's gospel would have difficulty with that message. James and John once asked Jesus to call down destruction upon a town that had treated them badly. Peter would struggle with Paul over the admission of Gentiles to the Christian community. Perhaps in those moments they remembered Jesus telling them the story of Jonah. And perhaps we need to remember it when we struggle to integrate the reality of God's unlimited mercy into our thought and actions.

The universe *is* made of stories, *not* atoms. May our stories be stories of mercy, stories of turning back to God, stories of true discipleship. May our stories become a part of the great story of Christ's redemption of the world.

Questions for Further Discussion:

1. How would you apply the story of Jonah to your own life?
2. Where in our world do you think the message of God's mercy needs to be heard today? Why?

15
THE LIGHT OF CHRIST CASTS NO SHADOW
Presentation of the Lord (B)

> • Malachi 3:1–4
> • Hebrews 2:14–18
> • Luke 2:22–40

Light and shadow. Whether you are pagan or Christian, or just interested in weather predictions, these are the symbols of this day.

We celebrate the Presentation of the Lord with candles and song as we recall how Joseph and Mary brought Jesus, the Light of the World, the light that would overcome the shadows of night, to the Temple to be consecrated according to Jewish custom. But long before the arrival of Christianity, in the cold north country of Europe, ancient peoples were conscious of the perennial struggle in nature between light and shadow. At this same time of year they celebrated the pagan feast of Imbolc, marking the midpoint between the dark shadows of the winter solstice and the light of the spring equinox. Perhaps in some way this ancient awareness of the tension between light and shadow prepared the way for their later acceptance of the Christian celebration of Candlemas Day, a feast celebrated with procession and song, with the blessing, lighting, and distributing of candles (always from beeswax).[5]

The designation of this feast as Candlemas Day developed slowly. From the earliest days of Christianity, the Church celebrated "the fortieth day after Epiphany," indicating that Epiphany was the original celebration of Christ's birth. In the latter part of the fourth century the feast was moved to February 2nd, reflecting the change to December 25th as the feast of Christ's nativity. In the East this day was celebrated as a feast of the Lord, while in the West it was traditionally thought of as a feast of Mary, often referred to as the Purification of the Virgin Mary. The new title of today's feast the Presentation of the Lord (changed after Vatican II), shows that now it is more correctly thought of as a feast of the Lord.

Gradually the celebration of this feast took on the form that we now experience. The procession was introduced by Pope Sergius in the late eighth century. The blessing of candles did not come into common use until the eleventh century. When German settlers arrived in Pennsylvania in the 1700s, they brought with them a tradition of celebrating Candlemas Day,[6] a day when candles were blessed and distributed to the people as a sign of light, a beacon of hope in the long winter darkness.

The German settlers who brought the tradition of Candlemas Day to America also brought with them another ancient legend or superstition involving the conflict between shadow and light: the notion that the weather on Candlemas Day was a forecast of how the weather during the next weeks would be. Thus, the early English saying:

> If Candlemas be fair and bright,
> Winter has another flight.
> If Candlemas brings clouds and rain,
> Winter will not come again.

And from the Germans:

> For as the sun shines on Candlemas Day,
> So far will the snow swirl until May.
> For as the snow blows on Candlemas Day,
> So far will the sun shine before May.

And the Germans brought with them another tradition—Groundhog Day. An early Pennsylvania "Dutch" diarist recorded on February 4, 1841:

> Last Tuesday, the 2nd, was Candlemas day, the day on which, according to the Germans, the Groundhog peeps out of his winter quarters and if he sees his shadow he pops back for another six weeks nap, but if the day be cloudy he remains out, as the weather is to be moderate.[7]

People have been gathering in Punxsutawney, Pennsylvania since February 2, 1886, for the official celebration of Groundhog Day. At 7:25 AM, on Gobbler's Knob, Punxsutawney Phil, a pampered groundhog (also known as a woodchuck) weighing 15 pounds, is pulled from his heated burrow under a simulated tree stump to make his prediction. According to records kept since 1887, Phil has been right in this prognostication only 39 percent of the time.

This day gained further notoriety a few years ago when the classic film *Groundhog Day*, starring Bill Murray, was released. In this film we can find a contemporary reflection on the struggle between shadow and light. Bill Murray plays the role of a slightly jaded television weather man who is sent to Punxsutawney to cover the annual prognostication. Murray, who openly displays his boredom with Groundhog Day, mysteriously finds himself reliving Groundhog Day over and over and over. At first, he uses the never-ending repetition of Groundhog Day to indulge his every appetite, since no matter what happens he starts over again the next morning when the alarm goes off at 6:00 AM. Finally, having exhausted himself in pursuit of sex, food, reckless adventures, and love, he turns to doing good for others. Gradually Murray sees the light and turns from the shadow world of self-indulgence to a life of caring for others. Once he does, he finds true love and is able to move on to the next day of his life, which he does with new joy and meaning.

No matter how you approach it, this day is about shadow and light. It is the light of Christ in our lives that makes the difference between a meaningless cycle of events and a life of unlimited meaning. The light of Christ casts no shadow. It casts no shadow, for it penetrates us. And when it does, it does not matter what the weather may be for the next six weeks, or months, or years. The light of Christ has brought us eternal springtime.

Questions for Further Discussion:

1. How would you describe the struggle between shadow and light in our world today?

2. If you have seen the movie *Groundhog Day,* what was its message to you?

16
THE AGE OF NO SECRETS
Fifth Sunday in Ordinary Time (B)

> • Job 7:1–4, 6–7
> • 1 Corinthians 9:16–19, 22–23
> • Mark 1:29–39

Today's readings are about secrets. Or, stated differently, the readings are about a great truth which was once a secret but is no more. The great truth, now revealed, is this: Our God is a God of compassion, a God who wants to be with us and to suffer with us.

We see this truth explicated (albeit dimly) in the story of Job. In this reading, Job laments that life seems a drudgery. Job has suffered "months of emptiness and nights of misery" (Job 7:3). He is filled with restlessness; he is without hope and he seems convinced that he will never see happiness again.

These are words to which each of us can relate in some way; they describe an experience of desolation as familiar today as when the book of Job was written. They raise the perennial question of the meaning of suffering: Why do I suffer? Why do the innocent suffer right along with the not so innocent? Every authentic religion must confront these questions.

But to appreciate Job's lament, and to hear Job's answer to the perennial question, you have to know the *whole* story. If you haven't done so, I would strongly urge you to go home today and read, or reread, the little book of Job. It is a classic.

The book begins with the pious and upright Job enjoying great prosperity. But one day Satan, after "going to and fro on the earth," comes to the Lord and proposes that Job be tested. Take away his prosperity, Satan posits, and he will *surely* blaspheme God. And so it happens. Job loses everything—his property, his children, his good health. He is in a miserable state but *still* he does not complain against God. Instead, he turns to his friends for condolence. In a series of speeches they argue that his suffering *must* be punishment for some wrongdoing. Job must repent of whatever he has done wrong. But Job can find nothing for which he should repent. Job eventually reaches the conclusion that even the just must suffer, that we cannot probe into the depths of the divine omniscience. His conclusion is summed up in the words, "the Lord gave, and the Lord has taken away; blessed be the name of the Lord" (Job 1:21).

When we suffer, Job's words are somewhat consoling. But we know there is yet more. We know that God is a God of compassion. To understand compassion, it helps to start with the Latin roots. It comes from two words, *cum*, meaning "with" and *patior* or *passio,* meaning "to suffer." Thus, compassion means to suffer *with* someone. As followers of Christ, we believe that God suffers with humankind. Whenever we suffer as Job did, God is not an uninterested bystander; God is intimately involved in our suffering. That is the great truth that was still a secret in Job's time.

It was still a secret at the start of Mark's gospel. If you pick up any good commentary on Mark, you will hear about the "messianic secret." Throughout Mark's gospel Jesus will be shown healing and performing miracles, but there is usually a cautionary word to his followers: "Don't say anything about this. Keep it quiet." In today's gospel, it is the demons who are not permitted to reveal the truth about Jesus.

Why the secrecy on Jesus' part? I think it is because Jesus recognized that his followers might easily miss the truth about God's compassion. He knew that those who witnessed the healing of Peter's mother-in-law, the curing of those who were ill, the freeing of those possessed by demons—these people might see him merely as a healer, a miracle worker. Truly, compassion *does* involve acts of kindness and concern for others, but the core meaning is to suffer *with* someone, to be present to the other person, to help another bear suffering and thereby to learn better how to bear our own suffering. The disciples of Jesus would not fully realize this truth until they had witnessed his suffering on the cross and had encountered him as the risen Christ. Then the truth would be revealed. Then they would be living in the age of no secrets. Then they would know that, indeed, God is a God of compassion, who suffers with humankind.

It is when we get to Paul that we see there are no more secrets. Paul's writings are filled with the excitement of the gospel; he has the energy, even the intoxication, of the truth fully realized. When he is weak, he knows God suffers with him. Paul was one of the first great witnesses in the age of no secrets.

We live in that age as well, the age of no secrets. We too must witness to the truth about God's compassion. We must be the mediators of God's compassion to the world. But we can only witness to that truth if we know what compassion is.

Let me tell you a story of someone who modeled what compassion means.

The writer Irma Zaleski[8] tells the story of a friend of hers who, at the start of the Second World War, was a medical student in Warsaw, Poland, then occupied by Germany. The Soviet Army took over East Poland and her mother and brother were sent off to a concentration camp in Siberia. When this young woman heard of her family's plight, she escaped from the Germans and made her way back to her home town. There she began a quest to receive permission to join her family in Siberia.

The Soviet officials thought she was crazy and refused to give her permission. But she persisted and eventually was given what one Soviet official called "permission to die."

And so she traveled for hundreds of miles by freight train through the Russian winter until, after walking the last 20 kilometers through the snow, she arrived at the concentration camp. She brought with her a small bag of medicines. In the camp, she tended to her mother and brother until each of them died.

Then she tells of how, when she herself was deathly ill with typhoid, a priest, who was also a prisoner in the camp, would come to visit her every day, after working many hours in the cold. She said he would sit by her bed and talk to her. He never talked about religion. He never tried to convert her. They simply talked about Warsaw, about the streets they knew, about restaurants, and concerts they had attended. After she left the camp and returned to Poland, this woman said she would have died, were it not for that priest. *That* was compassion. *Not* preaching, *not* searching for religious reasons to explain the suffering. Just being present and suffering with the other person.

The woman was asked how she survived the horrible experience of the camps. She said she could not have survived if she had gone there to *save* her family. She survived, because she went there to *suffer* with them.

The real answer, then, to the question raised by Job is the Cross. The Cross is the clearest expression of God's compassion. When we look at the Cross, we are reminded that God is suffering with us. No religion can take away suffering. But the great consolation our Church offers is the sure knowledge that God is with us in our suffering.

When we encounter suffering in our lives, in our families, at work, we may be tempted to think that we suffer alone. But the rebuttal that comes from the Cross is this: our God is a God of compassion. God suffers with us.

Questions for Further Discussion:

1. When you suffer loss do the words of Job—"the Lord gave, and the Lord has taken away"—offer consolation? What is needed to be able to make these words our own?

2. In the story of the Polish woman in the concentration camp, what does it mean that she survived because she went there to suffer with her family?

17
YOURS ARE THE HANDS
Sixth Sunday in Ordinary Time (B)

- Leviticus 13:1–2, 44–46
- 1 Corinthians 10:31–11:1
- Mark 1:40–45

Don't you wonder what the disciples thought, or whispered among themselves, when Jesus healed the leper, when he touched a man considered impure? A leper at the time of Jesus was a complete outcast.

Scholars tell us that the many skin conditions that made a person unclean were probably not true leprosy. Nevertheless, they were associated with death, a form of living death, and the person who came in contact with such a condition was rendered impure.

I have to think that the disciples were shocked and deeply concerned by their master's actions. And I wonder if they didn't at least think, if not say, something like, "Lord, you just touched a leper, an unclean person—shouldn't you do something to purify yourself?"

I remember an experience I had quite a few years ago, back when the AIDS epidemic was just beginning. A man infected with the AIDS virus came to me for help in getting Social Security disability benefits. I knew the man had AIDS, but I met with him, helped him with his case and then, at the end of the interview, I did something which to me seemed somewhat compassionate: I reached out and shook the man's hand.

But then I did something very human. As soon as the man had left and the elevator doors had closed behind him, I slipped quickly into the bathroom and washed my hands with a lot of soap and hot water. I was willing to reach out to this contemporary unclean man, but only with great caution. My actions illustrate our human condition when it comes to dealing with outcasts. We are prompted by grace to reach out to others but our own human need for self-protection holds us back.

How different my approach was from Jesus' approach! And we might ask: *why* did Jesus touch this man? After all, he could have healed him from a safe, clinical distance.

I suspect Jesus touched this man to give his disciples, and us, a disturbing example. In effect, Jesus was saying: if I can touch this unclean man, this sinner, this outcast, who under the law must live apart from the community, then you too can touch, welcome, even *embrace* the outcasts you encounter.

And that is what the gospel challenges us to do today: find the outcasts in our families, in our work, in our community, and touch them! And we know these outcasts are everywhere. The black sheep of the family, the difficult person at work, the transient at the library. *All* are in need of a healing touch. If not the touch of our hands, then certainly the touch of our full presence, our smile, our kind and gentle words.

Christ depends on us now to touch the outcasts. In the words of a prayer attributed to St. Teresa of Avila:

Christ has no body now but yours,
No hands, no feet on earth but yours.
Yours are the hands through which he touches all the world.
Yours are the eyes through which he looks compassion
    on the world.
Yours are the feet through which he walks to do good.
Christ has no body now but yours.

In the book *Tuesdays with Morrie,*[9] which tells the story of a man dying from ALS (Lou Gehrig's disease), Morrie says that one of the consolations of becoming debilitated is that others now touch him. How tragic that he had to wait so long!

Why are we called to touch the outcast? Because salvation is experienced most fully in community: the community of a loving relationship between husband and wife, among family members, in a loving and caring religious community, in a society that truly has compassion for the outcast—this is where God's saving presence is experienced. God's love remains constant for the outcast, but the person on the margins struggles to experience it, and believe—in the face of all the evidence to the contrary—that it could possibly be *true.* God's love flows through our touch, reminding and reassuring those who feel unlovable that they are, indeed, deeply and intensely loved by God. We must be great touchers, great healers, great lovers.

But the leper in today's story reminds us that we too at times feel like outcasts. Each of us feels at some time separated from our community, and we feel the anguish of being separated from God. We too are in need of healing. The marvelous reality is that Christ continues to touch us. And he is not limited to the physical hands that touched the leper. Now Christ touches us in a mysterious way with the hands of his glorified body. He touches us when we turn to him in prayer, when we take the risk of reconciliation, when we receive him in the Eucharist. By our walking through these doors, we say to Christ, time after time, "If you choose, you can heal me." And he says back to us without reservation, "I do choose. Be healed."

Christ came into this world and left his imprint on everything he touched. Even death. Christ touched death itself and transformed it. When we come to the end of our time on earth, it is not death that awaits us, but Christ. When that knowledge touches the deepest part of our awareness, then we are truly healed.

Through this holy Eucharist we are about to receive, may we be more deeply healed; may we become more fully the hands, the eyes, the feet of Christ; may we be Christ to a suffering world.

Questions for Further Discussion:

1. Who are the outcasts of our day? Do you find it difficult to touch them?

2. Have you felt the touch of Christ healing you? How?

18
PARALYSIS OF SPIRIT
Seventh Sunday in Ordinary Time (B)

- Isaiah 43:18–19, 21–22, 24b–25
- 2 Corinthians 1:18–22
- Mark 2:1–12

Paralysis is a terrible thing. I have seen it many times in the clients I represent for Social Security disability benefits. I have seen paralysis caused by multiple sclerosis, spinal cord injuries, chronic fatigue syndrome. It is an absolutely terrible thing to see. But there is something more terrible than physical paralysis. More terrible yet is paralysis of the spirit.

When we heard Mark's gospel today, perhaps we felt pity for the paralytic, lying helpless on his mat, being lowered down by his friends through a hole in the roof so he might approach Jesus. But in truth, this is not the man to pity. Pity, instead, the scribes and those who thought as they did. The scribes and those who excluded the paralyzed man from the community are the ones deserving of pity. They were the ones suffering the most debilitating form of paralysis—paralysis of spirit.

The scribes were paralyzed by a firmly rooted conviction both logical and comforting. It was commonly accepted among Jewish authorities in Jesus' time that illness or suffering was caused by sin. If the man on the mat was paralyzed, it had to be because he, or perhaps even his parents, had sinned. And since he was a sinner, he had no business trying to reach the good rabbi, Jesus. His exclusion from the gathering was justifiable. He deserved to be alienated from their society.

The scribes' thinking has a kind of beguiling (if pretzel-like) logic to it. It presumes a direct connection between righteousness and blessing. If one is blessed, it must be because God is pleased with that person. If one is not blessed, God must be displeased. The person must have done something sinful and displeasing to God in order to warrant the affliction. Even someone apparently good and righteous suffering a misfortune must have some hidden transgression that warranted the result.

We are not immune from this thinking. We too are tempted to think that a person's misfortune was somehow *merited*. The homeless person asking for a handout *deserves* to be ostracized from our company, because he has *chosen* to be lazy and live off the system. The alcoholic or drug addict who has lost the ability to control his addiction *deserves* to be denied financial help or housing, because he has chosen his way of life. The gay man *deserves* to be abused because he has chosen a sinful lifestyle. There are probably still those who secretly harbor the belief that the AIDS virus is somehow a punishment from God for immoral behavior. All of these are but a few examples of how the paralysis of spirit that afflicted the scribes still grips our own attitudes.

Paralysis of spirit produces alienation. The paralytic in today's gospel was excluded from the community. He was not allowed to approach Jesus through the door but had to be lowered down through the roof. But even in his paralyzed state the man had something to teach the scribes and those who thought as they did. The man modeled the humility that is required by anyone seeking wholeness. He lay on his mat completely dependent on his friends. He had emptied himself of the self-righteousness of the scribes and those who presumed he was a sinner.

And Jesus rewards his humility. He frees the man from his physical bondage, restores his sense of wholeness and allows him to rejoin the community. The same probably cannot be said of the scribes and their fellow thinkers. They are the ones in authority who will continue in their paralysis, their paralysis of spirit. We will encounter them again and again as we move through Mark's gospel. They will be with us to the end, even on Good Friday, when their paralysis of spirit will have progressed to a deadly demand for Jesus' destruction.

Jesus came to set captives free. Not just those held in chains in a dark prison or paralyzed by physical disease. But more importantly—and expansively—to free those imprisoned by their own deadening presumptions. We must be mindful of the terrible possibility of becoming paralyzed in spirit. Look around you today in your home, your place of work, your neighborhood, this parish, and ask yourself: who is being excluded because of my own paralysis? Is it one of my children? My spouse? Is it the immigrant? The gay person? Is it the religious woman with many God-given talents who is being excluded from equal ministry in the Church? Am I being excluded because of the paralytic mindset of someone in authority? These are honest questions that arise naturally from today's gospel.

And the gospel teaches this as well: it teaches that those who are excluded, those who are alienated, those who are kept out of the inner circle will find their way in. They will, if necessary, break a hole in the roof and be lowered down before our amazed eyes. In the early days of the Church, someone was assigned the task of standing outside the place of worship to watch for Christ's return. Perhaps we should be doing something similar today: keeping our eyes on the "ceiling" of our Church, watching to see who is trying to break through.

Being freed from paralysis of spirit is a joyful experience. We all have been through it and will likely do so again. Perhaps no one is freed all at once. Rather, it might be said that our Christian life is a steady process of being freed. We need each other in this process. We need each other's honesty, each other's support and encouragement. And at the center of that freeing process stands Jesus who cuts through all the paralysis and says, "Stand up, take your mat and go to your home" (Mark 2:11). Go home to the community of Christians who have also been freed from paralysis of spirit.

Questions for Further Discussion:

1. Have you encountered paralysis of spirit in your life?
2. How do we free each other from such paralysis?

19
IT'S A BEAUTIFUL DAY IN THE NEIGHBORHOOD
Eighth Sunday in Ordinary Time (B)

- Hosea 2:16b, 17b, 21–22
- 1 Corinthians 3:1b–6
- Mark 2:18–22

One of my heroes died at about this time three years ago, and I want to say a few words in tribute to him. I do so because this man expressed in his life much of the richness of today's readings. By that I mean he modeled the gentle, loving, intimate God of Hosea. And he modeled the love of God that is the new wine of today's gospel, a wine that can only be stored in fresh wine skins.

You might not immediately think of this man as a hero. He was not a leader in war, not a great sports figure, not a great leader on the world scene. He was, instead, a humble, gentle, soft-spoken man who was at home with children. He was a Presbyterian minister; a man who came to fame on television but who never spoke of God on the air. He was a dear friend in every child's neighborhood. I am speaking, of course, of Mr. Rogers. Fred Rogers died February 27, 2003, at the age of 74 from stomach cancer.

I pay tribute to Mr. Rogers because he was, in a sense, a prophet like Hosea. If we think of a prophet as someone who speaks an important truth to us at a particular moment in history, a truth that we need to hear, then Mr. Rogers was a prophet. He appeared at a critical moment in history—the start of the television age, when that new medium, which has had such a powerful and pervasive effect on our culture, was just beginning. The truth he proclaimed is this: The medium of television need not be something that demeans children, that teaches children to be aggressive, that frightens children; it can be a medium that builds respect, strengthens and reassures. Indeed, that it can be a medium through which children learn to love themselves and others.

Mr. Rogers began his first children's television show in 1954 and he did so, he said, because of his dissatisfaction with what was being offered children in those early days. In place of aggressive and cynical TV fare, now so commonplace, Mr. Rogers created the kind of gentle, secure, imaginative neighborhood that every child needs. He imagined a neighborhood where children could be themselves and be loved for it. He taught children to love themselves and to love others. He taught children that even when a family is not perfect, when there is divorce or even death—subjects he dealt with on his show—they were still loved. And in doing all this, he planted the seeds for a positive image of God.

Although he never preached about God, Mr. Rogers probably did more for children's image of God than anything else on TV. It is said that children form their first image of God from their experience of their father and mother. For many children, Mr. Rogers was a surrogate father. And every time he stepped through the door, put on his familiar sweater and sneakers, and sang those words, "It's a beautiful day in this neighborhood," he helped form the consciousness of children, helping them to image a God who is faithful, kind and reassuring.

I think the prophet Hosea would have liked Mr. Rogers. Hosea also knew about the faithfulness, the tenderness and loving kindness of God. And Hosea knew about children. He had three of them. He uses images of children to speak about the love God has for Israel. In the eleventh chapter of Hosea, the prophet speaks these words for God:

> When Israel was a child, I loved him,
>   and out of Egypt I called my son....
> Yet it was I who taught Ephraim to walk,
>   I took them up in my arms;
>   but they did not know that I healed them.
> I led them with cords of human kindness,
>   with bands of love.
> I was to them like those
>   who lift infants to their cheeks.
>   I bent down to them and fed them
>   (Hosea 11:1, 3–4)

Hosea spoke those words 2700 years ago. We are still struggling to realize their meaning.

Hosea knew the joy and tenderness of intimate family life. But he also knew the anguish of marital discord. Hosea's wife, Gomer, was unfaithful and Hosea had to deal with suffering and separation. At times, Hosea could have used a neighbor like Mr. Rogers. But from his struggles with married life Hosea learned the ways of God.

What Hosea learned from his own family life he proclaimed at this particular moment in history: God is a faithful lover. The book of Hosea describes the relationship between God and Israel as one of gentle, intimate attachment. The prophetic message of Hosea is that even when Israel is unfaithful, even when Israel betrays the covenant of love, God is faithful. And Hosea's message is one of hope, for he prophesies in our first reading that God will continue to call Israel into the desert and will speak to her heart. And Israel will respond then as she did in the days of her youth.

The knowledge of God proclaimed by the prophet Hosea is the new wine of today's gospel. Or we might say it is the old wine which Hosea knew but which has been renewed, reconstituted, rejuvenated by Jesus Christ. So powerful is this new wine, this knowledge of the intimate, loving closeness of God, that it cannot be confined to the narrow categories of understanding God that the Pharisees had. It is this intoxicating new wine that so enlivened the early apostles that people thought they were drunk, even though it was early in the day. And it is this new wine, this clear knowledge that God is faithful, loving, intimate, tender, soft-spoken, that so graced the image of Mr. Rogers.

We come to Mass today and every Sunday to receive that new wine. But it cannot be stored in old wine skins. Every time we come here, we must come with fresh wine skins—I mean with hearts and minds that have been prepared to receive the new wine; hearts and minds that have been prepared through prayer, devotion, sacrifice, caring for our neighbor.

Soon we will start the great season of Lent. What a perfect time to prepare fresh wine skins. We will do that best if we take to heart the words of Hosea and let ourselves be led by God into the desert so that God may speak to our hearts. In the silence of our Lenten desert, we will come again to know that God is faithful, loving, tender, soft-spoken. And on Easter morning, filled with the new wine, we will rejoice in knowing that it is, indeed, a beautiful day in this neighborhood.

Questions for Further Discussion:

1. Do you agree that Mr. Rogers conveyed an image of God that was positive, a God who is faithful, kind and reassuring? Why or why not?

2. Is Lent a time to prepare your heart like a fresh wine skin? How will you do it?

PART FOUR

Lent

HOMILIES 20–26

We must remember the original meaning of Lent, as the *ver sacrum*, the Church's "holy spring," in which the catechumens were prepared for their baptism, and public penitents were made ready by penance for their restoration to the sacramental life in a communion with the rest of the Church. Lent is then not a season of punishment so much as one of healing. There is joy in the salutary fasting and abstinence of the Christian who eats and drinks less in order that his mind may be more clear and receptive to receive the sacred nourishment of God's word, which the whole Church announces and meditates upon in each day's liturgy throughout Lent. The whole life and teaching of Christ pass before us, and Lent is a season of special reflection and prayer, a forty-day retreat in which each Christian, to the extent that he is able, tries to follow Christ into the desert by prayer and fasting.

Thomas Merton, *Seasons of Celebration*[1]

20

LENTEN SPONTANEITY
Ash Wednesday (B)

- Joel 2:12–18
- 2 Corinthians 5:20–6:2
- Matthew 6:1–6, 16–18

Here is an exercise to help you appreciate Lent from the perspective of today's gospel: try to remember a time when someone did something kind or thoughtful for you. It has to be something done spontaneously, without any compulsion or expectation of reward. It cannot be something done as a return favor for something you did. While you are thinking about it, I will give you an example from my own experience.

There is a generous man in our community, whose name I will not mention, who several years ago did something thoughtful for me in a truly spontaneous way. I met this gentleman at the early morning celebration of *Las Mananitas* on the feast day of Our Lady of Guadalupe. He was wearing an attractive Mexican serape which prompted me to comment on how beautiful it was. He immediately slipped it over his head and handed it to me saying, "Take it. It is a gift for you." In that spontaneous act of generosity we see what Lent is about. Lent is about recovering our spontaneity!

Spontaneous acts of generosity are what Matthew is getting at in the gospel we just heard. Matthew records Jesus addressing the three traditional practices of Lent: almsgiving, prayer, and fasting. He shows us the nonspontaneous way of doing these things. In the first example, alms are given to the poor in order to win the praise of others; prayer is done ostentatiously in public, again, to win the praise of others; finally, fasting is done in a way that attracts attention and, presumably, the approval and praise of others.

What is wrong with each of these acts? They are all premeditated, they all lack spontaneity. The practices we begin on Ash Wednesday and continue throughout Lent are designed to increase our spontaneity, a human quality that went into decline when we abused the greatest gift God has given us: the gift of our free will. God wants to strengthen and restore our free will to its pure state during Lent. When we do things like fasting, prayer, and almsgiving in order to gain approval from others, or respect, or admiration, our will is not free the way God intends it to be.

Sponte, from which the word "spontaneous" derives, refers to a manifestation of the will free from compulsion.[2] If you give to the poor fund because you feel compelled to do so, you are not exercising your free will. By the same token, if you come to Mass with the expectation of being admired, again your act of worship is not a manifestation of pure free will. The same is true for any fasting or penance you take on during Lent. If you do those things because you feel some pressure to do so, or because you expect some reward, either in this life or in the next, then your free will still needs purifying.

That is a high standard but it is the standard set by Jesus in the gospel. And he sets the standard high for a good reason: Jesus knew that we are better people when we do things freely and willingly than when we feel coerced or compelled to do something. Jesus not only taught this, he *lived* it. There was no compulsion, no hope of reward or honor, that brought Christ into our world. He came of his own free will. And he did so in order to restore and purify our free will.

Our free will, our freedom to choose, is the greatest gift God has given us. It was given to us, not to be used arbitrarily, but so that we might voluntarily choose God. When our ancestors, whom we think of as Adam and Eve, chose badly, sin was the result. Christ's saving acts made it possible for us to once again use our free will to love, serve, and obey God, which is how we find true happiness.

So, whatever you have chosen to do this Lent, whether it be fasting, almsgiving or prayer, do it spontaneously. Do it without counting the cost or the credit. Do these things in the way Jesus did: with pure free will.

Questions for Further Discussion:

1. Have you thought of Lent as a time to increase your spontaneity? How might you do this?

2. Have you ever been the beneficiary of a spontaneous act of generosity? Explain.

21
THE BUSINESS OF LENT
First Sunday of Lent (B)

- Genesis 9:8–15
- 1 Peter 3:18–22
- Mark 1:12–15

I was sitting by my window, reflecting on today's readings and watching a flock of sparrows feasting at our bird feeder. I enjoy watching them as they hop about in the bushes, lining up to take turns at the tray, fluttering away at the slightest hint of danger. But as I watched, something unexpected happened, something sudden and violent. A small hawk darted in out of nowhere, snatched a sparrow from midair and landed in the snow nearby where he began feasting on his prize.

The intrusion of this sharp-eyed, steel-clawed raptor brought to mind a similar experience that Thomas Merton records in *The Sign of Jonas*.[3] Merton, while meditating in the garden house attic after dinner on February 10, 1950, was observing a flock of starlings, when:

> like lightning, it happened. I saw a scare go into the cloud of birds, and they opened their wings and began to rise off the ground and, in that split second, from behind the house and from over my roof a hawk came down like a bullet, and shot straight into the middle of the starlings just as they were getting off the ground. They rose into the air and there was a slight scuffle on the ground as the hawk got his talons into the one bird he had nailed.
>
> It was terrible and yet beautiful thing, that lightning flight, straight as an arrow, that killed the slowest starling.

After that, Merton found it difficult to pray but he concludes: "I think that hawk is to be studied by saints and contemplatives; because he knows his business. I wish I knew my business as well as he does his."[4]

On this first Sunday of Lent we would do well to study the hawk, to know the business of Lent the way a hawk knows his business. The hawk was doing what to him came naturally. He was focused and disciplined in the way God intended him to be. During Lent we strive to be the kind of people God intended us to be. We seek to be as focused as the hawk, to return to God with the keen, single-minded focus of a hawk in winter.

The opening chapters of Genesis point to a time when we humans were single-minded in our love of God. Back then, our focus was God alone. What follows after the misuse of our God-given freedom, expressed in the account of Adam and Eve's expulsion from the garden, is the story of a people out-of-focus, a people who repeatedly miss the mark, who stray from the business of loving God with whole-hearted dedication.

Chapters 6-8 of Genesis give us the richly imaginative story of the great flood, of Noah, the ark, all of it a colorful account of how God has worked to return humankind's focus to God alone. Using a common memory among ancient peoples of a great flood, the author of Genesis interprets this natural disaster as the devastating consequence of sin, of humankind's missing the mark. But the reading is also about hope, for God enters into covenant with all creation and even sets a rainbow in the clouds as a natural reminder of God's promise of restoration. God would restore our focus, not by destruction, but by love—love incarnate in Jesus Christ.

What the flood waters in Noah's time could not accomplish, the waters of baptism did. St. Peter sees the waters of the great flood as prefiguring the great flood of grace that would come with baptism. Not the destructive waters of a flood but the cleansing waters of baptism would be the means for making possible a single-minded concern for God.

The short gospel passage from Mark reveals a Jesus who, like us, was tempted to lose his focus. Unlike Matthew and Luke, Mark does not give us the details of the temptations Jesus faced, but we know them well: the temptations to focus on physical needs, power and prestige, rather than God. Like the hawk, Jesus knew his business well; Jesus never lost his focus, never missed the mark. From the temptation in the desert to Calvary, Jesus kept his focus on the prize: our salvation. We are the beneficiaries of that loving focus.

I offer you the hawk in winter as a symbol of your Lenten practice this year. The hawk knows his business well, and so must we. We must use every opportunity, whether it be fasting, prayer, or almsgiving, to focus more keenly on God. The hawk focused in order to survive in an unforgiving environment. Our milieu may not be as harsh but the need to be focused and attentive is just as real.

We must do all we can during Lent to stay focused, to be single-minded, to hit the mark. But at the end of the day we are mindful that it was the single-mindedness of Jesus that made it possible for us to claim the prize of eternal life.

Mindful of that truth, let me leave you with one other hawk image. A few years ago, at twilight, I came upon a small hawk, apparently lying dead in one of my flower beds. It appeared that he had flown into one of the large windows on the south side of my house. I picked up his limp carcass, tossed it into the garbage receptacle and replaced the lid. A short while later, out of curiosity, I came back for a closer look at the hawk. When I lifted the lid on that tomblike receptacle, the hawk, very much alive, came rocketing out and soared off into the heavens!

Questions for Further Discussion:

1. Can you picture Lent as being like a hawk focusing on a target? How will you maintain that focus this Lent?

2. Can you think of other images of Lent that are meaningful for you?

22
FUNDAMENTAL THINGS APPLY
Second Sunday of Lent (B)

> • Genesis 22:1–2, 9a, 10–13, 15–18
> • Romans 8:31b–34
> • Mark 9:2–10

On Thanksgiving Day, 1942, in the midst of World War II, Warner Studios released the movie *Casablanca*, a classic film that a year later would win an Oscar. That movie gave us the timeless song "As Time Goes By." The lyrics include these words, "The fundamental things apply, as time goes by."

This weekend, with parts of the world engaged in yet another war, we might ask, "What *are* the fundamental things that apply?" Each of us might offer a different answer. But I want to suggest something fundamental which, for Catholics, *always* applies, something so obvious we might overlook it. The fundamental thing for Catholics, in times of war and in times of peace, is the Mass.

I say the Mass, because today's gospel contains a metaphor of what is fundamental in every Mass: communion and sacrifice. The disciples follow Jesus to the top of a mountain where they see him transfigured. So luminous is his appearance that his clothes become dazzling white. The disciples are deeply drawn to this transfigured Christ. They adore. They worship. Peter even proposes something permanent—three tents in which to preserve the moment. Peter sums up his feelings in these words, "Rabbi, it is good for us to be here" (Mark 9:5).

The experience of Peter, James and John is like our own experience of communion. We are drawn to Christ present in the consecrated bread, the body of Christ. We find comfort there. We want to remain there, to preserve this moment of communion. The experience we have of Christ really present in the bread is like witnessing Christ transfigured before our eyes. Do we not find ourselves saying, like Peter, "It is good for us to be here"?

But then, notice what happens. After this deeply affective experience of Christ transfigured, Jesus leads the disciples back down the mountain. And, most importantly, he begins to talk to them about rising from the dead. We can infer from this that he was also talking about his own suffering, about the cross, about sacrifice. The disciples had experienced communion; now they had to learn about sacrifice.

And that points us to what is fundamental in the Mass. The Mass is about communion but it is also about sacrifice. These fundamental things always apply.

What I am going to say about these two distinct, but not separate, aspects of the Mass, I take from Father Edward Foley, a Capuchin priest who is a theologian, a teacher, and musician at Catholic Theological Union in Chicago.[5] Father Foley says that in many ways we have obscured the sacrificial nature of the Mass, as if the Mass were no different from a communion service. He points out that there are fruits of the Mass that are entirely different from the fruits of communion. And if we focus only on communion, without allowing the sacrifice part of the Mass to enter our imagination, then the Mass may, in Father Foley's words, become like a liturgical happy meal.

The imagery of the Mass is about sacrifice. We find it in the offertory, in the breaking of the bread, in the eucharistic prayer and in the cup of Christ's blood that we receive. The imagery of the Mass points to sacrifice and draws us more deeply into a life of sacrifice. Father Foley says that Christ's sacrifice is "gift exchange," meaning Christ comes to us as gift but we in turn must give ourselves back to him as self-sacrificing gift. That is the fundamental thing we still struggle to apply in our lives.

Father Foley believes there are two powerful forces at work in the Mass. One is centripetal—that is, one that centers us. It is a force that draws us in. We sing, "Gather us in, the meek and the lowly...." We are drawn to communion. We rest in Christ's comforting presence. And like the disciples, we would like to preserve that moment, to keep it permanent.

But there is a second force at work in the Mass. It is a kind of centrifugal force that sends us out. It sends us back down the mountain. So that we, having received the gift of Christ's sacrifice, are compelled by this force to go out into our world and give ourselves as well.

Father Foley cites the theologian David Powers in identifying three fruits we receive from the sacrifice of the Mass. They are: the ability to stand unflinchingly for the truth, the strength to stand for nonviolent justice, and an openness to hear the call to self-sacrificing mission.

First, "to stand unflinchingly for truth." Across the whole spectrum of issues—abortion, stem cell research, cloning, the death penalty, issues of war and peace—the Mass empowers us to stand unflinchingly for truth. But we cannot stand for the truth without searching for it. If we have not read Pope John Paul II's encyclical *Evangelium Vitae*, our stand for truth on human life issues may be spirited, but it will lack the clear ring of truth. If we oppose war in Iraq and Afghanistan, or even if we support it, but are unfamiliar with Catholic teaching on just war principles and nonviolence, then our stand for truth will lack the depth of Church teaching.

The sacrifice of the Mass can give us renewed strength to stand for nonviolent justice in our world, whether it be in our families, our neighborhoods or on the world scene. This fruit enables us to see that all people are included in the Body of Christ. And if one part of the body suffers, we are affected as well.

There is an alternative view of Christ's transfiguration that has always attracted me. This view holds that Jesus was *always* transfigured, that he was *always* dazzling in his glory, but no one could see it. The experience on the mountaintop was, then, about the disciples seeing Jesus for the first time as he always was. For a brief time, their eyes were opened. They would again be opened at the resurrection.

Perhaps, then, Christ is now transfigured in each of us, in every person around us, in the poor, in those we now despise and even hate. Perhaps a fruit of the Mass might be to begin to see all people, especially those we are taught to hate, as transfigured; to see each person made dazzling in appearance by the incarnate Word. Being able to see that way is the beginning of compassion.

Finally, a fruit of the Mass is a deeper awareness that we are being commissioned for a life of sacrifice. Like the disciples coming down the mountain, we still puzzle over what it means to rise from the dead. By now we should know: it means self-sacrifice, which leads to resurrection. It means exchange of gifts, giving back to Christ the gift he gives us.

The poet Robert Frost said all that he had learned about life could be summed up in three words, "It goes on." Or we might say, "time goes by." There will be times of war and times of peace. But through it all, fundamental things apply, as time goes by.

Questions for Further Discussion:

1. Are you aware of two forces—centripetal and centrifugal—at work in the Mass? How would you describe them?

2. In what way are you commissioned for a life of sacrifice in the Mass?

23
THE WAY OF COSTLY GRACE
Third Sunday of Lent (B)

- Exodus 20:1–17
- 1 Corinthians 1:22–25
- John 2:13–25

It is said that Jesus came among us to comfort the disturbed and to disturb the comfortable.

We hear many stories in the gospels of Jesus giving comfort and, I have to confess, I would prefer to preach about Jesus the Comforter than Jesus the Challenger. But on this third Sunday of Lent we are faced with a very challenging gospel. It challenges us to choose between the way of cheap grace and the way of costly grace.

Jesus comes to the Temple for Passover. There he encounters not his Father's house but a marketplace, filled with sheep and oxen, sellers of doves, money changers—a privileged class of Jewish merchants who were there to grease the wheels of Temple worship. Those coming to the Temple to offer sacrifice could not use common Roman currency to purchase a suitable animal. They had to exchange their secular coins for Temple coins in order to make a purchase. The money changers made a profit in the transaction. Some scholars think it may have been the money changers cheating the poor that evoked Jesus' anger. Others say it was simply his disgust at seeing the holiest place of Jewish worship turned into a place of commerce.

But perhaps what lay at the heart of Jesus' indignation was that God the Father was being taken for granted. The merchants and money changers had worked out a comfortable arrangement between the worship of God and their own material need, perhaps even their greed. If they were stealing from the poor or were placing their own material success ahead of God, they did so in disregard of the commandments we heard in the first reading. In their comfortable relationship with the Temple, they had chosen the way of cheap grace.

In contrast, Jesus models the way of costly grace. For a brief time (minutes, hours, we don't know how long), Temple worship was brought to a halt. Without money changers, there could be no Temple worship. Jesus had dared to substitute himself for the Temple worship. He declares, "Destroy this temple," meaning his own body, "and in three days I will raise it up" (John 2:19). And those whom he offended would do just that—destroy his body. In a few weeks we will hear this evidence brought against him. By speaking truth to the money changers, and being willing to accept the consequences of his actions, Jesus had chosen the way of costly grace.

The terms "cheap grace" and "costly grace" were coined by the twentieth-century-Lutheran theologian and minister, Dietrich Bonhoeffer, who was describing an attitude found among seemingly religious people not only at the time of Jesus but equally so today: an attitude that presumes a person can serve God without sacrifice.

Bonhoeffer, who was ordained at about the time the Nazi party came to power in Germany, was committed to making Christianity a reality in the world. Living the Christian life, and not merely talking about it, is the key to Bonhoeffer's message. Like Jesus in today's gospel, Bonhoeffer was committed to the truth and was willing to accept the consequences of his own integrity. He had this to say about "cheap grace" versus "costly grace":

> Cheap grace is the preaching of forgiveness without requiring repentance, baptism without church discipline, communion without confession, absolution without personal confession. Cheap grace is grace without discipleship, grace without the cross, grace without Jesus Christ, living and incarnate.

Costly grace is the treasure hidden in the field ....

Costly grace is the gospel which must be sought again and again. The gift which must be asked for, the door at which a man must knock.

Such grace is costly because it calls us to follow, and it is grace because it calls us to follow Jesus Christ. It is costly because it costs a man his life, and it is grace because it gives a man the only true life.[6]

Cheap grace is what wearies the pastor of any parish. Cheap grace is characterized by an attitude which treats the Church like a 7-Eleven convenience store, a place for a quick stop where we can pick up a little grace before hurrying on to other more important things. Cheap grace presumes that the Church and its ministers must be there for me, even though there is little sacrifice or commitment on my part.

Costly grace is what every Christian is called to, for it is the life of Christ. Costly grace calls for sacrifice. It demands that we declare the truth and be willing to accept the consequences. Jesus Christ is the true source and model of costly grace. But recent times have given us additional models. We think of Archbishop Romero, who was assassinated March 24, 1980, because of his opposition to the military regime in El Salvador. And we think of the Lutheran minister Dietrich Bonhoeffer. Bonhoeffer opposed Hitler and the Third Reich from the very beginning. In July 1939, Bonhoeffer was in New York City, where he could have sat out the war in safety. He chose, instead, to *return* to Germany where he would actively oppose the great lie that was Nazism. Throughout the war he was involved in the underground opposition to Hitler, including an unsuccessful coup attempt. Bonhoeffer was eventually arrested and, less than a month before Germany surrendered, he was executed. *That* is costly grace.

We do not have to give our life as Bonhoeffer did to experience costly grace. Little opportunities happen all the time. If we follow Christ, if we live lives of honesty and integrity in our families, at work, in our parish, then we can expect to suffer the consequences of costly grace. Yet in doing so, we experience a blessing, we gain new life.

Bonhoeffer experienced the new life that comes with costly grace. A fellow prisoner described him as being, "all humility and sweetness; he always seemed to diffuse an atmosphere of happiness, of joy in every smallest event in life....He was one of the very few men that I have ever met to whom God was real and close...."[7] When his executioners came for him, Bonhoeffer whispered to a fellow prisoner, "This is the end. For me the beginning of life."[8] Bonhoeffer expressed what we must all come to know: that to follow Christ on the way of costly grace is the beginning of life. May we choose the way of costly grace this Lenten season.

Questions for Further Discussion:

1. Can you think of other people who have chosen a life of costly grace? What do you think made it possible for them to make such a choice?

2. Can you think of examples of cheap grace?

24
BECOMING AN ORDINARY MAN
Fourth Sunday of Lent [Laetare Sunday] (B)

· 2 Chronicles 36:14–16, 19–23
· Ephesians 2:4–10
· John 3:14–21

There is an old Zen saying that goes: "When an ordinary man attains knowledge, he is a sage; when a sage attains understanding, he is an ordinary man."

That saying comes to mind when I think of Nicodemus, one of the most fascinating figures in John's gospel. He first appears in the third chapter of John when he "came to Jesus by night" (John 3:2). Coming to Jesus in the dark of night is by itself significant, for John often uses the motif of light contrasted with darkness (representing evil, untruth and ignorance) to denote those who come to believe in Jesus and those who choose not to. Nicodemus, it would seem, is one of those who as today's gospel says, "do what is true" and thereby "come to the light" (John 3:21).

Nicodemus was an ordinary man who had attained knowledge. He had become a sage. One source says that he "almost certainly belonged to the highest governing body of the Jewish people composed of priests (Sadducees), scribes (Pharisees) and lay elders of the aristocracy."[9] Nicodemus was clearly one of the elite among Jewish leaders, a man of authority, and well educated in the Hebrew Scriptures. Yet, even with his great knowledge, he did not understand. Jesus says to him at one point, "Are you a teacher of Israel, and yet you do not understand these things?" (John 3:10). Nicodemus' mode of understanding, which may have served him well up until then, did not help him in approaching Jesus. He was still in the mode of knowing about God rather than being *known* by God. He is reaching out to the truth, using the best of his ability for rational thinking, but all of it to no avail. Coming to believe in Jesus is not so much an encounter of the mind but of the heart. It would take heart-knowledge if Nicodemus were to move to the level of understanding.

Did Nicodemus ever come to that level of understanding that would make him an ordinary man? There is some basis for speculating that perhaps he did. After today's encounter in the third chapter of John, we meet Nicodemus again in chapter seven. There, in a tense scene that in an ominous way prefigures Good Friday, the Temple police are sent to arrest Jesus, only to be stymied by the authority of what they hear. When the authorities continue to plot against Jesus, it is Nicodemus who speaks up for him (John 7:50). At some likely risk to himself, Nicodemus says to those seeking Jesus' death, "Our law does not judge people without first giving them a hearing to find out what they are doing, does it?" (John 7:51). With that, the furor dissipated and Jesus went to the Mount of Olives. Nicodemus may not have reached the level of understanding to which Jesus was calling him, but he did intervene and his knowledge may have averted Jesus' death—at least for the time being.

John's gospel gives us one more opportunity to speculate whether Nicodemus came to understand with the heart. In the nineteenth chapter of John, it is Nicodemus who, along with Joseph of Arimathea, received from Pilate the body of Jesus and prepared it for burial. Nicodemus, who is still described as the one who came to Jesus by night, brought "a mixture of myrrh and aloes, weighing about a hundred pounds" which he used to embalm the body (John 19:39).

I am drawn to believe that Nicodemus did, in the end, understand Jesus, and *did* become an ordinary man. By ordinary man I mean someone who, despite great learning and a position of authority, does the *natural* thing that circumstances demand. And does it spontaneously, without circumspection. With still some risk to himself, Nicodemus undertook the heart-wrenching task of burying a friend and, perhaps, someone he had come to know as more than a great teacher. There is something in the ordinariness of Nicodemus' actions in this last segment that testifies to a deep transformation. Nicodemus had moved, in my judgment, from learned sage to ordinary man. He had attained understanding.

Nicodemus can be an inspiration for us to reflect more deeply on our own spiritual growth. Perhaps we need to ask whether we are still at the stage of wanting to know about God—head-knowledge, rather than understanding of the heart. Do we need to move to another level of faith? And how do we get there? The key for Nicodemus, and most likely for us as well, seems to be an unrelenting quest for the light of Christ. We find that light in prayer, in meditation, in reflection on scripture, in the sacraments—in all the means our Church offers us to become ordinary people. And when we find ourselves caring for Christ as Nicodemus did—not necessarily with aloes and myrrh, but with our talent and time in service to others—then we, like Nicodemus, have become ordinary men and women.

Questions for Further Discussion:

1. What does it mean to be an "ordinary" man or woman?
2. Is it possible to have great knowledge about God and still not know God? How does a change in such a person come about?

25
A GRAIN OF WHEAT
Fifth Sunday of Lent (B)

> • Jeremiah 31:31–34
> • Hebrews 5:7–9
> • John 12:20–33

The news was all about war. The news was about conflict, of battles fought, soldiers and civilians killed. A great army encircled an ancient city. The news was about siege and surrender.

The city was Jerusalem; the army was the army of Babylon, ancestor to the nation of Iraq. It was the sixth century BC. Jerusalem would fall and its people would be sent into exile. Israel would be occupied until a more powerful military force came along.

But the *real* news was *not* news of war. Wars in this region had been going on for centuries. The real news was being recorded by an anguished, gentle man, named Jeremiah. The news he recorded, the good news that he spoke for God, was what we heard in the first reading:

> But this is the covenant that I will make with the house of Israel after those days, says the LORD. I will put my law within them and I will write it on their hearts; and I will be their God, and they shall be my people.
>
> (Jer 31:33)

That is the good news from another time of war.

Come forward in time another six centuries to the land of Palestine. It is occupied by the most powerful military force in the world at that time—Rome. And even as a Pax Romana prevailed, there was news of war on the edges of the empire. The news was of war and rumors of war.

But, once again, the news of war was not the real news. The real news was being recorded by John, or someone from John's community. The real news, the good news, was what we heard in the gospel:

> The hour has come for the Son of Man to be glorified. Very truly, I tell you, unless a grain of wheat falls into the earth and dies, it remains just a single grain; but if it dies, it bears much fruit.
>
> (John 12:23)

The good news, the announcement that Jesus' hour had come, was not expressed in millions of words through various media. Instead, it was expressed in a simple, humble metaphor: a grain of wheat that falls to the ground and dies. A grain of wheat: a symbol that is humble, yet powerful in its message.

Today the news is again of war, of battles, of cities besieged. Our media are filled with the news of war. But, once again, the good news does not come to us through the usual media; it comes through the medium of metaphor: a grain of wheat that falls to the ground and dies. I have placed in front of the altar a small bowl of wheat to remind us of the real news on this Fifth Sunday of Lent. The real news, the good news, as we again approach the season of Easter, is conveyed through a grain of wheat. Soon we will be invited once again to enter more deeply into the mystery of Christ's dying and rising. The grains of wheat here in front of you can carry that message far more eloquently than any words I might speak. The news mediated by these grains of wheat is this: the new covenant spoken of by

Jeremiah has been realized in Jesus. Jesus is the new covenant now written on our hearts.

Jesus is the grain of wheat that falls to the ground. Like the grain of wheat, Jesus accepts his suffering and death willingly. He falls to the ground simply because it is the will of God the Father. And from that surrender to death comes new life. That surrender produces the fruit that is Christ's Church. *We* are that fruit. *We* receive that life. That is the real news, the good news.

Jesus says that when we, in our lives, imitate the grain of wheat, God's name is glorified. And then we hear the words spoken from heaven, "I have glorified it and will glorify it again" (John 12:28). How will it be glorified again? Certainly, at the resurrection. But there is another way in which God's name is glorified. It is glorified in us, in your life and mine. Whenever we become like a grain of wheat through self-denial, detachment, self-sacrificing mission to others, new life emerges and God is glorified.

We really have no choice but to imitate the grain of wheat. Through our baptism we have become inserted into Christ; we are deeply imbedded in Christ, inextricably so. We cannot be separated from him. Christ's life is now lived out in us. We cannot avoid imitating his surrender to God. For some that surrender happens quickly; for most of us it takes a lifetime and more. But knowing that it will happen gives us hope.

The news of war can have a disproportionate impact on our lives. It can become like a narcotic that insidiously works its way into our hearts and minds. It can excite, sadden, stimulate, and sometimes leave us grieving. But what the news of war can never do is displace what is written in our hearts. What is written in our hearts is Christ. His presence there assures us that the good news—not the news of war—will prevail.

I invite you after Mass to come up and take a few grains of wheat from this bowl. Let them be an antidote to the feverish news of war. Let them remind you of Christ who went down into the ground, like a grain of wheat so that we might have life. And let them give you courage and hope that the good news of Christ will, in time, replace the news of war.

Questions for Further Discussion:

1. In the midst of news of war and other troubling events, are you able to hear the good news? How do you do it?

2. Is the good news written in your heart? Explain.

26
CHRIST, SWORDLESS ON A DONKEY
Palm Sunday (B)

> • John 12:12–16
> • Isaiah 50:4–7
> • Philippians 2:6–11
> • Mark 14:1–15:47

We have just heard the reading of the passion, but to fully appreciate the passion we have to first deal with the palms. In the processional gospel from John we hear that when the crowds heard that Jesus was coming to Jerusalem they took palm branches and went out to greet him; they greeted him like a king.

I am sure you have heard the story of the emperor who had no clothes. A pair of swindlers convinced the emperor and his court that they had made him the most beautiful set of clothes imaginable, even though no one could see them. His majesty processed through the streets in his nonexistent clothes and, in a fabulous example of mass illusion, all the people pretended he was fully clothed. The illusion was broken finally when one small, innocent child piped up and declared, "The emperor has no clothes."

A twist on that story can be found in today's Palm Sunday procession gospel where we meet a very different kind of king. This king had no sword. Not only that, this king enters his capital city, the seat of power, riding not on a prancing stallion but on a humble, little donkey. The gospel says, "Jesus found a young donkey and sat on it" (John 12:14). Why did someone not stand up and shout, "The king has no horse! The king has no sword!"

I suppose we can excuse the crowds surging out from Jerusalem. We know what they were looking for. They went out to greet a conquering hero-king. You can hear it in their shouts, "Hosanna! Hosanna!" which is Hebrew for "Save now!" It is almost precisely the same as "God save the king!" The psalm that the people sing is,

"Blessed is the one who comes in the name of the Lord," taken from Psalm 118–last of the "Hallel Psalms"–a psalm intimately connected with Temple worship but also a conqueror's psalm. When Simon Maccabaeus returned to Jerusalem after freeing Israel from the Syrians, the crowds sang the same psalm Jesus now heard. In the triumphant spirit of the moment, no one seemed to notice that this king had no sword.

Why did Jesus himself not confront the crowd and their illusion? Why did he not say, "Look, I am a king without a sword. Don't you get it?" Some of us may remember the lyrics from the musical *Jesus Christ Superstar:* "Why waste your breath moaning at the crowd?/Nothing can be done to stop the shouting/If ev'ry tongue were still the noise would still continue/The rocks and stones themselves would start to sing/Hosanna...."[10] Jesus could not have quieted the crowds even if he had tried.

But the disciples? Why didn't *they* shout, "The king has no sword!" They seem to have been under the same illusion as the crowd. We know that some of them did have swords. Simon Peter certainly did. They had been with him all this time and still they carried swords. But then Jesus does something more meaningful than any argument. He uses a symbolic gesture, a living metaphor. He climbs onto the back of a donkey and begins his entry into Jerusalem. But still the disciples don't get it. The author of John's gospel readily admits this. He says it was only after Jesus rose from the dead and was glorified that they understood the significance of his riding swordless on a donkey. Then, and only then, the disciples remembered Zechariah, chapter 9, verse 9:

> Rejoice greatly, O daughter Zion!
>   Shout aloud, O daughter Jerusalem!
> Lo, your king comes to you;
>   triumphant and victorious is he,
> humble and riding on a donkey,
>   on a colt, the foal of a donkey

Now they realized that Jesus had shown them what a unique Messiah he was. If they had remembered their own Hebrew Scriptures, they woul d have realized that when a king goes to war, he rides a horse; when he comes in peace, he rides a donkey. Jesus came as the king of peace but, in the excitement of the moment, everyone missed it.

But we should not be too hard on the disciples or the crowds. We too suffer from the same illusion at times. Who among us can truly say, "I get it." If we truly believed in a king without a sword, could we tolerate the spending of billions of dollars on weapons of mass destruction while every day children around the world are starving? Could we tolerate the flood of handguns that every year kill thousands of even well-fed children?

How will we ever come to believe in a swordless king? We are no different from the disciples. It is the experience of the glorified Christ, the resurrection that enables us to see our king as he is. When the paschal mystery, the dying and rising of Christ, has thoroughly worked its way into our thinking, into our prayer, into our attitudes, then we will see our king as he is. Perhaps this should be our prayer as we enter Holy Week.

Until we as a people of God fully assimilate the mystery we are about to recall, we will continue to see a procession of conquering kings on horses and carrying swords. The poet Harry Kemp put it this way:

I saw the Conquerors riding by
With cruel lips and faces wan:
Musing on kingdoms sacked and burned
There rode the Mongol Genghis Khan;

And Alexander, like a god,
Who sought to weld the world in one:
And Caesar with his laurel wreath;
And like a thing from hell, the Hun;

And leading like a star, the van
Heedless of upstretched arm and groan,
Inscrutable Napoleon went
Dreaming of Empire, and alone....

Then all perished from the earth,
As fleeting shadows from a glass.
And, conquering down the centuries,
Came Christ the Swordless on an ass.[11]

Questions for Further Discussion:

1. Why do we find it difficult to believe in a king without a sword?

2. As the poem suggests, has Christ riding "swordless on an ass" had more effect on the world than all the conquerors who went before him?

PART FIVE

Triduum

HOMILIES 27–29

It is only because I can see God entering the darkness of human suffering and evil in creation, recognizing it for what it really is, meeting it and conquering it, that I can accept a religious view of the world. Without the religious dimension, life would be senseless, and endurance of its cruelty pointless; yet without the cross it would be impossible to believe in God.

Frances Young, *The Myth of God Incarnate*[1]

27
WE'RE ALL DEACONS NOW
Holy Thursday: Evening Mass of the Lord's Supper (B)

- Exodus 12:1–8, 11–14
- 1 Corinthians 11:23–26
- John 13:1–15

Years ago people used to carry (indeed, some folks still do) a little card in their wallet or purse which read, "I am a Catholic. In case of an accident, please call a priest." I have heard of a card which was a spoof on that more serious statement. It read, "I am a very important Catholic. Please call a bishop."

It is unlikely anyone would ever have a card that read, "I am a Catholic. Please call a deacon." Deacons do not have the faculty (that is, the power) for forgiving sins or anointing the sick and the dying. So a deacon could do no more than hold your hand and give you a blessing.

But this Holy Thursday reading from John with its dramatic scene of Jesus washing the feet of the disciples is a clear statement that Jesus did not distinguish between important and not-so-important people. Jesus demonstrated in unmistakable fashion that if you want to be important, then be a servant of all.

On January 24, 2004, our diocese (of Salt Lake City) ordained twenty-five new deacons. This coming spring we will ordain one new priest. I have heard of other dioceses where the ratio of newly ordained deacons to priests has lately been as high as 50 to 1 What are we to make of these ratios? Is it a sign of the times, which we are obliged to regard carefully?

If it is a sign of the times, then perhaps it can be interpreted as a sign that the Holy Spirit is moving us to become more of a servant church. After all, that is what a deacon is—a servant. The very word *deacon* comes from the Greek *diakonos*, meaning to serve. Christ himself was the first deacon, for he says in Mark's gospel, "the Son of Man came not to be served but to serve" (Mark 10:45). In the Greek, the literal translation is something like, "not to be deaconed to, but to deacon." There is no clearer picture of Christ the Deacon than in tonight's gospel from John.

But the sign of the times is not the number of deacons being ordained but the ministry of service they represent. The deacon is to live and minister in such a way that others will come to recognize their own call to serve, not be served. Perhaps we can say we are all deacons now.

We are all deacons now, for it is in serving others without regard for our own selves that we come to imitate Christ most closely and thereby become true sons and daughters of God. The deacon is to take seriously the words of Jesus: "For I have set you an example, that you also should do as I have done to you" (John 13:15). Jesus' modeling of service, of what it means to be a deacon, has special meaning in the context in which it occurred. Without mentioning the familiar words of the Eucharist, John does say that the ritual foot washing took place during the supper. The call to service is an integral part of Eucharist. If we miss the important aspect of service that flows out of Eucharist, then we are missing a key element of what it means to become the body of Christ. We become Christ's Mystical Body through receiving him in communion and by what we do after the dismissal. We leave the table of the Lord refreshed, reinvigorated, and ready to accept our calling to be deacons in our contemporary world.

We are all deacons now. So go and serve one another. Serve according to your own talent, your own capacity. But serve faithfully, for we are all deacons now.

Questions for Further Discussion:

1. Do you see in the ministry of a deacon a sign to others to also serve as Christ taught us to serve?

2. How is service connected to our celebration of the Eucharist?

28
THE LANGUAGE OF FAITH
Good Friday (B)

> • Isaiah 52:13–53:12
> • Hebrews 4:14–16; 5:7–9
> • John 18:1–19:42

Jesus loved to tell stories. Week after week, we have heard them: "One day a farmer went out sowing....A man had two sons....A rich man had a manager...." But today it is not Jesus telling a story; today Jesus *becomes* the story. And, indeed, it is the greatest story ever told.

But what *kind* of story is it?

That depends on who is hearing the story.

The account we have just heard mentions an inscription that was placed on the cross, written in Hebrew, Latin and Greek, indicating the presence of three distinct groups who witnessed this story. What kind of story was it for each of them?

For those who read Hebrew—the Jewish authorities—this story was a riddle, a puzzle, a conundrum. They knew Jesus, they had heard his message, they had seen his miracles. They were expecting the Messiah. Many of them must have thought at some point that Jesus of Nazareth might be the Messiah. But now it was clear he was not; not the one who would come in power to restore Israel. It must have been disconcerting for many who read Hebrew to see this popular Jewish leader reduced to apparent powerlessness at the hands of the Romans. For them, the story was a disappointing riddle, a sad puzzle, a shameful enigma.

For those who read Latin, the Roman soldiers, this story was a comedy. They knew about power, about kings. They knew how the powerful behaved. And here in front of them was a helpless little man, dressed up in mock regal robes, wearing a crown of thorns and not denying to Pilate that he was a king. The whole idea must have struck those who read Latin as being terribly ironic, a farce, a subject for dark humor. And so the readers of Latin laughed at Jesus, humiliated him, cruelly mistreated him. For them this story was a comedy.

For those who read Greek, the story was a tragedy. The Greeks knew tragedy. Their greatest writers have left us classic tragedies: stories of Achilles and Hector, of Oedipus, of Narcissus. In a tragedy, a noble character has a flaw—such as pride or envy—that leads ultimately to his destruction. That must be how those who read Greek interpreted this story: a noble Jewish man with the flaw of claiming to be a god. That is what caused his destruction. To the readers of Greek the story was a tragedy.

But the important question is: what kind of story is it for us?

We do not hear this story today in Hebrew, Latin or Greek. Its meaning comes to us, instead, through the language of faith. The language of faith is planted in us at our baptism and is perfected throughout our lives. It is perfected through prayer, through devotion, through the sacraments and through suffering. The author of Hebrews says of Jesus, "he learned obedience through what he suffered" (Heb 5:8).

The more the language of faith is perfected in us the better we are able to grasp the meaning of this story.

The story we have heard is not a riddle. God forbid, it is not a comedy. It is not a tragedy. It is, instead, a love story. It is the greatest love story of all time. It is a love story in which Jesus is the main character. None of the other figures is even a supporting actor. It is Jesus who is in control. He is the one who dominates the scenes. Jesus is the one who goes forward to meet his captors; he announces who he is; he holds back the sword of violence; he confounds the powerful Pilate with his answers; he goes to the cross willingly. Jesus moves through this story like a lover determined to win the hearts of humankind. And as the language of faith is perfected in us, we know that he succeeded.

But here is why it is the greatest love story ever: it is not historically limited. It is not like *Romeo and Juliet*. It continues in you and me. Christ now lives in us and loves in us. We must be the Christlike lovers of those we meet. That is why what we have heard is the greatest love story of all time. It continues through all time. Now we are the actors in that love story.

Good Friday is a somber day in the Triduum. But at the same time it is a day shot through with hope, because we know how this story ends. It ends in glory, in resurrection. It has an ending appropriate to the greatest love story of all time.

Questions for Further Discussion:

1. How do you think those who witnessed the events of Good Friday interpreted what they saw?

2. Do you see the story of Good Friday as a love story?

29
REJOICE, HEAVENLY POWERS!
Easter Vigil (B)

- Genesis 1:1–2:2
- Genesis 22:1–18
- Exodus 14:15–15:1
- Isaiah 54:5–14
- Isaiah 55:1–11
- Baruch 3:9–15, 32–4:4
- Ezekiel 36:16–17a, 18–28
- Romans 6:3–11
- Mark 16:1–7

One of the finest blessings for a deacon on this holy night is his traditional charge to attend to the Easter candle. And when that deacon is asked to preach, his task is incredibly simple. The work has already been done for him by the rich interplay of symbols that touched our senses from the moment the priest and his ministers appeared at the back of the darkened church. The deacon need only point to and perhaps draw out some of the meaning of what has already been experienced.

The theme of this Easter Vigil is expressed in the opening words of the Exsultet which a deacon is most privileged to sing. It begins, "Rejoice heavenly powers!" Rejoice, because tonight darkness has been overcome by light. No, not overcome—darkness has been transformed, darkness has been so invaded by the invisible light of Christ that it is revealed as equally blessed. So radiant is the splendor of Christ's resurrection that night no longer carries a negative connotation; the night truly blessed has become our joy!

We began in darkness, symbolizing what life was like before the light of Christ leapt into our world. We symbolize that saving act by striking a spark from cold flint, a reminder of how Christ sprang forth from the cold stoniness of the tomb. That single spark ignites the Easter fire, which slowly spreads through the church, overcoming the darkness. The first object to receive the new fire is the Easter candle, which we bless and carry forward, evoking memories of the pillar of fire that went before the Israelites in the wilderness. The deacon intones, "Christ our Light!" three times, the pitch rising each time, perhaps a subtle suggestion of our Lord's rising from the dead.

Then comes the incensing of the Easter candle, recalling the Old Testament sacrifice of the Temple and the altar of incense where Aaron was instructed to "offer fragrant incense on it; every morning when he dresses the lamps he shall offer it, and when Aaron sets up the lamps in the evening, he shall offer it, a regular incense offering before the Lord throughout your generations" (Exod 30:7–8).

But the symbols of new fire, spreading light, and incense are not enough to evoke in us the true meaning of this night. The keynote of the great symphony of joy that is the Easter Vigil comes from the Exsultet, sung by the deacon at the ambo. More than a hymn, this Easter proclamation is a true sacramental, preparing our hearts to receive the great flood of grace that inundates us in the Easter Eucharist. It is a hymn of praise, joy, triumphant jubilation, and it is a gospel. That is why its proclamation is preceded by a blessing of the deacon and the incensing of the book or scroll on which the words are written, just as occurs when the gospel is read. So ancient are the words—some say as ancient as the fourth century—that no one knows for sure who composed them. They are words which every deacon should aspire to sing, for by tradition they belong only to the *deacon,* not to priest, bishop or even the pope. The Exsultet is the culmination of the paschal candle ritual, of which the deacon has charge.

The Exsultet you heard sung this evening contains profound theology and is organized much like the liturgy of the Eucharist. It begins with three poetic commands to rejoice, much like we hear on Gaudete Sunday, the fourth Sunday of Lent. Heavenly powers, all creation, earth "in shining splendor," and Mother Church are each commanded to rejoice! With such insistence on rejoicing, no one can remain a passive observer at this liturgy.

Then, in words that remind us of the "Pray, brothers and sisters" at the start of the Eucharistic prayer, the deacon invites you, "dearest friends," to join in asking God for mercy that he may sing his Easter praises. For the new deacon undertaking to sing the solemn praises of this great hymn for the first time, this may be the most heartfelt prayer he has made.

The light which is the central symbol of this night comes not just from the Easter candle; it comes as well from the long account of salvation history that we hear in both the Old and New Testament texts. The Exsultet prepares our hearts and minds to receive this light of God's revelation in Scripture by recalling the history of Israel leading up to Christ's resurrection. Thus we heard: "This is our Passover feast." "This is the night when first you saved our fathers: you freed the people of Israel from their slavery." "This is the night when the pillar of fire destroyed the darkness of sin!" If you follow the progression of images, you see them culminating in Christ who on this night "broke the chains of death and rose triumphant from the grave."

Then comes one of the most important pieces of theology in the Exsultet. The deacon sings, "O happy fault, O necessary sin of Adam, which gained for us so great a Redeemer!" Now it is not just the night that has been made blessed; it is sin itself which is seen in a new light. The sin of Adam—that *felix culpa* (happy fault)—has been redeemed, for this necessary sin led to the coming of Christ and his saving passion, death, and resurrection. Without suggesting that sin is unimportant, we see that sin must yield to the power of Christ's resurrection, so joyfully recalled on this night.

Finally, the Exsultet moves to the point where, again in similarity to the Eucharistic prayer, the deacon offers to God the Easter candle. The deacon, who began the rite with the lighting of the paschal candle, now sings, "Accept this Easter candle, a flame divided but undimmed, a pillar of fire that glows to the honor of God." He prays that its light will mingle with the light of heaven whose joy we anticipate in this most glorious of temporal liturgies.

The paschal candle rite, of which the Exsultet is the culmination, is the finest of sacramentals. May it be for you this night a true sacramental, disposing your heart and mind for the grace of this night. And may the light of the Easter candle be like the Morning Star which never sets in your life. In the days to come, may you find its flame still burning, its peaceful light penetrating every corner of your life.

Questions for Further Discussion:

1, Which of the many symbols of the Easter Vigil are most meaningful to you?

2. What does it mean when we say that the Exsultet is a sacramental?

PART SIX

The Easter Season

HOMILIES 30–39

The Lord of the empty tomb
The conqueror of gloom
Come to you.

The Lord in the garden walking
The Lord to Mary talking
Come to you.

The Lord in the Upper Room
Dispelling fear and doom
Come to you.

The Lord on the Road to Emmaus
The Lord giving hope to Thomas
Come to you.

The Lord appearing on the shore
Giving us life for ever more
Come to you.

Celtic Easter Blessing

30
BEYOND ALL BOUNDARIES
Easter Sunday (B)

- Acts 10:34a, 37–43
- Colossians 3:1–4
- John 20:1–9

A little cartoon in yesterday's issue of the *Salt Lake Tribune* is the starting point for this morning's homily. I suppose if you fall asleep during the homily, you can simply find the cartoon and you will have the homily.

The cartoon strip is called "Non Sequitur," and it shows a man sitting in his room, reading a newspaper, his dog sitting nearby. The man is looking over his shoulder at the doorway which is being bricked in by a woman, presumably his wife. He must have asked why she was filling in the doorway with bricks, for the woman answers, "Because my therapist says I need to work on establishing my boundaries."

And that is what Easter is about. It's about boundaries—boundaries established by human sinfulness that are now forever taken away by the risen Christ.

Our human condition can be described as one of living within boundaries, boundaries that hem us in, that circumscribe our lives. We live within boundaries that keep us from the loving relationship with God we were intended to have. And we create boundaries in our lives, just like the woman in the cartoon, boundaries that separate us from others.

Easter is about boundaries being far extended, even taken away. It is about Christ breaking through the boundaries of sin and death; it is about Christ breaking through the boundaries of the tomb so that we might live in full union with God.

To appreciate the full meaning of Easter, we have to go back to a time of no boundaries. We must go back to when God and humankind lived in perfect harmony, without any boundaries, original or self-established. We enter that time of no boundaries when we read the first chapters of Genesis. There we learn that God created humankind to live in harmony with God.

But then something happened. Sometimes we speak of it as original sin, or the Fall. Or we might think of it as a mysterious boundary that entered the lives of each one of us, dividing us from

93

God, from each other and from our real selves. Last night at the Easter Vigil we heard a long series of readings telling us of God's efforts, through centuries of sacred history, to overcome that boundary. God sent Moses and the prophets to teach the people of Israel how to get beyond those boundaries and to live once again in intimate relationship with God. The prophets spoke of a savior who would come to restore the relationship we once enjoyed with God. One of those prophets was Micah. He spoke of a time of restoration, a time when "the boundary shall be far extended" (Mic 7:11).

We believe that prophecy was fulfilled in Jesus Christ. And that brings us to the gospel. It begins with a grieving woman, Mary of Magdala, bound by fear and darkness as she makes her way to the tomb. There she discovers that the boundary of the tomb has been taken away. The tomb is empty. Jesus has broken through the boundary of death. Christ has risen!

This is the truth we proclaim at Easter: Christ has broken through the boundaries of sin and death once and for all. The boundaries that once divided us have been far extended.

But our Church does not simply give us this truth in the abstract. Part of the genius of the Catholic Church is that we know truth comes to us arm in arm with beauty. Beauty enters our imagination through all the senses. It comes to us through the richness of liturgy, especially the Triduum liturgy, which is why your pastor encourages you to participate in the Triduum. Coming to church only on Easter Sunday is a little like reading only the last book of the trilogy of the *Lord of the Rings*. You get the ending but you miss a lot that can make the ending more meaningful.

The liturgical experience of boundaries began on Holy Thursday, when, at the end of Mass, the altar was stripped, the Blessed Sacrament removed, the lights lowered. We left the church in silence. Our ritual action evoked the sense of events crowding in upon our Lord as he left for Gethsemane and all that would follow.

And then Good Friday. The boundary of sin and evil drew closer as we heard the passion read and as we reverenced the cross. We can recall Good Fridays when even the weather cooperated, with dark clouds and cold rain restricting our movement and casting a kind of gloom over the day. Then the boundaries seemed almost tangible.

But then, last night as we gathered at the front of the church for the start of the vigil, we sensed a change coming in the liturgy. A kind of excitement came over us. Suddenly beauty began to unfold all around us. A spark of new fire pushed back the darkness. The light spread from candle to candle, pushing back the boundary of darkness still more. Incense rose like silent prayer, delighting our senses. We felt our awareness of God's majesty in the Easter event expanding our consciousness.

But it was not just the beauty of light, of smells and sound, that extended the boundary at last night's Vigil. It was something else. Something far more precious. It was the beauty in the faces of our catechumens and candidates who, for the first time, stepped across the boundary and were baptized, received first communion and confirmation. For them, last night was truly a time of no boundaries. Indeed, they are the real beauty of our Church, which comes so closely connected to truth.

This morning we rejoice that Christ is risen. Christ has broken through the confines of death, making it possible for us to live without boundaries. We rejoice in that truth. And as we rejoice, we pray that we will live not just today but every day as Easter People, as people who know no boundaries. Do not let the boundaries creep back upon you. Keep them far extended.

Questions for Further Discussion:

1. Have you experienced Christ breaking through the boundaries you may have set in your life?

2. What is the most beautiful part of Easter for you?

31
HOW WE COME TO FAITH
Second Sunday of Easter (B)
(Low Sunday)

> • Acts 4:32–35
> • 1 John 5:1–6
> • John 20:19–31

With today's reading from the Gospel of John, a great drama comes to an end. It is as though the curtain drops on the final scene of a drama we might call, "How We Come to Faith." John's telling of the story begins on Christmas Day with the words from the prologue, "In the beginning was the Word, and the Word was with God, and the Word was God" (John 1:1). It ends with Jesus' words, "Blessed are those who have not seen and yet have come to believe" (John 20:29). The curtain drops, the lights on the stage go out and the drama shifts from the stage to you and me seated in the audience.

The final scene of this drama, "How We Come to Faith," is played out in the twentieth chapter of John's gospel. That scene portrays four ways that the earlier followers of Jesus came to have faith in him. First, there is the "other disciple," presumably John, who outran Peter but deferred to him in entering the tomb. When the "other disciple" entered the tomb, he saw that it was empty. He saw the burial garments neatly rolled up, and, the gospel says, "he saw and believed" (John 20:8). The "other disciple" represents those who came to faith simply by seeing the empty tomb.

The second person in the twentieth chapter who experienced faith in the Risen Lord is Mary Magdalene. The gospel records that at first Mary did not recognize the Risen Christ; she thought he was the gardener. She pleads, "Tell me where you have laid him" (John 20:15). But then Jesus said to her, "Mary!" He simply spoke her name and she believed. Mary represents those who have heard the Lord call their name and have believed.

Third, we have the group of disciples in today's gospel, huddled together in fear behind locked doors who saw and heard the risen Lord when he appeared and said, "Peace be with you" (John 20:19). The gospel says, "Then the disciples rejoiced when they saw the Lord" (20:20). They represent those who came to faith by seeing the risen Christ.

And finally, there is the fourth representative, Thomas, the Twin, who was not with the other disciples when Jesus appeared. He declared that he would not believe unless he could actually touch the wounds of Christ. A week later he was given the opportunity. Jesus appeared and invited Thomas to examine his hands and his side. But contrary to some popular belief, Thomas did not require a physical probing of the Lord's wounds. When he heard Jesus say, "Do not doubt but believe" (John 20:27), Thomas answered with the profoundest expression of faith in the Gospel, "My Lord and my God" (John 20:28). This Jesus who stood before him was both *Kyrios* and *Theos,* Lord and God. Thomas represents those who struggle with doubt, who look for some tangible sign, who must wrestle with doubt before they come to faith. In a sense, Thomas represents all of us.

There is a recurring reference to Thomas in John's gospel that symbolizes his struggle for faith. Three times Thomas is referred to as "the twin." The symbolism of twins expresses conflict, brokenness, and division. Think of the conflict between the twins, Jacob and Esau, in Genesis over their father's birthright, of Jacob's separation and exile. But twins also symbolize the movement back toward reconciliation and unity. Again, recall how Jacob and Esau are reunited, how they embraced, despite Jacob's fears that Esau had come to do him harm.

Who was the twin of Thomas? The gospel does not say. But here I would mention an interesting tradition that Father Raymond Brown mentions in his scholarly study of John's gospel. He mentions a tradition that Thomas was spoken of as a twin of Jesus, because he resembled him in personal appearance.[1] If you allow yourself to accept that tradition for a moment (and it is only a tradition with a small "t"), then this final scene in the great drama takes on special poignancy. Thomas has been separated not only from his community, but more importantly, he has been separated from his twin, Jesus. His struggle with doubt can be likened to Jacob's wrestling with an angel the night before he reconciled with Esau. Like Jacob, Thomas emerges wounded—he has been called "Doubting Thomas" for twenty centuries—but he is now reconciled with Christ as Lord and God. He is no longer a separated twin, he is one with Christ. We believe that Thomas the Twin was never separated from Jesus again. Again, it is part of our tradition that Thomas went on to become the apostle to India. There is still a vital Christian community there which claims to trace its origins to Thomas.

As the curtain falls on this drama, the lights go down and the drama shifts to you and me. The final words of John's gospel are spoken to you and to me: "Blessed are those who have not seen and yet have come to believe" (John 20:29). We are blessed this morning, we are happy, because we believe, even though we have *not* seen. We should not feel embarrassed if, like Thomas, we have to struggle for our faith, if we find ourselves asking for signs. Jesus did not reprove Thomas for his seeking a sign. We, too, are twins who from day to day, even hour to hour, find ourselves feeling separated from the risen Lord. But then comes that moment of reconciliation, of unity, when we are no longer separated twins, but one in Christ. In that struggle, St. Thomas is our patron and model.

Questions for Further Discussion:

1. What do Jesus' words, "Blessed are those who have not seen and yet have come to believe" mean to you?
2. Have you had doubts like Thomas? How have you resolved them?

32
PROMISE KEEPER
Third Sunday of Easter

> • Acts 3:13–15, 17–19
> • 1 John 2:1–5a
> • Luke 24:35–48

In the Muslim tradition I am told there are over one-hundred names for Allah. One of the principal names is Mercy. One part of Muslim religious practice is simply repeating the many names of God as a meditation. That is a practice we might want to consider grafting onto our own religious practice. If we were to do so, I would suggest one possible way of naming God —Promise Keeper.

I choose Promise Keeper as a name for God, because that is one clear meaning to be drawn from today's gospel. God *is* a promise keeper. That truth is attested to in the Hebrew Scriptures and is beautifully conveyed in today's readings. God made a promise to Noah that never again would every living thing on the earth be destroyed by flood. A rainbow in the clouds was to be the sign of that promise (Gen 9:13). And God kept that promise.

God promised Abram that if he left his own country, his kindred, and his father's house and entered an unknown land, God would make of him a great nation, with offspring so numerous they would be "like the dust of the earth" (Gen 12:1–3; 13:16). God changed Abram's name to Abraham and promised he would be the ancestor of "a multitude of nations" from which kings would come (Gen 17:5–6). God promised to be Abraham's God and to give him the land of Canaan. The sign of that promise would be circumcision. And God kept that promise.

God promised Moses that the people of Israel would be led out of their slavery in Egypt and into a land flowing with milk and honey (Exod 3:8).When they were camped in the wilderness of Sinai, still far from that promised land, God again made promises. Through Moses

God promised to make the people of Israel God's "treasured possession," a priestly kingdom, and a holy nation. (Exod 19:5-6). The sign
of that promise would be the law, the Ten Commandments. And God
kept that promise.

Even when the people of Israel disobeyed and wandered far
from God, the promises did not cease. In the depths of their despair
during the Babylonian captivity, God sent the prophet Isaiah with a
new promise. God promised to come like a shepherd who feeds his
flock and gathers the lambs in his arms (Isa 40:11); God promised to
cause righteousness and praise to spring up before all the nations (Isa
61:11); God promised to send a son who would be from the House of
David (Isa 9:6-7). The sign of that promise would be a young woman
who would bear a son, Immanuel—God is with us (Isa 7:14). And God
kept that promise.

With that history of God's promise keeping in their memory,
those who followed Jesus were well-disposed to trust in his promise
that the Son of Man would be raised on the third day (Luke 9:21).
But, like their ancestors who either did not grasp the significance of
God's promises, or did not believe them at a deep enough level, the
disciples in today's gospel appear to have wandered into that dark
region of doubt and dismay we all know at some time. When Jesus
appears to them, they are described as startled, terrified, troubled,
questioning. Only when Jesus shows them his hands and feet and eats
with them do they become incredulous with joy and amazement. The
promise of resurrection was too much for them to believe in; it took
Christ's presence and his return to table fellowship with them to convince them that God is, indeed, a promise keeper.

Now, we are the ones who have been given a promise. This time
it is the promise of eternal life for each of us . St. Augustine puts it
this way:

> We have been promised something we do not yet possess, and
> because the promise was made by one who keeps his word, we
> trust him and are glad; but insofar as possession is delayed, we
> can only long and yearn for it. It is good for us to persevere in
> longing until we receive what was promised, and yearning is over;
> then praise alone will remain.[2]

It seems, then, there is only one thing we can do while we await
the fulfillment of God's promise of eternal life: praise God!
Augustine goes on to say in his meditation that the time before
Easter—Lent—is a commemoration of what we experience in this life;

the time after Easter is for celebrating the happiness that will be ours in the future. Before Easter, fasting and prayer are appropriate; now, constant praise is our only option. The Easter Alleluia is now the sign of our trust in God the Promise Keeper.

The gospel we are given on this Third Sunday of Easter is convincing and reassuring. It is convincing because it shows us ordinary people behaving just the way we do. We too know of the promises God has made down through the centuries. We know how those promises were kept. But owing to our human frailty and lack of faith, we still do not put our full trust in God's promises. Like the disciples, we still approach the promise of eternal life with questions and troubled hearts, perhaps even terrified at times. It takes a lifetime to overcome the obstacles created by life on the other side of Lent. Yet every Easter our Alleluias reveal that we are coming to believe more and more in God the Promise Keeper.

Add the title Promise Keeper to your list of names for God. When you say your prayers tonight, add Promise Keeper to the names you use to call on God. May the name of God as Promise Keeper reassure you and enliven your praise this Easter season.

Questions for Further Discussion:

1. Have you thought of God as Promise Keeper? Would meditating on this name be meaningful for you?

2. Why is the Easter Alleluia the appropriate sign of God keeping a promise to us?

33
JESUS, THE GOOD SHEPHERD; JESUS, OUR TRUE MOTHER
Fourth Sunday of Easter (B)
(Mother's Day)

> • Acts 4:8-12
> • 1 John 3:1-2
> • John 10:11-18

If you could be an animal, instead of a human, what animal would you choose to be?

This is an exercise sometimes used as an icebreaker at meetings to get people loosened up. I have heard people choose to be powerful lions, or sleek gazelles, or high-flying eagles. Whenever I have done this, I usually think of myself as one of those big work horses, the kind that pull the Budweiser beer wagon.

When I asked that question, how many of you chose a sheep as the animal you would identify with? Probably not many. But if we are to find meaning in today's gospel, we have to think, at least for a moment, from the standpoint of sheep. And that's okay. It is sheep, after all, that Jesus prefers in today's gospel, not lions, or eagles or horses.

To appreciate the imagery of the gospel, you have to know a little about the role of the shepherd at the time of Jesus. Scholars tell us that at the time of Jesus, several shepherds might bring their flocks of sheep at night to a sheepfold, a square marked off on a hillside by a stone wall; the sheep would enter and leave the stone enclosure through a gate in the wall. A shepherd might spend the night at this gate, protecting the sheep and seeing that they did not stray. In the morning, the shepherd would lead his sheep out, calling each by a special name that he might have for that sheep. Each sheep knew its name and recognized the voice of the shepherd. It would not follow a stranger.

This understanding of sheep and shepherd helps us to better understand our own relationship with Jesus. Jesus says, "I am the good shepherd. I know my own and mine know me" (John 10:14). It is not sheep that Jesus knows, but rather each one of us individually and personally. Indeed, he knows us better than we know ourselves.

And like the good shepherd, Jesus, every day, calls us by name and leads us out of the relative safety of the sheepfold. He speaks a word to us that enables us to go forth into the freedom of life in Christ.

What is the word that Jesus speaks to us, when he calls us each by a name known only to him? We allude to this word during the Mass when we say, "Lord, I am not worthy to receive you, but only say the word and I shall be healed." What is that healing word that Jesus speaks to us?

A wise person said to me recently that the fruit of Lent for her was to realize more fully than ever before how much we are loved by God the Father. Is that not the word that Jesus speaks to us as he calls us into lives of greater freedom? The word that frees us and enables us to leave the stone enclosures of our lives is Love—love of God the Father for each one of us. Without a deep and abiding awareness of that love, we remain in our own comfort zone, we stay in the sheepfold and never experience the true freedom on the green hills and mountains where we are no longer timid sheep but children of God. Whatever it is that holds us back—be it a life of harmful addiction, prejudices, our fears and worries, our too busy lives—all of these are left behind when we hear the voice of the Good Shepherd, saying "Come out! Be free! My Father loves you!" Saints, I suppose, hear this voice constantly and clearly.

The image of Jesus the Good Shepherd is a good one, even though today most of us know very little about sheep and shepherds. But there is another image that, in a way, complements the image of shepherd and is appropriate for this day—Mother's Day. It follows naturally to speak of our Lord as Jesus the Good Mother.

Jesus as Mother has a firm basis in our tradition. In the Old Testament book of Hosea, God is imaged in a way that reminds us of a tender mother. The prophet Hosea says: "When Israel was a child I loved him....It was I who taught Ephraim to walk, I took them up in my arms" (Hos 11:1-3).

Later, in our more recent tradition, Julian of Norwich, the great fourteenth-century mystic, spoke of Jesus as our "true Mother." She contrasts "human motherhood" with "spiritual motherhood" and says that just as from our natural mothers we receive our physical birth, so from Jesus our true being arises. Our earthly mother brings us forth into pain and death; Jesus, our true Mother, births us for "joy and endless life." Our natural mothers nourish us at the breast; "our precious Mother Jesus," Julian says, "feeds us with himself...and does so with the blessed sacrament." Our earthly mother held us tenderly to herself; Jesus our True Mother leads each of us to himself, holding us tenderly, leading us through the wound of his side into the godhead and the joys of heaven.[3]

We give thanks on this day for all mothers, for all that they are to us but especially for the way that mothers image for us the tender, caring love of Jesus. The images of mother and shepherd are easily blended. Our mothers are the first to speak to us the word of God's love; even in the womb, that word is heard. To a mother, her child is everything; she lives, breathes, and sleeps her child. And so it is with the love of God for us. God hovers over us like a true mother.

Earthly mothers give their lives for their children, caring for them, searching for ways of reaching them. Is this not like the Good Shepherd who, the gospel says, "lays down his life for the sheep"? Is it not fair to paraphrase St. Luke by asking, "What mother among you, if she has a hundred children and loses one of them, does not leave the ninety-nine and follow the lost one until she finds it?..."

Jesus is the Good Shepherd. Jesus is our True Mother.

The Jesuit Gerard Manley Hopkins closes his untitled sonnet with these lines:

> Christ plays in ten thousand places,
> Lovely in limbs, and lovely in eyes not his
> To the Father through the features of men's faces.[4]

And we might add: "Lovely as well through the features of our mothers' faces."

Questions for Further Discussion:

1. Is Julian's imagery of Jesus as our True Mother meaningful to you? In what way?

2. What are some of the things that keep us from responding to the call of the shepherd to come out?

34
DON'T BECOME A PRISONER TO YOUR OWN IMAGES
Fifth Sunday of Easter (B)

- Acts 9:26–31
- 1 John 3:18–24
- John 15:1–8

Federal district judge Bruce Jenkins, a judge for whom I have a great deal of respect, once cautioned lawyers about the danger of becoming prisoners of their own images. He gave, as an example, lawyers who image the practice of law as being like war. The lawyer who becomes a prisoner to this image can very easily begin to act as though the courtroom is a combat zone. Such a lawyer begins to think in these terms: "Never give the other side an inch." "Fire back when fired upon." "Take no prisoners." And on and on, until the courtroom becomes a very uncivil place. This kind of imprisonment may explain why in the last few years the Utah Supreme Court has had to create a committee on lawyer civility whose task is to come up with a code of civility for lawyers. That is what can happen when lawyers become prisoners of their own images.

But, of course, lawyers are not the only ones who can become prisoners of their own images. The same thing can happen in our religious life. We too can become prisoners of images that will profoundly affect the way we conceive of our relationship with God. The image we have of God, of Christ, and of our relationship with God can affect the way we worship, the way we pray, and the way we relate to each other.

One image of God I have sometimes discovered in some Catholics, and more so among RCIA inquirers, is the image of God as being distant. Sometimes the image is of a God who is like a stern judge, far away, watching our every move, and just waiting to pass judgment on us, a judgment that we fear will be unfavorable. When we become prisoner to such an image, our prayer, our worship, our everyday life, become distorted. We think of God as someone unapproachable, someone who must be placated or appeased, someone from whom we must beg a lighter sentence. We live with a kind of fear that we may not quite make the grade. If this were an appropriate image, Jesus would have said, "I am the true lawyer, and my father is one tough judge." But, of course, he didn't say that.

Or we may have an image of God as being someone like the head accountant of a business, someone who keeps a careful record of the good we do and who will, at the final accounting, determine whether we have earned enough grace to enter heaven. If we become a prisoner to such an image, we might conceive of our relationship with God as one in which Jesus negotiates a better deal for us, someone who adjusts the books so that we can earn enough credits to be assured of eternal life. If this were a good image of our relationship with God, Jesus might have said, "I am the true bookkeeper and my father is the chief financial officer."

But, of course, he did not.

Jesus did not use *any* of these images. Instead, he said, "I am the true vine, and my Father is the vine grower.... Abide in me, as I abide in you.... I am the vine, you are the branches" (John 15:1-5). This is an image we can not only embrace but can become prisoner to; it is an image that can enliven our life as followers of Christ.

First of all, notice that Jesus says he is the *true* vine, meaning that there must be other vines which are false. Whether this is interpreted as referring to Jewish religious practice at the time, or whether we think of it as referring to one of the many false gods that compete for our attention today, we can infer that there is always a temptation to become grafted into a false vine, a vine that will not give life. Jesus is saying that when branches are joined to him much fruit is produced. A good examination of conscience for today might be to ask: What vine am I grafted into? If I am not bearing fruit, do I need to examine the vine I have chosen to be part of?

You do not have to be much of a botanist to appreciate the richness of the vine-and-branches imagery. We know that there is a dynamic flow of life in every plant. Nutrients and water flow from the vine to the branches; sunlight and moisture flow back to the vine. And from this flowing back and forth, fruit is produced. The same is true in our relationship with Christ. By being connected to Christ, like branches to a vine, the life-giving energy of the Trinity enters us. We may call this flow uncreated energy, grace, or we may call it, simply, love. The end result of this reciprocal flow of love is good fruit: the fruits of prayer, good and virtuous lives, peace, compassion, zeal in caring for others. The types and varieties of such fruits are infinite.

But the richest fruit that is produced in us is a growing awareness that images of a distant God are no longer adequate. The image of vine and branches is one of intimacy and closeness, pointing to the reality of the incarnation: God is with us, God has taken on our nature. We are now as close to God as a branch is to the vine.

There is, of course, a hint of pain in this gospel, for it speaks as well of pruning. Jesus says, "my Father is the vine grower," and he speaks of pruning away branches that do not bear fruit as well as pruning good branches that are bearing fruit, so that they might produce more and better fruit. Pruning is happening all the time during our life in Christ. We do not fully understand it, but somehow the pain we experience is a necessary part of making us capable of bearing good fruit. We experience pruning in our own individual lives and in our life as part of the Church.

In the past few years our Church has gone through a painful period of pruning. I mean, of course, the national scandal over some priests accused of sexual misconduct and abuse. Our Church has had to adopt very strict measures for dealing with this scandal. We are undergoing at this stage of our history as American Catholics a very painful pruning process, but it is a pruning we believe will ultimately produce more and better fruit.

Scandal is painful for all of us, but do not let it make you a prisoner to any image that does not adequately express the mystery of our life as Catholic Christians. Do not become a prisoner to an inadequate image of God, the Church, or the priesthood. We take courage from the image Christ has given us in the gospel: I am the vine, you are the branches. Live in this image. Live in it and bear much fruit.

Questions for Further Discussion:

1. What are some ways you have seen of people becoming prisoners of their own images?

2. Do you see signs of pruning going on in the Church? In your own life?

35
THE TWENTY-FIFTH ANNIVERSARY OF FATHER COLIN BIRCUMSHAW'S ORDINATION
Sixth Sunday of Easter (B)

> • Acts 10:25–26, 34–35, 44–48
> • 1 John 4:7–10
> • John 15:9—17

There is a line in William Blake that applies to today's gospel. It applies to Father Colin as we celebrate this weekend the twenty-fifth anniversary of his ordination to the priesthood. And it applies to all of us on this sixth Sunday of Easter. The line says, "we are put on the earth for a little space that we may learn to bear the beams of love."

We hear Christ say in the Gospel, "As the Father has loved me, so I have loved you" (John 15:9). The idea of God the Father loving the Son is easy to accept; so too is the thought of Jesus loving the Father. After all, there is no imperfection to come between them. But today's gospel adds something that is truly astounding—breathtaking, really, if you think about it. Jesus says that we are loved in the same way as he is loved by God, the Father. That's powerful stuff—to think that our Lord loves us with the same intensity, the same depth, fullness, persistence, the same extravagance that the Father loves the Son! As we used to say in the 1970s, when Father Colin was ordained: that blows your mind!

We spend our lives trying to grasp the reality of this staggering parallel. Our condition may be compared to someone who has spent a long time in a dark cave. Maybe you have had this experience. As you come out of the cave, as you approach the entrance, the light is incredibly intense. You find yourself covering your eyes. The brightness is too much, you are unable to bear the beams of light. It is the same way as we struggle throughout our lives to bear the beams of divine love.

Most of us do not have the capacity for a direct and immediate experience of that love. It must be mediated to us. We must be *gradually* transformed throughout our lives so as to bear the beams of love.

Father Richard McBrien, who has written a classic commentary on Catholicism, says, "the encounter with God is a mediated experience...."[5] Ours is a mediated religion. Our lives are a long process of mediated awareness, coming to us through the sacraments, through prayer, through loving relationships, through contemplation and the growing realization that we are loved with the kind of love spoken of in the gospel.

How is our encounter with God mediated? Every person and every experience mediates that encounter in some way. But I am convinced that the real heavy lifting falls to our priests. Again, Father McBrien says that "the function of the priest as mediator is not to limit the encounter between God and the human person, but to focus it more clearly for the sake of the person and ultimately for the sake of the community of faith."[6] This weekend we celebrate with Father Colin twenty-five years of being a priest, twenty-five years of mediating God's love.

The words in today's gospel were first spoken to priests. The life of a priest, any priest, but in particular one who has been ordained for twenty-five years, is about the faithful mediation of Christ's love. Everything that Father Colin has done during his twenty-five years of priestly ministry has had as its ultimate purpose the transformation of believers so that they may bear the beams of love. Every hour spent in reconciliation, the time spent in counseling, in preparing homilies, in prayer, in celebrating the Eucharist, presiding at weddings, at funerals, all of these have had as their purpose that transformation of hearts and minds necessary for an encounter with the divine.

St. Gregory Nazianzus in the fourth century, while still a young priest, said this:

> We must begin by purifying ourselves before purifying others; we
> must be instructed to be able to instruct, become light to illuminate,

draw close to God to bring him close to others, be sanctified to
sanctify, lead by the hand and counsel prudently....

[Who then is the priest? He is] the defender of truth, who
stands with angels, gives glory with archangels, causes sacrifices
to rise to the altar on high, shares Christ's priesthood, refashions
creation, restores it in God's image, recreates it for the world on
high and, even greater, is divinized and divinizes.[7]

Some might not choose such rich language to describe the ministry of our priests. But the words are apt; they capture the essence of
what it means to be a priest, to be a minister consecrated to mediating the richness of Christ's love, the same love that Christ shares with
the Father.

I move now from the great and saintly Gregory of Nazianzus to a
more common figure—Groucho Marx. Groucho is sometimes credited
with saying, "Ninety percent of success is just showing up." Father Colin,
your twenty-five years of being a priest have been a success, in large part,
because you have shown up, time after time, after time. When you were
appointed to serve at the Josephinum, you showed up; when you were
appointed to serve as a pastor, you showed up; when you were called in
the middle of the night to minister to a dying parishioner, you showed
up; whatever the need, no matter how menial, you showed up. Twenty-
five years ago you made an appointment with yourself to be here on this
day to celebrate your ordination, and you have kept that appointment.
You have showed up. We are all the better for your having done so.

What has enabled Father Colin, or any priest for that matter, to
be a mediator of divine love? If you attend the reception after Mass
and look through the pictures accumulated there, you will note some
changes in Father Colin's appearance over twenty-five years. When
you look at the pictures, you may remark: look he had a beard then.
Or, look how slender and handsome he was then. But there is something else I would call your attention to: it is the altar banner at Father
Colin's ordination as deacon and at his first Mass. It proclaims the
words of John's gospel, "So if I, your Lord and teacher, have washed
your feet, you also ought to wash one another's feet" (Jn 13:14). It is
humble, unassuming service to the community of faith, to the
Church, that has made it possible for Father Colin to be a mediator,
a channel, of God's love. You see, you cannot be a channel of God's
love unless you are emptied, unless you have experienced *kenosis*–that
emptying out of oneself St. Paul describes in his letter to the
Philippians, where he says: "Let the same mind be in you that was in
Christ Jesus, who, though he was in the form of God, did not regard

equality with God as something to be exploited, but emptied himself...." (Phil 2:5-7). That is the attitude that makes anyone, priest, religious, or lay person, a true mediator of God's love.

Father Colin has discouraged gifts on this occasion. The reason for that is clear. He has received a gift which makes all other gifts pale in comparison. He has been given the gift of Christ's friendship as it is promised in today's gospel: "You are my friends if you do what I command you" (John 15:14). Our gift to Father Colin is to articulate and affirm that his twenty-five years of priesthood have made him a friend of Christ. May that friendship deepen; may Christ's joy be in you, Father Colin, and may it be complete.

Ad multos annos. [to many more years]

Questions for Further Discussion:

1. What does it mean that we are put on earth to learn to bear the beams of love?

2. Do you agree with Groucho that 90 percent of success is just showing up? In what way?

36
THE GREATER CHRIST
Ascension of the Lord (B)

* Acts 1:1–11
* Ephesians 1:17–23
* Mark 16:15–20

One of the complaints I have heard made against Christians is: "Your God is too small." Usually what is meant by that objection is our tendency to confine God within our carefully worked out concepts and forms. We certainly need to be aware of our natural tendency to "domesticate" God, to keep God confined within the limits of our dogma and doctrines. Of course, such an objection arises out of ignorance. But it is not just the non-Christian challenger who is often ignorant; often it is we ourselves who are unable to describe a God who is big, a God who transcends our limited means of expression.

Today, on this feast of the Ascension, I want to speak about what I would call, "the Greater Christ"[8] which, I hope, will whet your appetite for thinking of Christ in a much bigger way than you ever have before.

I would begin by asking: Where did Christ go after he ascended into heaven? The first reading from Acts says, "a cloud took him out of their sight" (Acts 1:9). We know that Christ is not in the clouds somewhere. The gospel from Mark says he "sat down at the right hand of God," which is another way of saying he returned to God his Father. But we know that these are simply images which the early Church used to describe the ascension in ways that would be understandable to people of their time; they do not mean that Christ now sits on a physical throne somewhere.

I want to suggest today that it is perhaps better to say that Christ never left us at all. His physical body disappeared from sight, but Christ remained. *How* did he remain? Certainly, among us as Church, when we gather in his name. Certainly, in the poor as you have heard me mention often before. Certainly, in the Eucharist where he remains quintessentially present. But there is another way that Christ remains with us, and it is an ancient understanding in the Church which has not gotten the attention it deserves: Christ remains with us in nature as the Cosmic Christ.

All of the other ways I mentioned that Christ remains with us fit within a framework of history. But it is also acceptable to think of Christ within a framework of nature that surpasses history. Thinking in terms of the Cosmic Christ does not take away from our understanding of Christ the Redeemer, the savior of souls. Rather, it gives us a powerful new paradigm for viewing nature, and possibly for resolving the ecological crisis that faces our planet.

Some solid support for an approach to nature that is Christ-centered is found in the epistles of the apostle Paul, starting with the first reading from Ephesians. There, Paul prays that those who hear his words will recognize God's great power which was put to work in Christ "when he raised him from the dead and seated him at his right hand in the heavenly places" (Eph 1:20). He concludes: "And he has put all things under his feet and has made him the head over all things for the church, which is his body, the fullness of him who fills all in all" (Eph 1:22). In Colossians Paul hymns this truth even more beautifully:

> He is the image of the invisible God, the firstborn of all creation;
> for in him all things in heaven and on earth were created, things
> visible and invisible, whether thrones or dominions or rulers or
> powers—all things have been created through him and for him.
> He himself is before all things, and in him all things hold

together. He is the head of the body, the church; he is the beginning, the firstborn from the dead, so that he might come to have first place in everything. For in him all the fullness of God was pleased to dwell, and through him God was pleased to reconcile to himself all things, whether on earth or in heaven, by making peace through the blood of his cross.

(Col 1:15–20)

All things—not just persons like you and me—were saved by Christ. All things, "whether on earth or in heaven": every tiny organism, every star and planet, everything that can be found in creation. The entire cosmos was included within the ambit of Christ's saving passion, death and resurrection. The rebirth and renewal we experience at a personal level as Catholic Christians will, we believe, extend beyond the Church and encompass the entire cosmos. That is the "Greater Christ" which our faith tradition allows us to envision.

This understanding of "the Greater Christ" has the potential to radically alter our attitude toward nature. It can make nature as important a scene for the grace of Christ to operate within as is our own parish community. Nature becomes the focus of our efforts at social justice for "He [Christ] is present not only in the human victims of world history but in victimized nature too."[9] We move, then, from adoring Christ present in the Eucharist to reverencing Christ as also present in the air, water, land, and all creatures.

Such a reverence can be the starting point for a vital "eco-spirituality."[10] In speaking of the sinful attitudes which cause so much environmental degradation, Father Charles Cummings says in his book *Eco-Spirituality:*

These sinful attitudes can be changed, by the grace of God, through a process of religious conversion. The roots of our ecological crisis are ethical and spiritual; the corrective should be sought on the same level. Before and beyond the task of restoring nature, there is the task of healing human hearts and reconciling human minds that are narrow and closed. If our minds and hearts are fully open to nature, neighbor, and God, there can be a gradual global transformation comparable to a new creation. Eco-spirituality believes that spiritual healing will lead to ecological healing.[11]

When we begin to see the entire cosmos as Christ-pervaded, then we see that our God is not small at all, and we pause in reverence before the greatness that is Christ.

Questions for Further Discussion:

1. Is it helpful to you to think of the "Greater Christ," i.e., Christ present in nature as the Cosmic Christ?

2. Do you agree with Father Cummings that there can be a "transformation comparable to a new creation"? What can we as Catholics do to help bring about that transformation?

37

THAT THEY MAY BE ONE
Seventh Sunday of Easter (B)

- Acts 1:15–17, 20a, 20c–26
- 1 John 4:11–16
- John 17:11b–19

A bishop celebrates Mass with a small group of striking miners and expresses his solidarity with them.

Inspired by Renew, an adult faith-formation program, a small group of Catholics meets each week to pray, discuss Scripture and look for ways to serve their community.

A small group of Catholics, Lutherans, and Episcopalians gather during Lent for discussion and prayer.

A priest from Tanzania with $40 in his pocket travels to Utah as part of a new religious order and serves a small congregation on an Indian reservation.

What does each of these examples have to do with today's gospel? They are all ways in which Christ's prayer to the Father—"Holy Father protect them in your name that you have given me, so that they may be one, as we are one" (John 17:11)—is being answered.

Jesus knew the difficulties his little band of followers was facing. In his last words to be spoken before the start of his passion, Jesus was aware of the forces that would challenge the unity of his followers. John makes note of this by his reference to "the one destined to be lost," Judas, whose betrayal is seen as necessary, "so that scripture might be fulfilled" (John 17:12). That the early Church itself recognized the need to preserve its unity is shown by the first reading where Peter stands up before a group of believers (one hundred twenty persons) and presides over a selection process to replace Judas with Matthias. Thus, the group of twelve apostles is restored and, as the

"New Israel," is ready to be sent into the world to carry out the mission Christ had entrusted to them: making the world one in Christ.

You don't have to be much of a church historian to know that the same forces which assailed the unity of the early Church are still with us. Most of us have a broad understanding of the fragmenting of the Christian community that has gone on over two millennia. Every month when I attend my Interfaith Works meeting and look around the table at all the faces of so many good people, Christian and non-Christian alike, who remain divided and alienated from each other, I am reminded of how far we have yet to go. The schisms, divisions, splinterings, reformations—whatever you want to call them—are very real to us now at the start of the twenty-first century.

But just as the reminders of disunity are apparent, so too are the reminders that the prayer of Christ is being answered. Today a descendant of Peter continues to pray and work for unity among Christians and all people of good will. In his encyclical *Redemptoris Missio* (The Mission of the Redeemer), Pope John Paul II acknowledges that "the mission of Christ the Redeemer entrusted to the church is far from completed."[12] But he senses "a new urgency of mission activity" so that the mission of the church, the mission stressed by the Second Vatican Council, "that they all may be one" (John 17:21), may be accomplished.

The mission of the Church outlined in *Redemptoris Missio* brings us back to the examples I gave at the outset. Early on in the encyclical the pope, in speaking of the importance of witness, says:

> The evangelical witness which the world finds most appealing is that of concern for people, and of charity toward the poor, the weak, and those who suffer. The complete generosity underlying this attitude and these actions stand in marked contrast to human selfishness. It raises precise questions which lead to God and the gospel. A commitment to peace, justice, human rights and human promotion is also a witness to the gospel when it is a sign of concern for persons and is directed toward integral human development.[13]

You might wonder why social justice would play such an important role in the mission of the Church. The reasons should be clear to us as we view the divisive struggles going on in our world, most of them caused in some part by poverty, war, and oppressive governments that ignore fundamental human rights. Reports on the news, as well as lesser-known reports by such organizations as Amnesty

International, show us that no country, not even our own, is exempt when it comes to denying social justice. And we cannot expect to have unity and peace when justice is denied.

Pope John Paul II describes small Christian communities as the starting point for a new society based on a civilization of love.[14] Those who have been part of the Renew program and the small communities it fostered can attest to the real possibilities for unity and revitalization of the larger parish this movement has produced. The small groups that have continued now for several years demonstrate real vitality and commitment. They have the potential for becoming, as the pope suggests, "a leaven of Christian life." They are another way in which Christ's prayer for unity is being answered in our own time.

Dialoguing with our brothers and sisters of other religions is another expression of our mission as Catholics. On this point, the pope declares:

> There is no conflict between proclaiming Jesus Christ and inter-religious dialogue. The two are distinct and intimately connected; they should not be confused or regarded as identical.
>
> Followers of other religions can receive God's grace and be saved by Christ apart from the ordinary means of salvation.
>
> Dialogue should be done in the conviction that the ordinary way of salvation, as willed by Jesus Christ, is the Church.[15]

This short passage from the encyclical is key to meaningful dialogue with other religions. While being faithful to our belief that Christ is the means of salvation, it acknowledges that the grace of Christ touches all people, offering them the same wholeness we seek.

Finally, in a chapter entitled, "Leaders and Workers in the Missionary Apostolate," Pope John Paul II emphasizes the fundamental importance of churches sharing missionaries with other churches in need. He mentions how Pope Pius XII encouraged bishops to offer some of their priests for temporary service in the churches of Africa.[16] We have seen this work both ways: we have a diocesan priest serving in Africa and have also had two priests from Tanzania serving in this diocese of Salt Lake City. It sounds contradictory, but then, as the pope notes, the "Holy Spirit remains the principal agent" for the accomplishment of the mission to unite all of God's people. Who knows where the Spirit will go.

There is one final point I would mention from the encyclical. It says: "The call to mission derives from the call to holiness."[17] The Pope says that missionaries—those who respond to Christ's prayer that all might be one—should be "contemplatives in action." He concludes: "The future of mission depends to a great extent on contemplation...."[18] That is an intriguing thought. Let us pray that we would all become "contemplatives in action" and thereby hasten the day when Christ's prayer will be completely answered.

Questions for Further Discussion:

1. Can you point to ways in which Christ's prayer for unity is being answered? What can we do to encourage unity?

2. What does it mean to be a "contemplative in action"?

38
HOLY SPIRIT: DESIGNER OF THE WEB OF LIFE
Pentecost Vigil (B)

- Genesis 11:1–9
- Romans 8:22–27
- John 7:37–39

Jesus was one of those people on whom nothing was lost. Jesus had that priceless gift of being able to see the close affinity between things happening around him and the life of God. This was especially so when it came to nature—the way a seed grows in secret, the ways of foxes and birds of the air, the way lilies and fig trees grow. In all things Jesus saw a correlation with the life of God. The images Jesus used are some of the most brilliant facets of gospel beauty. They sparkle with a brightness that is fresh, original and clear. More than metaphors, they show us a connection between the natural and the spiritual world. Thus, it is no surprise to hear in John's gospel tonight Jesus likening the Holy Spirit to "rivers of living water" flowing out of the believer's heart.

I want you to hold in your mind for a moment that powerful image of "rivers of flowing water" and then consider another image from nature that has the possibility of deepening our understanding during this Pentecost vigil. Recently I have become fascinated by one of our country's great natural treasures, the Florida Everglades. I have had the opportunity to make brief visits to the edge of the Glades and have had an introduction to this complex ecosystem, both from what I observed and from the writings of others more familiar with them. In the great mystery of this intricate web of life called the Everglades, I find a reflection of the mysterious and creative activity of God's Spirit at work in our world.

Now let me return to that thought of "rivers of flowing water" which I asked you to hold in your mind. To understand the Everglades you have to start with the life-giving movement of water, falling as rain on Lake Okeechobee to the north, overflowing its banks, and moving steadily, almost secretly, southward, feeding a river of saw grass that is the frame on which the Creator has woven a beautiful tapestry of life.[19] With that in mind, is it not easy to see how the Holy Spirit, that great river of divine life that has its source in the Trinity, must spill over its banks, suffusing the world with love and giving supernatural life to everything it touches? Like the hidden filtering of water through the Everglades, so the Spirit moves—secretly, silently, touching hearts, restoring, consoling, comforting, reassuring, instructing— all for one purpose: to give divine life!

In its natural state, the Everglades, like any ecosystem, are balanced and ordered, with life ebbing and flowing according to a rhythm of nature that will always be a mystery and a source of awe for those who have eyes to see. There is a life spirit moving through this unique corner of creation that evokes in our imagination an understanding of the Holy Spirit descending on the apostles and weaving a web of holy life in the early Christian community. As Father Alfred Delp—the Jesuit priest hanged by the Nazis during World War II— wrote from his prison cell:

> The Holy Ghost is the breath of creation. As in the beginning the Spirit of God moved on the face of the waters, so now—but in a much closer and more intimate way—God's spirit reaches the heart of man bringing him the capacity to grow to fulfillment.[20]

The Holy Spirit is like a breath of creation, moving on the waters of a great river of flowing water, touching individuals as well as communities, expanding our capacity to grow to fulfillment.

From a distance, the Everglades may seem just a swamp; up close, they are a marvelous interplay of species—plants and animals, insects and birds, fish and reptiles. From a distance, our world, especially that part dominated by humans, may appear to be a disaster. Up close, in the intimate view of the Spirit, it is a divine work of art being carefully crafted into something worthy of its Creator.

There is, of course, only one force that has threatened the delicate balance found in the Glades—the greedy hands of modern man. The flow of water which has sustained life in the Glades over countless generations has been diverted and polluted, drying up wetlands and poisoning the food chain. I was saddened to learn during my most recent visit that one of the last Seminole villages to be abandoned was abandoned because a high mercury content made the fish inedible. Can we not also see how our community life suffers and even dies when the flow of living water we call Spirit is obstructed or tainted?

But the river of flowing water in both its natural and spiritual forms can never be entirely stopped. It can be impeded, obstructed, slowed at times, but never halted completely. There is hope to be found in what is hidden from the eyes of casual observers. As more and more clean water is allowed to flow into the Glades, life in all its forms and varieties is secretly renewed. So too are we when we are open to the possibility of renewal that comes as the Holy Spirit flows into our hearts; we discover an abundance of life as beautiful as the natural world of the Everglades.

Questions for Further Discussion:

1. What other images of nature come to mind when you think of the Holy Spirit and Pentecost?

2. What are some ways that we impede or obstruct the flow of that great river of life, the Holy Spirit?

39
COME, HOLY SPIRIT, PERFECT IN US THE LANGUAGE OF THE KINGDOM
Pentecost (B)

- Acts 2:1–11
- Galatians 5:16–25
- John 15:26–27; 16:12–15

Buenos dias. Guten morgen. Bonjour.

With that, I have exhausted the foreign language greetings I can give you this morning. If I were to try really hard, work for days with a lot of help, I might even be able to preach to you in one of those languages. But you probably would not understand me. Unless, of course, I had the gift of the Holy Spirit, mentioned in the first reading from Acts. Then it would not matter what language I spoke, for each of you would hear me in your own language.

The reading from Acts, with its reference to Parthians, Medes, and Elamites, all hearing the Galilean Christians in their native language, is a post-resurrection story that speaks of a special unity in the early Church. It reminds us that the Holy Spirit, the Advocate, the Spirit of Truth, always speaks in the language of unity. We may hear the gospel proclaimed in many different languages, but if we are listening, we hear the Holy Spirit speaking in words that connote unity.

To fully appreciate this remarkable account in Acts, you have to go back to Genesis, to the eleventh chapter, where we hear the dramatic story of the tower of Babel. In the tower of Babel story, the author of Genesis grapples with the question: why do people speak different languages? Why are we many, not one? Why are there inhabitants of Mesopotamia, Judea, and Cappadocia, all of them speaking a different language?

The author of Genesis answers these questions with a highly symbolic story. According to the text, the whole world once spoke the same language, using the same words. Language was a gift from God, a gift of unique beauty through which truth was revealed. That truth bore fruit in unity.

But the story of Babel, like the story of Adam and Eve, is one of rebellion; it is a story of human willfulness and ultimate separation. As the story goes, overachieving humans began to build a tower, a tower so high it would reach the sky. The Lord, not pleased with this display of hubris, resolved to put an end to this ego-driven building project. The Lord declares: "Come, let us go down, and confuse their language there, so that they will not understand one another's speech" (Gen 11:7). The people of the tower are then scattered over the earth. They become the Parthians, Medes, and Elamites. They speak many different languages. Truth too is fractured and scattered.

The scattering of peoples, the proliferation of languages, and the dispersal of truth set the stage for what we hear in Acts. The confusion and the scattering that took place in Genesis is now reversed in Acts. Something has happened to reverse what happened at Babel. That something, of course, is Easter. The graced events of Christ's life, starting with the incarnation and completed in his passion, death and resurrection, have restored the order lost in ancient times. Where once there was confusion, now there is clarity; where once there was a fractured people, now there is unity; where once there was a scattering of truth, now there is a restoration by the Spirit of Truth.

Jesus, the Word of God, came into the world to teach us the grammar and the vocabulary of a new language: the language of the Kingdom of God. Every word in this new idiom expresses the truth of unity restored between God and humankind. We, however, are slow learners. And so, we were given the Holy Spirit, the Spirit of Truth, who perfects our understanding and gradually makes us fluent in the language of the kingdom.

This language is not necessarily embodied in spoken words or symbols. More often it is discovered in small acts of human kindness. As our inner ears become more attuned, we begin to appreciate this language of the Holy Spirit as it works its way into our consciousness. Sometimes we are surprised by it. I recall a time when, as a college student in Europe, a friend and I, living on a shoestring, visited Paris. Hungry and feeling somewhat alienated by our lack of French, we wandered into a patisserie and began admiring the rich and delicate pastries on display. We knew enough of the language to understand that we could not afford the attractive items we pointed to. Finally the shopkeeper stopped, took a plate, filled it with pastries, and, smiling, gave them to us. We sat in that little shop for some time, feasting on delicacies we could not afford, and delighting in this little act of human kindness. Who said the French were rude? For a few brief moments, this act of kindness made us one with them.

In a few months we, the members of this parish, will be given a further opportunity to perfect our hearing of the Holy Spirit. For the first time in the more than one-hundred-year history of our parish, we will have a pastor whose first language is Spanish and whose culture is Latino. We will be called upon to demonstrate just how fluent we are in the language of the kingdom. How will we accept this change? Will we feel divided? Anglo from Hispanic? English-speaking from Spanish-speaking? None of that will happen if we remember that the language of the Holy Spirit, the language of the kingdom, has little to do with a particular idiom; it has *everything* to do with acts of kindness, acts of welcoming and reconciliation; it is heard not in *division,* but in *unity.* If the Holy Spirit is given half a chance we will likely experience the unity my friend and I felt in that French patisserie—we will be surprised by human kindness.

But the Holy Spirit may also speak in words that challenge us. If we listen and understand, we may be asked to go beyond separation and division. We may be asked disturbing questions that we would like to pretend we do not understand. Once, while visiting St. George, Utah, I stopped at a Mexican diner for something to eat. While waiting for the food to be prepared, I chatted in Spanish with the couple who operated it. And as sometimes happens when you are trying to converse in a language in which you are not completely fluent, I was asked a question in Spanish, to which I answered, *"Sí."* Yes. The couple began to laugh, and I began to laugh, because, it turned out, the question was: "Do you want to eat inside or out on the patio." My answer showed I did not really understand the question.

And, I suppose, that is sometimes what happens when we hear the Holy Spirit asking us disturbing questions. The questions are: Why are you not doing more to bring about unity in our parish, in our diocese? Why aren't you more disturbed by the lack of real community? I don't know about you, but the answer I sometimes give is *"Sí,"* meaning I really did not understand the question. Or didn't want to.

At Pentecost, the world was given a new language, the language of the kingdom, a language that was incarnated in our nature through Christ and is brought to perfection by the Holy Spirit. We cooperate with the Holy Spirit in perfecting our understanding through acts of charity, words of reconciliation, devotion, the sacraments and prayer. Ultimately, we must stand in silence before the mystery of how this perfecting is occurring in human history. So let me close with a kind of take off on something Father Colin referred to last Sunday. Father Colin mentioned the Sistine Chapel and the many tourists who come to admire the tremendous paintings by Michelangelo depicting the course of salvation history. In our efforts to understand what the Holy Spirit is doing in our world, we are like tourists in the Sistine Chapel: heads craned, trying to take it in, thinking about and commenting on what it all means. But, then, we hear the command of the "Shssshers," those Sistine Chapel guards Father mentioned, who go about saying "Shhssshh" to the noisy tourists.

As we struggle to make sense of our world, sometimes the Holy Spirit is just saying, "Shhsssh. Shhsssh...be still in the face of the mystery of life. Shhsshh...be still, Christ has made all things new. Shhsshh...be still and know that I am God."

Questions for Further Discussion:

1. What examples can you give from your own life of the language of the kingdom that the Holy Spirit teaches?
2. Do you ever hear the Holy Spirit saying, "Be still"?

PART SEVEN
Ordinary Time
HOMILIES 40–70

The rhythm of the liturgical seasons reflects the rhythms of life—with its celebrations of anniversaries and its seasons of quiet growth and maturing.

If the faithful are to mature in the spiritual life and increase in faith, they must descend the great mountain peaks of Easter and Christmas in order to "pasture" in the vast verdant meadows of *tempus annum,* or Ordinary Time.

Trinity Communications, *Catholic Culture: Ordinary Time*[1]

40

THE TRINITY, LIKE A ROSE, UNFOLDS IN OUR LIVES
Feast of the Holy Trinity (B)

- Deuteronomy 4:32–34, 39–40
- Romans 8:14–17
- Matthew 28:16–20

In the name of the Father, of the Son, and of the Holy Spirit. One thing I learned years ago is that there is no better way to get the attention of Catholics than to say those words. It works. At the start of a meeting, when everyone is milling about, chatting noisily, make the sign of the cross, say "In the name of the Father..." and Catholics immediately snap to attention.

Why is that? Of course, it has to do with our Catholic culture. Those little things that make us Catholic. I have heard of distracted Catholics walking down the aisle of a movie theater and absentmindedly genuflecting before sitting down. That's part of being Catholic.

But when we make the sign of the cross and repeat the words, "In the name of the Father..." we are evoking something very deep in our nature. We are giving expression to the unfathomable reality that our God is Three in One and that we, made in God's image, are trinitarian in our nature. How did we come to this belief, this doctrine? And what does it mean to us on this Trinity Sunday, right here in our own land of Zion, our own parish.

Our knowledge of the Trinity is like a rose. If you have passed the rectory in recent weeks, you have noticed some beautiful roses blooming in the flower garden. Maybe you have roses blooming in your own garden. But last winter there was nothing there but thorny stalks and a few brown leaves from last season. Someone may have looked at those uninspiring bushes and said, "That is a rose." But was it really? A horticulturist might have confirmed that it was a rose. A scientist might have done a DNA study and concluded it was a rose. But to the poet, to the young lover, *was* it a rose? Only when those pregnant buds of pink, and yellow and red break forth into their full beauty so that every passerby can see them and smell them, can we say, "Yes, that is, indeed, a rose."

And so it is with the Trinity. The first reading today is an eloquent and powerful statement of monotheism. Moses declares in unequaled eloquence that there is *one* God. There is *one* God *alone*, not polytheism, not one god among many, but one God who has chosen a ragtag bunch of Semitic nomads, brought them out of Egypt and made them a Chosen People. "So acknowledge today and take to heart that the LORD is God in heaven above and on the earth beneath; there is no other" (Deut 4:39). Monotheism, pure and simple.

But we are trinitarian.

The rose continues to grow.

The early Christians came to their belief in the Trinity not through abstract reasoning, not through mathematical formulas, not through the speculation of theologians but through their own experience. They knew God as Father, as Creator, as source of all that is. A little later in Deuteronomy, Moses asks the people about their God in this rhetorical question, "Is not he your father, who created you, who made you and established you?" (Deut 32:6). The answer for any faithful Israelite was a resounding "YES!"

But the early Christians, the ones to whom Paul was writing to in his epistle to the Romans, knew God not only as "Abba, Father," but also as Son. They had the experience of God as Son revealed in Jesus Christ.

But the rose continued to unfold.

Now they had the experience of God as Spirit. Paul sings in his letter, "When we cry 'Abba! Father!' it is that very Spirit bearing witness with our spirit that we are children of God" (Rom 8:15–16). Three in One; One in Three. Experience had led the Church to this knowledge. The rose had unfolded, revealing its full beauty to our senses.

But why is it important? Why do we have a feast day celebrating the Holy Trinity, the way we celebrate Easter or Christmas?

We celebrate in order to become more fully what we already are: a trinitarian people. In the first chapter of Genesis it is recorded, "Then God said, 'Let us make humankind in our image, according to our likeness...'" (Gen 1:26). God is Trinity. God is a household, a community of love. There is no "Mine and Thine" in God, only "I and Thou." God is not a solitary figure living alone in splendid isolation. And, my friends, we have that same nature. The Trinity is, then, a model for how we are to live. Our lives are a long process of returning to our true nature. Much of what we experience in this life as dissatisfaction or frustration comes from living out of harmony with our trinitarian nature. Because of our trinitarian nature, we are made to love; our nature urges us to live in loving relationship, and even communion, with all others. To the extent we enter fully into relationships with others, to the extent we are self-giving, to that extent we realize our true nature.

Father's Day offers us a rough example. Think of a father who strives throughout his life to be in perfect, loving relationship with his son or daughter; think of a son or daughter who returns that love unselfishly; think of the spirit of love that exists between them and how it affects everyone around them. That is a hint of Trinity.

We have in the doctrine of the Trinity an Eternal Rose—a reality that will continue to unfold and be appropriated by the children of God on a deeper level. We have only experienced the first hint of blossom. Our spiritual descendants will experience that reality far more deeply than we do. What a legacy we leave them as caretakers of this great truth entrusted to us.

There is a Greek word used to describe the life of God in the Trinity. It is *perichoresis* and means something like "to dance around each other." Imagine the household of God with the Father and Son in an eternal dance with the Holy Spirit as the love, the delight, the laughter between them. It is that kind of love, laughter, and delight we wish all fathers this day in their relationships with their children. May there be love; may there be joy and laughter. May there be a celebration of our trinitarian nature.

Questions for Further Discussion

1. Why is it important that we are trinitarian and not simply monotheists?
2. How would you describe the unfolding of the Trinity in your own experience?

41
ECCLESIA DE EUCHARISTIA[2]
Body and Blood of Christ (B)

- Exodus 24:3–8
- Hebrews 9:11–15
- Mark 14:12–16, 22–26

Every few months I go into our local hospital and donate a pint of blood. As I lie back watching the collection bag slowly filling, I often reflect on how vital blood is to life and the sacredness with which it is regarded in every culture. Even in our modern age, to my knowledge no one has come up with an artificial substitute for blood. Thanks to medical science, we know a lot about the complex, life-giving nature of blood. Although ancient people did not have this knowledge, they had a deep respect for this mysterious liquid.

The Hebrew tradition closely associated blood with life. Indeed, the root words for "blood" and "life" are paired in Hebrew as well as other ancient languages.[3] In the book of Deuteronomy the people of Israel are instructed, "Only be sure that you do not eat the blood; for the blood is the life, and you shall not eat the life with the meat" (Deut 12:23). Since blood was equated with life, we can better understand why it had such atoning value in Hebrew sacrifice. Thus, the priestly writer in Leviticus says, "For the life of the flesh is in the blood; and I have given it to you for making atonement for your lives on the altar; for, as life, it is the blood that makes atonement" (Lev 17:11). Since blood was life, it was especially efficacious in ritual sacrifice. We have a reminder of this in the first reading from Exodus which describes how Moses, after constructing an altar, collected the blood of bulls, half of which he sprinkled on the altar and the other half on the people.

With that as a background, we can better appreciate the amazement Jesus' followers must have felt at the Last Supper when for the first time he spoke the words we heard in Mark's gospel: "This is my blood of the covenant, which is poured out for many" (Mark 14:24). We could easily substitute "life" for "blood," giving us, "This is my *life* of the covenant, which is poured out for many." Jesus was telling his followers that it was his life that would now bring about atonement, not the blood of bulls. Jesus was prepared to make the most efficacious sacrifice possible, the offering of his own life, not on an altar of stone but on the wood of the cross.

But it was not just a new understanding of blood as sacrificial element that Jesus gave to his disciples. He gave a new understanding of sacrifice itself. Jesus raised to a new level of meaning the notion of sacrifice. It is a meaning we still struggle to understand. The Holy Father, John Paul II, has given us an important document for probing more deeply the meaning of sacrifice in his encyclical letter, *Ecclesia de Eucharistia.* In the very first sentence the Pope picks up the theme I just introduced you to. He says, "The Church draws her life from the Eucharist."[4] This is the heart of the mystery of the Eucharist. But it is life derived *not* from a bloody sacrifice to appease an angry God, but the utter gift of one's self to another without counting the cost.

If we can grasp this understanding of sacrifice, then we see why the Eucharist is the center of everything for us. Every truth of our Catholic faith has its roots in the Eucharist. Pope John Paul II says, "The Church was born of the paschal mystery. For this very reason the Eucharist, which is in an outstanding way the sacrament of the paschal mystery, *stands at the center of the Church's life.*"[5] For example, the Trinity is all about sacrifice, or self-giving: the Father pours out himself to the Son, the Son to the Father, and the Holy Spirit the same, all in a marvelous *perichoresis,* or divine dance. The Eucharist, then, is not just something the Church does; the Eucharist *is* the Church. *Everything* finds meaning in the Eucharist.

If everything finds meaning in the Eucharist, then that has to include our individual lives as well. Every bit of our lives is part of the sacrifice intrinsic to the Eucharist. Not just the conscious offering of our prayers during the celebration of the Eucharist at Mass, but every moment of sacrifice, whether deliberate or simply imposed by the unavoidable circumstances of life, is a part of the Eucharist. Every sickness, frustration, failure, humiliation, setback, disappointment—everything we suffer—is part of the living sacrifice of the Eucharist. Sometimes we say, "That really took the life out of me..." or "I sweat blood over that." When we have those moments—and everyone does—we are being further "eucharistized" by life. The hope for us as Catholics is that we will come to see those moments not as meaningless suffering but as part of the ongoing sacrifice of Christ in the paschal mystery.

The one moment of our lives which must also become a little Eucharist is, of course, our own death. In the Eucharist we encounter the majesty of death—Christ's death.

But our own death will find its majesty in the Eucharist as well. By learning the hard but liberating lessons of sacrifice which the Church strives to teach us through such documents as *Ecclesia de Eucharistia,* we take ownership of our own deaths. Penetrated by the wisdom of that teaching, we will be able to say with St. Paul, "Where, O death, is your victory? Where, O death, is your sting?" (1 Cor 15:55). Death too will have been transformed by Eucharist.

Questions for Further Discussion:

1. Are you able to see any suffering you experience as the ongoing sacrifice of Christ?
2. What does it mean to be "eucharistized" by life?

_____

42

LAW BREAKER VERSUS LAW MAKER
Ninth Sunday in Ordinary Time (B)

- Deuteronomy 5:12–15
- 2 Corinthians 4:6–11
- Mark 2:23–3:6

There is a saying among lawyers that if you have the facts on your side, you hammer on the facts. If you have the law on your side, you pound on the law. And if you have neither the facts nor the law on your side, you just bang on the table.

The Pharisees and Herodians, who make their ominous appearance at the close of today's gospel, must have thought they had a good case against Jesus. We heard in the first reading from Deuteronomy a clear statement of the law: "Observe the sabbath day and keep it holy, as the LORD your God commanded you" (Deut 5:12). We know from the Old Testament that the Sabbath law was a serious matter. The ancient Israelites were enjoined to keep the Sabbath, even in times of plowing and harvest. The death penalty could be imposed for disobeying the Sabbath; historians even attribute the loss of important battles and the destruction of Israelite cities to Jewish refusal to fight on the Sabbath.

By the time of Jesus, the rabbis had developed a complex set of restrictions to prevent violation of the Sabbath. It is said that the rabbis had built a fence around the law to preserve it. Thus, the picking of heads of grain by Jesus' disciples infringed against the rule that made it unlawful to reap, thresh, winnow, and/or grind on the Sabbath. Healing on the Sabbath was only permitted in cases of danger to life.

Those who began to plot against Jesus must have thought that they not only had the law on their side, but the facts as well. The gospels reveal a Jesus who seemed to *prefer* healing on the Sabbath. Peter's mother-in-law was healed on the Sabbath. When he first preached in the synagogue in Capernaum, Jesus drove an unclean spirit out of a man on the Sabbath. In all, the gospels record eight Sabbath miraculous healings, six of which caused controversy precisely because they occurred on the Sabbath.

On its face, it sounds as though the enemies of Jesus had a pretty strong case. But in truth we know they had no case at all. Why? Because the Pharisees and Herodians were not confronting a law-breaker; they were confronting the *lawmaker*. The man whom they now plotted against was the one, St. John tells us, through whom all things were made, including the Sabbath. The Son of man, Jesus—true God and true man—is Lord even of the Sabbath. In acting and speaking as he did, Jesus was simply being faithful to who he was. What would happen to him was the consequence of that authentic action.

Why then did Jesus, a faithful Jew who went regularly to synagogue, openly disregard the carefully constructed fence which the Jewish authorities had placed around the Sabbath? Did he do it to be hurtful to the Pharisees? Was he protesting against the law or trying to provoke the Herodians? No, that was not the motivation for his actions.

In disregarding the fence placed around the Sabbath, Jesus was *restoring* the Sabbath to its rightful place as intended by God: a day of rest and joy for all creation. Jesus was restoring the Sabbath to be a benefit for all creation. He was not doing this in defiance of the Pharisees; restoration of the Sabbath for all creation was part of Christ's mission to make all things new in himself.

If we see in today's gospel just an interesting little contest between Jesus and his critics, then we miss something critical for our Catholic understanding. In a sense, Jesus was showing us the *sacramental* nature of the Sabbath. Using language usually applied to our understanding of the seven sacraments, we might say that the Sabbath is now an outward sign restored by Christ to give us grace. Or, to use the sacramental language of Pope Paul VI, "a reality imbued with the hidden presence of God."[6] Is that not what the Sabbath is? Or should be— an especially holy moment in time created by God to give us life in the form of rest and joy?

Our weekly Sabbath rest is sacramental in nature. Like a sacrament, our rest is a sign that points to something. Our physical resting points to a deeper spiritual resting in three ways. First, our resting from work on the Sabbath commemorates God's rest at creation. We rest in the beatitude that we are created by God, in God's image, loved constantly, intensely, dynamically—a love that by its nature cannot end. The Sabbath is a sacred moment to rest in, rejoice in, even revel in this great objective reality.

The Sabbath points to the reality of our being saved by Christ; a moment in time, a day when we rejoice that we are no longer slaves, that we too have been brought out of Egypt by the strong hand and outstretched arms of Christ. In the Eucharist we are about to celebrate on this our Sabbath, we rest for a time, a few brief minutes, and find real joy in this knowledge.

Finally, the Sabbath points to the *eschaton*, the end times, when as a community of faith, we reach the final consummation where there will be total restoration and rest. In our Sabbath moments we experience renewed hope that the promises God has made will be fulfilled; that hidden within the suffering and tragedy of our contemporary world, Christ is at work, in the Holy Spirit, bringing all creation to union with God.

We should not be too critical of those in the Jewish establishment whose plotting casts a shadow over today's gospel. We ourselves often fall short in keeping the Sabbath holy. But the shadow of Pharisees, Herodians and even Calvary itself cannot obscure what we know through faith: Christ has restored all things for us, even the Sabbath. Let us today find rest and joy in this sacred time.

Questions for Further Discussion:

1. What does our Sabbath—Sunday—mean to you? Is there any way you would like to change your observance of Sabbath?

2. Do you think of the Sabbath as being sacramental in nature? In what way?

43
VOLUNTARY DISPLACEMENT
Vigil of Saints Peter and Paul

> • Acts 3:1–10
> • Galatians 1:11–20
> • John 21:15–19

Tomorrow we celebrate the Feast of Saints Peter and Paul. It is the only saint's day (with the exception of feasts of the Blessed Virgin Mary and All Saints Day) that takes precedence over a Sunday in Ordinary Time. My thoughts on the vigil of that feast come from a little book entitled,

Compassion: A Reflection on the Christian Life,[7] which has given me a term to describe the lives of Saints Peter and Paul. The term is "displacement." A dictionary definition of displacement is "to move away from an ordinary and proper place;" in other words, to leave a place that is familiar, a place in which we are comfortable and at home. It is part of our nature to resist displacement. Most of us are not naturally attracted to displacement. We would prefer to stay as much as possible in our ordinary and proper place.

Both Peter and Paul probably would have preferred to stay in their ordinary and proper place: Paul as a brilliant Pharisee, Peter—a fisherman. But something compelled each of them to accept voluntary displacement—not just to leave the comfort of their customary life, but to embrace a new way of life, even to the point of death. What compelled them to do this? *Compassion.* Both Peter and Paul had undergone life-transforming encounters with the risen Lord. The result of that encounter was compassion, a willingness to accept voluntary displacement and to suffer with and for others.

Peter and Paul are models of compassion for us on this vigil feast. It is *compassion,* that divine quality in each of us that grows in awareness through an encounter with the risen Lord, and compels us to not only accept displacement but voluntarily to seek it out. A priest leaves the comfort of his bed to go to a hospital to care for a dying man. A parishioner leaves a place that is ordinary and proper to accept a ministry of service to others. Whenever we respond to the call of Christ to move beyond our comfort zone, to stretch a little more, we are accepting voluntary displacement.

The authors of the book *Compassion* say that "voluntary displacement as a way of life rather than as a unique event is the mark of discipleship."[8] A Greek word we might associate with voluntary displacement is *kenosis,* to be emptied out. And the great hymn of displacement is found in Philippians where Paul says that Jesus, "though he was in the form of God, did not regard equality with God as something to be exploited, but emptied himself, taking the form of a slave, being born in human likeness" (Phil 2:6-7). Jesus is the model *par excellence* of voluntary displacement. Peter and Paul were disciples formed according to that model.

Again, the authors of *Compassion* say this:

A greater displacement cannot be conceived. The mystery of the incarnation is that God did not remain in the place that was proper for him but moved to the condition of a suffering human being. God gave up his heavenly place and took a humble place among mortal men and women. God displaced himself so that nothing human would be alien to him and would experience fully the brokenness of our human condition.[9]

From the flight into Egypt to Calvary, Jesus' life was a life of displacement. It is no wonder, then, that he would say, "Foxes have holes, and birds of the air have nests; but the Son of Man has nowhere to lay his head" (Luke 9:58). Christ's life was a continual movement out of the proper and the ordinary to a place of suffering and sacrifice. What moved him to voluntary displacement? *Compassion.*

Compassion flowing from an encounter with the risen Lord cannot be contained; it *must* be manifested in voluntary displacement. All of the great religious figures of our Christian tradition witness to this truth: Peter, our tradition has it, left his familiar Galilee for Rome where, as Jesus intimated (John 21:18-19), he stretched out his hands in a martyr's death. The same with St. Paul. Benedict went to Subiaco; Bruno to Rome; Francis to Le Carceri; Ignatius to Manresa; Mother Cabrini to all corners of the Americas; Charles de Foucauld to the Sahara; Dietrich Bonhoeffer from the safety of a teaching career in New York to Nazi Germany where he died a martyr; Archbishop Romero from the security of an apolitical episcopate to death at the altar of his cathedral. This list goes on and on.

Must we, then, imitate these models of displacement? Is it *necessary* that we make a dramatic change in our lives. Probably not, although we should not rule out the possibility. What is probably more appropriate is to be aware of the displacement that happens in our lives all the time. Whenever we experience displacement there comes with it a call to create a more compassionate community.

Let me give you one example that comes to mind. For many years, the Sisters of St. Benedict operated a Catholic hospital in Ogden, Utah. It was a place, a way of life that was familiar to them, an ordinary and proper place. But there came a time when St. Benedict's Hospital was sold and the sisters were forced to reevaluate their ministry. Surely, that was an experience of displacement. But the sisters listened and discerned the voice of God calling them to create a more compassionate community. Thus, they moved into other ministries, they formed a foundation to support programs caring for children, they became more active in the parish. Displacement always brings with it an opportunity for creating a more compassionate community.

From their own voluntary displacement, Peter and Paul began the work of building a more compassionate community. We are the beneficiaries and heirs of that legacy. We honor them today by renewing our zeal for a more compassionate community.

Questions for Further Discussion:

1. Have you experienced voluntary displacement in your life?
2. Has it made you more compassionate?

44
GOD LOVES A GOOD STORY
Feast of Saints Peter & Paul

> • Acts 12:1–11
> • 2 Timothy 4:6–8, 17–18
> • Matthew 16:13–19

Today's Feast of Saints Peter and Paul is a special occasion for many reasons. First, it is the only saint's day, with the exception of feasts of the Blessed Virgin Mary and All Saints, that takes precedence over a Sunday in Ordinary Time. Second, it is an occasion to recall some of the foundational stories of our Christian tradition, stories that are still alive with the excitement and newness of the early Church.

A few years ago Father Andrew Greeley, priest, sociologist, and novelist, wrote an article for the *New York Times* entitled, "Why Do Catholics Stay in the Church? Because of the Stories."[10] And you know, I think he had it right. Stories are at the heart of what it means to be Catholic. And so we should be excited by today's readings. In the first reading, we hear one of the great stories of the New Testament—the story of Peter's dramatic rescue from prison. And in the background, we hear the voice of St. Paul, also no stranger to prisons and dramatic rescues. On this Feast of Saints Peter and Paul, we know what is meant by the saying, "God created humans because God loves stories."

Why do you suppose the early Church preserved this remarkable story of Peter in all its suspense and drama? Certainly, it had to do with preserving an account of what happened to the apostles in the early days of the Church. This story must have been told in dimly lit rooms time and time again. But I think there is another reason this story is preserved so faithfully. I think it is because it is of the same genre as the foundational story of our faith. I mean the gospel story, the passion narrative: the suffering, death and resurrection of our Lord. Because, you see, this story, like the Easter story, has these essential elements: freedom lost, suffering endured, freedom regained, a return home, and then, a commitment to freeing others. These elements, I am convinced, form the basis for every truly edifying story, whether it is in sacred scripture or in literature. Great stories like the story from Acts are timeless, because they touch chords deep in our hearts, and we are reminded of what we all deeply desire—to be set free, to return home, and to free others.

Look at the story in today's reading from Acts and see if does not have the elements I mentioned: Peter loses his freedom, he suffers, he is miraculously freed, (his escape occurs in stages—past the first guard, then the second), he is free to return home to family and community, and he spends the rest of his life freeing others by proclaiming the gospel, even at the expense of his life.

This same story is playing out in each of our lives, even though we may not be fully conscious of it. We begin life as children, free from care, free from worries and anxiety, trusting, living in the moment, content with simple joys. Is it any wonder why Jesus said we must become like little children? But then what happens? Freedom is lost. Gradually, with adulthood, we lose that spontaneity, that zest for life, that joy and freedom. For most it is a life of cares, concerns, the tedium of everyday life. In the words of Thoreau, "Most men live lives of quiet desperation." And for the even less fortunate, it can be captivity to self-destructive habits, to drugs, alcohol, the many addictions we hear so much about.

But in every person's life there comes a moment of freedom. For some, that freedom may be momentary, fleeting, while for others it may continue for a lifetime. What frees us? What really frees us? I don't mean the limited experiences of freedom. You know the answer: It is Christ. It is the experience of the risen Lord, the Christ. That is what ultimately frees us. Many good experiences in life can give us a provisional, tentative experience of freedom, but true freedom comes only through Christ. And we know when we have experienced that true freedom, because we are drawn to free others, through teaching, writing, preaching, through the lives we live.

Now we move to another level of understanding freedom. Go back for a moment to the readings and ask *why* was Peter in prison in the first place. The answer is found in today's gospel where Jesus asks his disciples, "Who do people say that the Son of Man is?" (Matt 16:13). And Peter answers, "You are the Messiah, the Son of the living God" (Matt 16:16). It was *that* answer that sealed Peter's fate. Peter said "Yes" to Jesus while the society in which he lived said "No." That clash between the individual "Yes" and the societal "No" is what put Peter in prison. Our captivity begins when we say "Yes" to society and "No" to Christ; our freedom comes when we reverse the order and say "Yes" to Christ. It *is* that simple. And, paradoxically, when we say "Yes" and become captive to all the sacrifices that go with being a follower of Christ, then it is that we are most free.

This is the tremendous paradox of today's readings. This is the great mystery, the riddle of true Christian discipleship: because he said "Yes" to Jesus, Peter would always be free. No matter what he suffered, whether in Jerusalem or Rome or anywhere in between, Peter would always be free. Peter could have stayed in that prison for the rest of his life and he still would have been more free than his captors. And what is true for Peter is equally true for us. We come to freedom—by saying "Yes" to Jesus. You see, we are asked again and again, day after day, moment by moment, the same question put to the disciples: "Who do you say that I am?" When we say, "Yes, Jesus, you are the Son of the Living God," when we are able to live our lives in a way that is faithful to the profession of faith we make every Sunday, then we are free. That is what the gospel is about, that is what the greatest story ever told is about, that is what the story of our lives is about— saying "Yes" and being free. And once free, we can free others.

But it is not just in Scripture that we find this kind of story. The story of our salvation is somehow imbedded now in our nature. And from that nature, from time to time, comes a story with the same elements I mentioned—freedom lost, suffering, freedom gained, a return home, and a desire to free others. I was reminded of this the other day when I watched the movie *Rabbit-Proof Fence*. If you haven't seen it, go rent it. It is a marvelous film, a film that should be mandatory viewing in every Catholic school.

It is the story of three young aboriginal girls living in Australia in the 1930s, a time when government policy was to remove the light-skinned, half-caste aboriginal children from their homes and place them in dormitory schools where, it was expected, they would become servants, intermarry, and, as the director of the program put it, "the color would be bred out of them." And so the three girls— Molly, the oldest, about fourteen years of age; her half-sister Gloria, eight, and cousin Gracie, about four or five—are taken from their homes in the Outback and placed in the school. Freedom lost.

The girls suffer terribly, separated from their families, forbidden to speak their language, punished frequently. Finally one day, Molly has had enough. She convinces the other two to run away. And so they begin a journey over hundreds of miles of desolate country. Freedom regained.

They follow a fence that was constructed to keep rabbits from inhabiting farmland. Hence the name, "Rabbit-Proof Fence." It leads them eventually back to their home in the Outback, to their families and their familiar way of life. The girls return home.

But the story does not end there. Molly has a daughter and is *again* taken from her home and forced to live in captivity. She escapes, journeys home again, and now begins a lifelong campaign to end this horrible social experiment. Thanks to her commitment to freeing others, the law is eventually repealed.

In a few days we will be celebrating the great event of our American freedom, the Fourth of July. We are grateful for the freedom we enjoy as an American people, a freedom that is a hint of an even greater freedom offered to us by Christ. By the grace of this Eucharist we are about to celebrate, may we come to realize that true freedom and may it strengthen us to free others.

Questions for Further Discussion:

1. Have you experienced freedom lost? Freedom regained?
2. Why was Peter more free than any of his captors?

45
THE ILLUSION OF FACTS
Fourteenth Sunday in Ordinary Time (B)

> • Ezekiel 2:2–5
> • 2 Corinthians 12:7–10
> • Mark 6:1–6

You may have heard the story of the monk who was always quoting Scripture. For every situation that arose, the monk had a quote from the Bible. Finally the abbot grew tired of this and ordered the

Scripture-quoting monk to stay in his cell. The monk obeyed but as he trudged off to his cell, he muttered the words from today's gospel, "Prophets are not without honor, except in their hometown, and among their own kin and in their own house" (Mark 6:4).

Well, it happened that a few weeks later a donkey wandered into the monastery courtyard and refused to leave. Several of the monks tried to evict the unwelcome guest but were unsuccessful. Then the abbot came out and began pushing and pulling on the jackass but could not budge him. Finally the abbot paused to catch his breath, and as he looked up, he caught sight of the monk-who-quoted-Scripture peering out of the window of his cell. The abbot wiped the sweat from his brow and said to the monk, "I suppose you have some quote from Scripture that applies to this situation." The monk thought for a moment and then said, "He came to what was his own, and his own people did not accept him" (John 1:11).

We shall see in today's gospel that Jesus handled rejection better than the monk in the story. But first we must deal with the reasons for the rejection. I will suggest two reasons: the illusion of facts and the pitfall of familiarity.

In the fifth chapter of Mark, Jesus performs a series of tremendous miracles outside Nazareth. Today, in the sixth chapter of Mark, he has returned to his hometown of Nazareth and is among family, friends and neighbors. And how is he received? Rather badly, it seems. The gospel says, "And they took offense at him" (Mark 6:3).

Why? Why did those who knew Jesus best reject him? One possible answer is what I call "the illusion of facts." The townspeople did what people still do today—and perhaps we ourselves do at times—they added up the facts about Jesus and said, "So what? He's a carpenter, lower class, son of Mary. Why listen to him?" Today, there are more books available on the historical Jesus than ever before and still people say, "So what?" ABC-TV did a special recently on Jesus of Nazareth. I heard of one man who, after seeing it, said, "Before I was an agnostic; now I am an atheist."

Why this reaction to Jesus then and now? I suggest we react this way because Jesus Christ is greater than the sum of the facts. You cannot simply add up the facts about Jesus and come away with the experience of God Incarnate. The facts can help, but they cannot give the saving experience that comes from a living encounter with Jesus the Christ. The incarnation, the presence of a transcendent God becoming imminent in creation, is a new reality which, after two thousand years, is still not easily appropriated. The illusion of facts can obscure the Truth, even when it is right in front of us.

The illusion of facts can also obscure the truth about ourselves. Our media are filled with facts. We hear that scientists have decoded the human gene; that babies can be produced in a test tube; that sheep, maybe even humans, can be cloned in a laboratory. Under a barrage of such facts, the illusion can develop that we are no more than highly developed forms of biological material. Biological facts notwithstanding, we are made in the image and likeness of God, redeemed by Christ, sanctified by the Holy Spirit and destined for eternal life! That reality is so far greater than the sum of the facts it is mind-boggling. And it is liberating. Once realized, this truth can liberate us from needless anxiety and suffering. Think of the suffering that is inflicted on women who are beguiled by the illusion that their value depends on having a body like the latest most popular model or movie star. Think of the men who suffer under the illusion that their worth is determined by their physique.

The rejection of Jesus might also be traceable to the "pitfall of familiarity." To the people of Nazareth, this Jesus was so familiar, so ordinary, so common. Familiarity put a glaze over the townspeople's eyes and kept them from seeing the greatness of their native son.

We, too, can slip into the pitfall of familiarity. We have heard the words of Jesus so many times before. We have heard the stories before. Our senses too can glaze over. We can hear comforting words—John 15:9—"As the Father has loved me, so I have loved you; abide in my love," but experience no comfort. We can hear the disturbing words of Matthew 25:40—"Just as you did it to one of the least of these who are members of my family, you did it to me"—but not be disturbed by the news of an entire generation of Africans lost to the AIDS epidemic, while billions are spent around the world on weapons. The pitfall of familiarity is as real for us today as it was that day in Nazareth. The challenge for us is to break through the familiar, to make the good news new again, to know and proclaim Jesus to a world that has yet to know him.

But the gospel ends with a wonderful insight into Jesus. It shows us how Jesus handled failure and rejection. When Jesus says "prophets are not without honor, except in their hometown and among their own kin and in their own house..." he does so without a trace of cynicism. There is no self-pity, no bitterness. He simply states what is true and moves on. Proof of this is found in the sentence which follows today's gospel and really should be included in today's reading. Today's gospel ends, "And he was amazed at their unbelief." The next line is, "Then he went about among the villages teaching" (Mark 6:6). Jesus was not paralyzed by cynicism. And neither should we be. For Jesus, it was enough to do God's will, regardless of honor. And so it should be for us.

Questions for Further Discussion:

1. Why do you think Jesus was not accepted in his own hometown? Have you ever felt this way?

2. What is significant about the way Jesus handled rejection?

46
AMOS IN AMERICA
Fifteenth Sunday in Ordinary Time (B)

- Amos 7:12–15
- Ephesians 1:3–14
- Mark 6:7–13

When the lectionary gives us the prophet Amos as the first reading for the Liturgy of the Word, the lector is obliged to consult what the great prophet had to say. As Paul says in his letter to Timothy, "all scripture is inspired by God and is useful for teaching, for reproof, correction, and for training in righteousness" (2 Tim 3:16). I hope you will agree with me that the inspired words of Amos are still useful today for teaching, reproof, correction, and training in righteousness.

To appreciate today's gospel reading, we must begin with Amos the prophet. Mark shows us the Twelve being summoned and sent out to preach repentance. That, too, is what Amos was sent out to do. Amos lived during the rule of Jeroboam II (ca. 786-746 BC), who reigned as king of the Northern Kingdom when the country was divided between the Kingdom of Israel in the north and the Kingdom of Judah in the south. Although he prophesied in the north, Amos came from the south. His home was in Tekoa, a village southeast of Bethlehem.[11] He was, as our first reading indicates, "a herdsman and a dresser of sycamore trees" (Amos 7:14). It is believed that Amos began his prophetic activity in the Northern Kingdom around 752 BC.[12]

What Amos found when he began prophesying in the north were conditions not unfamiliar to us—a wealthy class living in affluence while the poor suffered. The conditions Amos confronted have been summarized in this way:

> [T]here was pride (6:13–14), plenty and splendor in the land, elegance in the cities and might in the palaces The rich had their summer and winter palaces adorned with costly ivory (3:15), gorgeous couches with damask pillows (3:12), on which they reclined at their sumptuous feasts. They planted pleasant vineyards, anointed themselves with precious oils (6:4–6; 5:11); their women compared by Amos to the fat cows of Bashan, were addicted to wine (4:1). At the same time there was no justice in the land (3:10), the poor were afflicted, exploited, even sold into slavery (2:6–8; 5:11), and the judges were corrupt.[13]

With a few changes, Amos would find essentially the same conditions in America in these opening years of the twenty-first century.

In the face of these conditions, Amos preached the same message Jesus gave his disciples: Repent! Amos the Prophet was a forerunner of those apostles Jesus would send into the same territory; he was a precursor of those missionaries who, in response to the call of Jesus, would preach repentance, reform, and a return to God. He preached repentance from an idolatrous attachment to material wealth at the expense of the poor. The reverberations of Amos' words can be heard in the Christian Scriptures, in tradition, and in the words of modern-day Christian prophets.

To those who chose idols in place of Yahweh, Amos warned of impending destruction:

> Alas for those who are at ease in Zion,
>   and for those who feel secure on Mount Samaria,
> the notables of the first of the nations,
>   to whom the house of Israel resorts!
> Alas for those who lie on beds of ivory,
>   and lounge on their couches,
> and eat lambs from the flock,
>   and calves from the stall;
> who sing idle songs to the sound of the harp,
>   and like David improvise on instruments of music;

who drink wine from bowls,
>   and anoint themselves with the finest oils,
>   but are not grieved over the ruin of Joseph!
> Therefore they shall now be the first to go into exile,
>   and the revelry of the loungers shall pass away.

(Amos 6:1, 4–7)

If we are serious about the instruction Jesus gave the Twelve—to preach repentance—we should be troubled by Amos' warning to a people living in affluence. Although we probably find some of the imagery quaint—men and women lying upon beds of ivory, drinking bowls of wine—the essence of Amos' charge applies to us as well. We are the most affluent country on the face of the earth today. And we have to ask: Has the message of Amos become outdated? Has God changed? Has God chosen to be silent? Does God no longer care about the idols of wealth, about the exploitation of the poor? For believing Christians, the answer has to be a resounding "No": God has not changed.

There are prophets among us today saying the same things Amos said. Like Amos they may appear to lack proper credentials. And they may be ignored for that reason. Amaziah, priest of Bethel, tried to silence Amos by pointing out he had no standing to speak as he did in the king's sanctuary. Amos acknowledges his lack of earthly authority, being only a herdsman and a dresser of sycamore trees, but he asserts an even more legitimate authority: the direct command of God to "prophesy to my people Israel."

We would do well today to heed the voices of Amos' spiritual descendants who, like him, may appear to have no earthly authority when they challenge conditions in our own country. Those who protest against globalization and the exploitation of the poor in third world countries, those who object to a tax system which favors the rich, those who continue a determined protest against the nuclearization of our world are cut from the same rough cloth that gave us the Prophet Amos. Like Israel, we may ignore their prophecy to our peril.

We would be foolish to think that the instruction Jesus gave to the Twelve to preach repentance is somehow limited to those in the inner circles of the Church, to those who are ordained or the official representatives of our Church. It is more likely that the urgent concern God has for repentance finds expression today in persons from callings in life just as lowly as shepherds and dressers of sycamores.

Questions for Further Discussion

    1. What would Amos be saying if he were among us today?

    2. Do you hear the voice of Amos in any modern-day prophets?

47

IN THE TRADITION OF DE LA SALLE
Sixteenth Sunday in Ordinary Time (B)

                                 · Jeremiah 23:1–6
                                   · Ephesians 2:13–18
                                   · Mark 6:30–34

When we hear in the readings today about sheep and about shepherds, we probably think of Jesus, the Good Shepherd. Or perhaps we think of the bishop, whose calling is to be shepherd of the people of his diocese. But a big part of being a shepherd, whether it be Jesus or a bishop, is *teaching*. The gospel from Mark today concludes, "and he began to teach them many things" (Mark 6:34). In that regard it can be said that we are all shepherds, for we are all called to teach, whether it be in one of our Catholic schools, a public school, in our religious education program, or just in our families, as part of our vocation as parents.

    If we are to teach well, we need a model. Today I want to introduce you to such a model. He is the founder of the Christian Brothers, a saint and patron of all teachers—St. John Baptiste de la Salle. De la Salle, who was proclaimed a saint in 1900 by Pope Leo XIII and the patron of all teachers by Pope Pius XII in 1950, has left us a body of classic texts on the vocation of teaching.[14] In his works are found approaches to teaching which have a place in the heart of each one of us as we respond to the call to be a teacher.

    De la Salle was born in 1651, during the reign of King Louis XIV, a time of great privilege for some and a time of grinding poverty for others. De la Salle might have spent his life as a member of the privileged class. Born into a wealthy family—his father was magistrate in Reims—de la Salle could have easily spent his life managing the family estate. Instead, he chose a life dedicated to educating the poor and to the formation of a community of lay teachers who would carry on his work. After being ordained a priest by the archbishop of Reims on Holy Saturday, 1678, de la Salle's vocation soon gravitated toward establishing schools for poor boys. Over time he would deplete his own personal wealth caring for the needs of the poor. But his efforts would result in the founding of schools in many parts of France and the start of an order of teachers which continues to this day.

What, then, are the values of St. John Baptiste de la Salle that can inform our teaching today? They are three. First, de la Salle emphasized that schools were communities of faith. Since faith is the core value, teachers were to be intent on acquiring it through prayer, meditation on the gospels and a deep realization of themselves as "ambassadors" of Christ to the students.

The question which we might pose to ourselves in every teaching context is: "Am I being an ambassador of Christ to those I am teaching today?" Such a question is premised on several things. First, it presumes a growing awareness of who Christ is. It demands a constant attention to the gospels and other works from our Catholic tradition that inform us about Christ, both his humanity and divinity. We cannot expect to be faithful ambassadors of someone we do not know on a deep and intimate basis.

Second, de la Salle urged his teachers to "overflow with abundant zeal." Such zeal would be prompted by an awareness that each child a teacher served was made in the image and likeness of God. By acting with zeal, de la Salle taught, teachers would draw down upon their students the Spirit of God. It was especially among the poor that de la Salle urged teachers to perfect their awareness of God's image and likeness.

The key to such zeal is a disciplined life of prayer. Without a prayer life suited to our individual gifts, we are unable to recognize the divine image—in ourselves, first of all and, by extension, in those we serve. But gaining such an awareness can be as difficult and as demanding as learning calculus or music. Learning to pray well does not come naturally to most of us. It requires knowledge, guidance, discipline, and, above all, a radical honesty. If we were to take de la Salle seriously on this point, we might have a full-time spiritual director on the staffs of our Catholic schools right along with an athletic director!

Reliance on the providence of God was another core value for de la Salle. Through his own sufferings over many years, sufferings often caused by religious figures he had to contend with in forming his schools, de la Salle came to experience at a deep level what it meant to rely on divine providence. I am sure there are many in Catholic education who have experienced firsthand the importance of this value. Certainly those who have been involved in Catholic education in our diocese since it was created have more than once experienced the "abandonment to divine providence" that de la Salle urged us to imitate.

Most of us, when we look back over our lives, can identify one or two particularly good teachers. They stand out in our memory more clearly than historical facts, the conjugation of Latin verbs or the Pythagorean theorem. They stand out as individuals who shepherded us through difficult courses but, more importantly, gave us not only knowledge but a better sense of our own worth. If we think about it, these memorable teachers in some way embodied the principles that de la Salle taught. Part of our responsibility as Church is to foster vocations to teaching that will continue the great tradition of teaching that St. John Baptiste de la Salle so epitomizes.

Questions for Further Discussion:

1. Do you see yourself as a teacher? If so, which of de la Salle's principles do you find most important?
2. Do you see the vocation of teaching as being as important as other vocations?

48
LEST CHRIST'S FLOCK GO HUNGRY
Seventeenth Sunday in Ordinary Time (B)

- 2 Kings 4:42–44
- Ephesians 4:1–6
- John 6:1–15

Ordinary things are like tools which, if you know how to use them, can shape the hearts of people in an extraordinary way. Lost coins, buried treasure, fig trees, rich and poor soil, barley loaves and fish—all of these were sharp tools in the hands of a master like Jesus. Jesus was a master at using these tools. He used them to move people from the ordinary to the extraordinary, from the natural to the supernatural, from the particular to the universal.

We have a splendid example of this in the sixth chapter of John, the gospel text we will be following for the next several Sundays. The ever-skillful Jesus starts out today talking about physical food—barley loaves and fish—but by the time this chapter ends he will have brought us to a more transcendent level, the level of understanding ordinary bread as Eucharist. He will have prepared us for a food that can relieve our spiritual hunger.

As Catholic Christians in the modern world, we have been commissioned to carry on the important task begun by Jesus that day on the hillside across from the Sea of Galilee. We carry on this mission for the reason expressed at the Council of Trent: "Lest Christ's flock go hungry...."[15] But our task today of evoking an understanding of Eucharist from chapter six of John is difficult, because for many the extraordinary has come to seem ordinary, and the ordinary, mundane. Too many who come to Mass have lost that sense of amazement at what happens here every time the Eucharist is celebrated. Perhaps many leave still feeling their hunger has not been relieved.

Hunger is an ordinary, natural experience. Jesus knew hunger. And so do we. Perhaps Jesus was feeling hunger himself as he rested on the mountainside after performing many signs and wonders. Jesus knew hunger—not just the hunger that grips the body—but the deeper hunger for meaning, for joy and assurance that only an intimate communion with God and neighbor can provide. In his teachings on the Bread of Life in chapter six of John's gospel, Jesus was preparing the hearts and minds of those who would be with him at the Last Supper and who would come to know him in the breaking of the bread. He was preparing them to see more clearly the extraordinary hidden in the ordinary.

The experience of hunger, at many different levels, is universal and timeless. We experience a hunger for meaning, for joy, for communion, just as did the people who were fed by Jesus. But that hunger may not always be satisfied by those of us who carry on the work of the disciples. We live in a far more complex world which offers an abundance of competing alternatives for easing spiritual hunger. In our electronic postmodern world, the task of feeding those who hunger at the deepest levels is not as simple as it was that day when the disciples handed out barley loaves and fish. If we are to nourish people, many of whom may be malnourished in the midst of plenty, we must use all the resources available to us.

Our Church today continues that mission of nourishing those who come to the Eucharist. And we do it for the same ancient reason, "lest Christ's flock go hungry...." We know that hunger can exist in the midst of plenty, that even those who receive food may still be malnourished. This is true of those who stand in line at Catholic Community Services for government commodities; it is equally true for those who stand in line to receive the body and blood of Christ in our own parish. It is part of our mission, then, as Catholics of the twenty-first century, to do an even better job of feeding those whose deepest hunger is expressed by coming here today for Eucharist.

We know that the feeding of those who come to the table of the Lord requires the best of our talents and resources. The way we prepare for, present, and participate in the Liturgy of the Eucharist determines whether we will leave our assembly nourished and strengthened to live full Christian lives. The eucharistic meal bears a resemblance to our ordinary experience of dining well. From our ordinary experience we know that if the guests at the meal are to appreciate fully what is being done for them, the event must appeal to them at many different levels. The food must be well-prepared, but the presentation is equally important. In the same way, our eucharistic celebration must appeal not only to the mind but to the senses as well.

Our Church gives us tools in the form of "instructions" for making this happen. One of the more recent set of tools is found in the *General Instruction of the Roman Missal,* or "the GIRM." Everyone involved in liturgy—and that means all of us who come to Mass, not just the choir and other ministers—would benefit by getting to know this little book. This morning I am going to highlight just one principle for enhancing the experience of being fed by the Lord at the table of plenty.

The guiding principle for celebrating the Eucharist well is to do all things "in such a way that it leads to a conscious, active, and full participation of the faithful both in body and in mind, a participation burning with faith, hope and charity...."[16] This is what the Church desires and this is what those who come to Mass have a right to by their baptism. By being vigilant in preserving the dignity of the liturgy, by taking special care for the beauty of the sacred place of worship, by encouraging good music, our celebration is made fruitful. The beauty of artwork, the harmony of voices in song and prayer, sometimes the scent of incense, the reverent gestures and graced movements—all prepare us to be fed by the Lord at an ever deeper level. The fruitfulness that comes from such a celebration is a heightened awareness that the extraordinary has indeed been revealed in the ordinary. Christ is recognized in words proclaimed by an ordinary person, the divine presence is felt in the bread and wine, and the weight of ordinary existence is lightened by the experience of communion with God and neighbor.

Questions for Further Discussion:

1. Is a conscious, active, and full participation in the Eucharist important to you? How do we make it possible?

2. Do you leave Mass feeling fully nourished? Most of the time? Some of the time?

49
VOICES OF A EUCHARISTIC CHOIR
Eighteenth Sunday in Ordinary Time (B)

> - Exodus 16:2–4, 12–15
> - Ephesians 4:17, 20–24
> - John 6:24–35

In his book *Mystical Women, Mystical Body,* Deacon Owen Cummings says: "Theology, however, involves the ability to listen across the centuries for the accent of truth and, having found it, to blend that accent with our own speech."[17] I had that thought in mind as I reflected on the Scripture readings for today's Mass. What "accents of truth" can we pick up by listening carefully to the readings today?

You do not have to be a great listener to pick up from the gospel reading that it has to do with Eucharist. Indeed, the sixth chapter of John's gospel, which we began reading last Sunday and which will continue through the twenty-first Sunday, is sometimes referred to as the "Bread of Life discourse." In the reading we just heard, Jesus says, "I am the bread of life." But what about the first reading from Exodus? Can we detect any "accents of truth" from that reading which will add to our appreciation of the Eucharist?

In Exodus we hear about the Israelites grumbling to Moses because they are hungry. In language that immediately suggests the Eucharist, the Lord says to Moses: "I am going to rain bread from heaven for you" (Exod 16:4). The manna which God freely showers down on the people reminds us of Eucharist, for it is bread for the journey, given by God through an intermediary, Moses. If God could work such a miracle for the Israelites, then surely the ordinary bread which we bring to the altar can become, through the actions of the priest, the body of Christ: our own special food for the journey. This is a truth which resonates well with us.

But as we listen carefully across the centuries we notice that in Exodus something fundamental to the Eucharist is missing. We do not detect any expression of praise or gratitude. Our Eucharist, which takes its name from the Greek word *eucharistein,* is "an action of Thanksgiving."[18] I have searched all of chapter sixteen of Exodus and can find no indication that the Israelites ever gave thanks for the "bread from heaven." In fact, there is no sign of a response of *any* kind to this great generosity of God. That absence of response begs the question of us: do *we* give thanks and praise to God for the Eucharist, or do we simply take it for granted as the Israelites apparently did when they received the bread from heaven?

And we have to ask: *Why* were they not more grateful? Why did they not praise God? My belief is that, to the extent that we are in relationship with the gift giver, we are truly grateful. When we receive some unsolicited item in the mail, we usually experience no gratitude. Similarly, when a gift is given perfunctorily to a large group by the head of an institution—e.g., the principal of a school gives the staff an $8.00 Christmas gift certificate to a grocery store (this actually happened to my wife)—this evokes little sense of gratitude. But a meaningful gift from a loved one fills us with real gratitude. Clearly, one of the voices we might be hearing over the centuries is a critical questioning. It asks whether in our own time we have the kind of relationship with God that produces praise and gratitude. Is the Eucharist something we come to expect, or is it an "action of Thanksgiving"?

When we listen to voices of the crowd in today's gospel we notice that the response to receiving a miraculous gift of bread is no different than it was in Exodus. The crowd following Jesus had only recently been the beneficiary of the miracle of the five barley loaves and two fish. Now, they have followed Jesus across the lake to Capernaum. But, from Jesus' words, it appears they are no more grateful than their predecessors. Jesus says, "Very truly, I tell you, you are looking for me, not because you saw signs, but because you ate your fill of the loaves" (John 6:26). Instead of thanksgiving, the crowd asks for another sign: "manna" or "bread from heaven" they say would satisfy them. Jesus then speaks the words that point to our understanding of Eucharist: "I am the bread of life. Whoever comes to me will never be hungry, and whoever believes in me will never be thirsty" (John 6:35).

The voices we have listened to thus far have not been encouraging. But they do serve as a backdrop for what comes next. It is the voices that are heard in the years—even centuries—following Jesus' death that we must listen to. Those voices form a eucharistic choir of praise and thanksgiving for what God has given us in this sacrament. The voices of St. Paul, the early church leaders, the saints and martyrs, the holy men and women down through the centuries, give us a harmonious chorus of gratitude. Many of those voices are those of men. But, as Deacon Owen Cummings demonstrates in his book, there were also beautiful, though often unnoticed, voices from women mystics who only now are being heard and appreciated.

The response of these women mystics—Hildegard of Bingen, Catherine of Siena, Thérèse of Liseux, and many more—is in sharp contrast to what we saw in the Israelites and the crowd following Jesus. These women respond to the true bread from heaven with voices that are both mystical and prophetic. They are mystical in that they proclaim the real presence of Christ in the Eucharist in terms of how they have been affected. They speak in terms of divinization, transformation, a burning desire for unity and thanksgiving. Hadewijch[19] of Antwerp is described as having "a profound sense of God's gracious generosity" which she refers to as "overflowingness."[20] And they speak of love as being the central force in their experience of Eucharist. It is a love that flows over into loving and caring for those around them.

There is a wonderful chorus of eucharistic voices to be heard as we listen across the centuries. They are voices which can question us, challenge us, and fill us with a desire to add our own voices to the great eucharistic choir. Through this eucharist may our voices harmonize with that choir.

Questions for Further Discussion:

1. Why do you think the Israelites and the crowd that followed Jesus did not show more gratitude?

2. What voices from the eucharistic choir do you hear as you listen over the centuries?

50
MANGIA!
Nineteenth Sunday in Ordinary Time (B)

- 1 Kings 19:4–8
- Ephesians 4:30–5:2
- John 6:41–51

Today's gospel continues what is known as the "Bread of Life discourse" from the sixth chapter of John's gospel. Two weeks ago we heard about the multiplication of loaves. In the two Sundays that follow we will continue to hear gospel readings that form the basis for our understanding of Eucharist.

One priest, in commenting on the "Bread of Life discourse," described a sumptuous scene involving an Italian family seated around the table. Mama comes in with a platter of steaming food and she exclaims, "*Mangia!*" Eat!

I would like to return to that scene today and try to tease a little more meaning out of it.

Imagine that among those seated at the table is a small boy—let's call him Luigi. Now, while everyone else is eating away, Luigi sits quietly, thinking. Suddenly he asks, "Why do we eat food?" Everyone pauses, but no one at the table can offer Luigi a satisfactory answer.

Luigi continues to ponder this question and one day he goes to a doctor, an Italian doctor, of course. The doctor is able to explain to Luigi how the body works, how food is digested and how the body is nourished.

Now, imagine that you are Luigi here at this eucharistic banquet we are about to enjoy and you ask, "Why do we eat the body and blood of Christ? Why communion? Why the Eucharist?"

This time I would like to tell you about another Italian doctor, the great Doctor of the Church, St. Thomas Aquinas, who asked that same question many centuries ago.

And St. Thomas came up with four reasons for why we partake of the Eucharist, all of them related to ordinary food.

First of all, Aquinas said, we consume ordinary food for nourishment. Unless we eat, we die. The same holds for the Eucharist. Unless we consume the Eucharist, our faith begins to die. And our faith can die. I saw recently that an estimated 70 percent of Catholics do *not* receive the Eucharist on a regular basis. The good doctor Aquinas might say that is one reason there is so little faith in your world.

Next, Aquinas said we receive communion in order to grow in faith. We know from experience that unless a child receives ordinary food, that child will not grow. The same is true with faith. And in that regard, each of us is still growing. None of us has reached maturity.

How do we measure growth?

For ordinary growth, we might use a measuring tape. On one of our basement walls there is a gradually ascending scale of pencil marks which trace my sons' growth over time. But when it comes to faith, I suggest that one way we measure growth is by the increased compassion we have for other people. Not a conservative compassion, but a compassion that makes us increasingly sensitive to and disturbed by the suffering of the poor, the disadvantaged, all those who suffer injustice. I am speaking of heightened awareness of the need for social justice.

Third, St. Thomas said ordinary food is needed to repair injury. When someone is sick or has been injured, we may give that person special food for healing and strengthening. Think, for example, of chicken noodle soup. Aquinas said the Eucharist does the same on the level of faith; it heals and repairs the injury caused by sin in our lives. Through a life of prayer we become more aware of our own sinfulness. Yet, if we are receiving the Eucharist regularly, a kind of quiet healing is going on in our souls.

Finally, St. Thomas said ordinary food brings us joy and pleasure. This is the answer to Luigi's question. It is a joy to eat good food, to converse with others and to share in the pleasure of a good meal. The same applies to our heavenly food, the Eucharist. We receive the Eucharist with joy and we take pleasure in the company of those who share this banquet with us.

The great spiritual writer Abbot Marmion said that joy is the echo of God's life within us. *The echo of God's life within us!* What a beautiful thought! From the moment we assembled today we began to participate in God's life. In a few moments we will receive that Life *par excellence* in the Body and Blood of Christ. Our hearts, minds and voices echo that life of God within us.

With that knowledge of what is about to happen to us when we receive the Eucharist, we can say with new enthusiasm, "*Mangia!*"

Questions for Further Discussion:

1. Have you experienced the effects of the Eucharist mentioned by St. Thomas Aquinas?
2. How do you measure growth in faith?

51
TRANSLATED TO LIFE
Assumption Vigil (B)

- 1 Chronicles 15:3–4, 15–16; 16:1–2
- 1 Corinthians 15:54b–57
- Luke 11:27–28

When Pope Pius XII proclaimed the dogma of the Assumption of Mary in 1950, he did so not on the basis of historical or biblical sources, but on the basis of a long tradition of Catholic devotion and piety. It was a proclamation in keeping with the axiom of Pope St. Celestine, *"Legem credendi statuit lex orandi"*–"the rule of prayer determines the rule of faith." And so the pope proclaimed as dogma what the Catholic faithful had long believed: Mary, "preserved free from all stain of original sin, when the course of her earthly life was finished, was taken up body and soul into heavenly glory, and exalted by the Lord as Queen over all things, so that she might be the more fully conformed to her Son, the Lord of lords and conqueror of sin and death."[21]

But, in a larger sense, it can be said that this dogma *does* derive from Scripture, for it is the culmination of a life of faith and obedience, starting with Mary's assent to the incarnation. Mary's lifetime of fidelity is what Luke records in tonight's gospel reading where Jesus declares, "Blessed rather are those who hear the word of God and obey it" (Luke 11:28). By her obedience to the Word of God, both the Word she bore in her womb and the words she heard from her Son, Mary became a model for all Christians and a type of the Church. The Vatican II document *Lumen Gentium* speaks of the "utterly singular way [Mary] cooperated by her obedience, faith, hope, and burning charity in the Savior's work of restoring supernatural life to souls."[22] And moreover, "taken up to heaven, she did not lay aside this saving role, but by her manifold acts of intercession continues to win for us gifts of eternal salvation."[23]

It is not difficult for me to appreciate what *Lumen Gentium* means by Mary's singular cooperation with her Son in bringing life to souls, because in my early days as a Catholic, Mary did just that. In the summer of 1967, at the age of 18 and newly graduated from high school, I came to love all things Catholic, especially Mary. Introduced to Mary by my godfather, I gloried in the devotions cradle Catholics had taken for granted since childhood—the rosary, the Angelus, scapulars, the Miraculous Medal, special feasts. I remember stealing a few minutes from my job of cutting grass for the county to pray in a country cemetery in front of a statue of the Blessed Mother. My own experience validated the axiom expressed by Pope St. Celestine: my prayer determined my faith. In those days I knew nothing about Augustine, Newman or Merton—only Mary. That would change, but my gratitude to Mary would not diminish.

The Assumption is, then, a great feast, for we celebrate what is to be the destiny of each one of us who hears the word of God and keeps it: resurrected life, rejoicing in God. What Christ has done for Mary, he also does for us. Each of us is given the promise of salvation and resurrection.

In the Eastern Church, the feast we will celebrate tomorrow is known as the Dormition of the Theotokos—the falling asleep of the God Bearer. The theme of the celebration is expressed in these words:

> In giving birth, you preserved your virginity!
> In falling asleep you did not forsake the world, O Theotokos!
> You were translated to life, O Mother of Life,
> And by your prayers you deliver our souls from death![24]

And:

> Neither the tomb, nor death, could hold the Theotokos,
> Who is constant in prayer and our firm hope in her
>   intercessions.
> For being the Mother of Life,
> She was translated to life by the One who dwelt in her virginal
>   womb![25]

We rejoice in knowing that Mary has been "translated to life." And we rejoice as well in the life Christ has given to us with the cooperation of one who heard the word of God and observed it.

Questions for Further Discussion:

1. What does it mean that the rule of prayer determines the rule of faith?

2. How is Mary a model for all Christians and a type of the Church?

52
OUR LADY OF THE ROCKIES
Feast of the Assumption (B)

- Revelation 11:19a; 12:1–6a, 10ab
- 1 Corinthians 15:20–27
- Luke 1:39–56

One of the more controversial topics relating to Mary is her role in mediating grace to our world. In the *Dogmatic Constitution on the Church [Lumen Gentium]* the Second Vatican Council affirms that the Blessed Virgin may properly be invoked as "Mediatrix."[26] The document hastens to add that this title must be understood as neither taking away from nor adding to "the dignity and efficacy of Christ the one Mediator."[27] Nevertheless, the title of mediatrix has been a difficult one for Catholics and others seeking to understand Mary's role in the economy of salvation. Catholic theologians have always been quick to point out that since Mary was a human person, not divine, she could not be a redeemer as Christ is. Nevertheless, there is agreement that Mary "cooperated" with her Son in the work of redemption.

Recently I came across a story that can give us a small insight into grace and how Mary might be seen as mediatrix. Without exploring in detail the difficult issues inherent in this topic, I believe this story is consistent with an understanding of grace developed by the great theologian Karl Rahner. It is the story of Our Lady of the Rockies.[28]

One author speaks of Rahner's understanding of the experience of grace as being "indistinguishable from the stirrings of the transcendence of the human spirit."[29] In other words, when the human spirit transcends the limitations of its concrete human situation, there is an experience of grace. I find that transcendence in the story of Our Lady of the Rockies.

In 1979 a man in Butte, Montana, vowed that if his ill wife recovered, he would build a statue in honor of Mary. He was thinking in terms of a statue a few feet high. When his wife recovered, he set out to fulfill his promise. But with the help of friends and coworkers, his vision expanded far beyond his original vision. Six years later, on December 20, 1985, a 90-foot statue of Mary was sitting atop the continental divide overlooking the city of Butte, 8,510 feet above sea level.

The story of how the people of Butte came together to accomplish such a feat is simply remarkable. Starting with only a few Catholics committed to the dream of one man, the effort grew to include thousands of people from all denominations and walks of life. Together, they blasted out of the rocky side of a mountain a site for the largest statute of Mary in America. For months they labored building a road to the site until, finally, with the help of an Air National Guard helicopter, they lifted into place a beautiful statue of Mary which is second in size only to the Statue of Liberty.

And here is where grace comes in. The struggle to build and put in place this statue of Mary gave new hope to a community that for many years had been experiencing some of the worst economic conditions in the country. Donations of time, money and equipment poured in from all over. The people of Butte found real meaning in the project. And when it was completed, they experienced some measure of the "transcendence of the human spirit," or—grace.

Today Our Lady of the Rockies is more than a beautiful statue on a mountain. She is a rallying point for many whose lives have been graced by her presence. A Women's Memorial Wall has been established on the outer walls of the chapel/observatory base where the names of women and mothers are inscribed. Already the wall contains 13,000 names from 1859 to the present, representing all 50 states and 20 foreign countries. A nondenominational, nonchurch-sponsored foundation has been formed whose purpose, as expressed in its mission statement, is:

> To recognize the Dignity of Motherhood and the sacrificial Love a Mother has for her child, without regard to Nationality or Belief, in a manner that honors All Women and lifts the human spirit in love, peace & joy, and to maintain the statue and support facilities in such a way that future generations will treasure Our Lady of the Rockies for what it represents.

Is it not fair to say that in some way Mary was a mediatrix of grace to the people of Butte, Montana?

Questions for Further Discussion:

1. What does it mean to speak of Mary as "mediatrix of grace"?
2. Can you think of other examples of "transcendence of the human spirit"?

53
UNLOCKING THE POWER OF THE EUCHARIST
Twentieth Sunday in Ordinary Time (B)

- Proverbs 9:1–6
- Ephesians 5:15–20
- John 6:51–58

We are fascinated with power.

We marvel at displays of power in nature—tropical storms that can destroy lives and property; earthquakes; forest fires, to say nothing of the power contained in the atom which we have learned to unleash, for good and for bad. But there is another kind of power not always apparent and visible. It is the power of life: life hidden in a tiny seed which grows into a giant redwood, life developing secretly in human cells as they divide and grow, and the life that comes from believing in someone, life that germinates in the human spirit, where it can grow and affect many lives.

Given this human awe in the face of power, we should not be quick to judge those who in today's gospel heard Jesus and then "disputed among themselves" (John 6:52). Their frame of reference as they puzzled over this charismatic rabbi, Jesus of Nazareth, was of other powerful religious leaders. Surely they thought of Moses and the wonders he had worked, both in Egypt and in the wilderness: the parting of the Red Sea, the production of water from a rock, and, what was probably most relevant, the manna which Moses gave to the hungry Israelites as they grumbled in the desert. At the start of chapter six of John's gospel, the manna from heaven must have been on the minds of every person who had witnessed, or heard of, how Jesus multiplied the five barley loaves and fed the five thousand.

But in today's gospel, Jesus' power is not spectacular—it is muted and mysterious. It is more akin to the power of life in a tiny seed or cell. He says, "I am the living bread that came down from heaven" (John 6:51). For us, these words have clear and immediate eucharistic overtones, but not for those who heard Jesus, including his disciples. Many experienced not awe and wonder, but dismay and confusion at Jesus' radical statements. Even the disciples would find this a hard saying; their understanding of it would grow as their belief in Jesus grew.

As Catholics, we tend to take for granted such words of Jesus as "Those who eat my flesh and drink my blood have eternal life" (John 6:54). But we should not overlook the real difficulty such statements caused orthodox Jews at the time of Jesus. Scholars tell us that "to eat someone's flesh" was a biblical metaphor for hostility.[30] Moreover, the drinking of blood was regarded as "an horrendous thing forbidden by God's law."[31]

But it was not just the repugnance of eating the flesh of the Son of Man and drinking his blood that put off some of those who heard Jesus. It must have also been disturbing to think that the power of God could somehow be contained in the flesh and blood of this Galilean Jew—charismatic, yes—but still just a man from Galilee. Here was someone who worked miracles, who intimated divinity, and who now suggested that his own flesh contained the power of life. We should not think poorly of those who quarreled among themselves over this hard saying.

That divine life can be contained in something as simple as bread and wine is *still* difficult for us to believe. Indeed, it has been one of the main differences among Christians for centuries. Yet, as St. Gregory of Nyssa said in the early centuries of the Church, God's taking form in the Eucharist is the surest sign of God's power:

> The fact that the all-powerful nature was capable of stooping down to the lowliness of the human condition is a greater proof of power than are the miracles, imposing and supernatural though these be....The humiliation of God shows the super-abundance of his power, which is in no way fettered in the midst of conditions contrary to its nature....The greatness is glimpsed in the lowliness and its exaltation is not thereby reduced.[32]

Given these very real difficulties with Jesus' proclamation that he is "the living bread," how is it that some would come to accept this truth and some would not? Perhaps more importantly, how do we come to a deeper understanding of this truth?

The key is *belief* in Jesus. Father Raymond Brown, in discussing the Bread of Life discourse, which refers to all of chapter six of John's gospel, points out that the passages that preceded today's gospel (Chapter six, verses 35-50) insist on the necessity of belief in Jesus. Father Brown says that "the gift of life comes through a *believing* reception of the sacrament."[33] He adds that the themes of the Bread of Life discourse are both sapiential—i.e. wisdom and revelation—and sacramental, i.e. the Eucharist. He summarizes:

> This is only a hypothesis, but we must remember that the juxta-position of the sapiental and the sacramental themes is as old as Christianity itself. The two forms of the Bread of Life Discourse represent a juxtaposition of Jesus' twofold presence to believers in the *preached word* and in the *sacrament* of the Eucharist. This twofold presence is the structural skeleton of the Eastern Divine Liturgy, the Roman Mass, and all those Protestant liturgical serv-ices that have historically evolved from modifications of the Roman Mass.[34]

This "juxtaposition" of the sapiental and the sacramental in the Mass is our division of the eucharistic celebration into the Liturgy of the Word and the Liturgy of the Eucharist. In hearing the Word pro-claimed and broken open through preaching we come to believe more deeply in Jesus. This believing in Jesus through hearing the Word then disposes us for "a believing reception" of the Eucharist.

There is a marvelous sanctifying interplay between Word and sacrament in the Eucharist. Our active and conscious participation in the Liturgy of the Word prepares us for a deeply meaningful recep-tion of the Eucharist. Eating the body and blood of Christ, his very flesh and blood, enables us to understand better what we came to believe through hearing. As the book of Proverbs urges in the first reading: "Come, eat of my bread and drink of the wine I have mixed! Lay aside immaturity, and live, and walk in the way of insight" (Prov 9:5). We advance in understanding through both the Liturgy of the Word and Eucharist. When we do so, we are better able to recognize the power of life that Jesus, the Living Bread, has given us.

Questions for Further Discussion:

1. What is the connection between the Liturgy of the Word and the Eucharist?

2. What does it mean when we say that the gift of life comes through a believing reception of the sacrament?

54
THE MESSIAH IS ONE OF YOU
Twenty-first Sunday in Ordinary Time (B)

- Joshua 24:1–2a, 15–17, 18b
- Ephesians 5:21–32
- John 6:60–69

This story concerns a monastery that had fallen upon hard times. It was once a great order, but as a result of waves of antimonastic persecution in the seventeenth and eighteenth centuries and the rise of secularism in the nineteenth, all its branch houses were lost and it had become decimated to the extent that there were only five monks left in the decaying motherhouse: the abbot and four others, all over seventy years of age. Clearly it was a dying order.

In the deep woods surrounding the monastery there was a little hut that a rabbi from a nearby town occasionally used for a hermitage. Through their many years of prayer and contemplation the old monks had become a bit psychic, so they could always sense when the rabbi was in his hermitage. "The rabbi is in the woods, the rabbi is in the woods again," they would whisper to each other. At one such time, as he agonized over the imminent death of his order, the abbot decided to visit the hermitage and ask the rabbi if by some possible chance he could offer any advice that might save the monastery.

The rabbi welcomed the abbot at his hut. But when the abbot explained the purpose of his visit, the rabbi could only commiserate with him. "I know how it is," he exclaimed. "The spirit has gone out of the people. It is the same in my town. Almost no one comes to the synagogue anymore." So the old abbot and the old rabbi wept together. Then they read parts of the Torah and quietly spoke of deep things. The time came when the abbot had to leave. They embraced each other. "It has been a wonderful thing that we should meet after all these years," the abbot said, "but I have still failed in my purpose for coming here. Is there nothing you can tell me, no piece of advice you can give me that would help me save my dying order?"

"No, I am sorry," the rabbi responded. "I have no advice to give. The only thing I can tell you is that the Messiah is one of you."

When the abbot returned to the monastery his fellow monks gathered around him to ask, "Well, what did the rabbi say?"

"He couldn't help," the abbot answered. "We just wept and read the Torah together. The only thing he did say, just as I was leaving—it was something cryptic—was that the Messiah is one of us. I don't know what he meant."

In the days and weeks and months that followed, the old monks pondered this and wondered whether there was any possible significance to the rabbi's words. The Messiah is one of us? Could he possibly have meant one of us monks here at the monastery? If that's the case, which one? Do you suppose he meant the abbot? Yes, if he meant anyone, he probably meant Father Abbot. He has been our leader for more than a generation. On the other hand, he might have meant Brother Thomas. Certainly Brother Thomas is a holy man. Everyone knows that Thomas is a man of light. Certainly he could not have meant Brother Eldred. Eldred gets crotchety at times. But come to think of it, even though he is a thorn in people's sides, when you look back on it, Eldred is virtually always right. Often very right. Maybe the rabbi did mean Brother Eldred. But surely not Brother Phillip. Phillip is so passive, a real nobody. But then, almost mysteriously, he has a gift for somehow always being there when you need him. He just magically appears by your side. Maybe Phillip is the Messiah. Of course the rabbi didn't mean me. He couldn't possibly have meant me. I'm just an ordinary person. Yet supposing he did? Suppose I am the Messiah? Oh God, not me. I couldn't be that much for You, could I?

As they contemplated in this manner, the old monks began to treat each other with extraordinary respect on the off chance that one among them might be the Messiah. And on the off, off chance that each monk might himself be the Messiah, they began to treat *themselves* with extraordinary respect.

Because the forest in which it was situated was beautiful, it so happened that people still occasionally came to visit the monastery to picnic on its tiny lawn, to wander along some of its paths, even now and then to go into the dilapidated chapel to meditate. As they did so, without even being conscious of it, they sensed this aura of extraordinary respect that now began to surround the five old monks and seemed to radiate out from them and permeate the atmosphere of the place. There was something strangely attractive, even compelling about it. Hardly knowing why, they began to come back to the monastery more frequently to picnic, to play, to pray. They began to bring their friends to show them this special place. And their friends brought their friends.

Then it happened that some of the younger men who came to visit the monastery started to talk more and more with the old monks. After a while one asked if he could join them. Then another. And another. So within a few years the monastery had once again become a thriving order and, thanks to the rabbi's gift, a vibrant center of light and spirituality in the realm.[35]

I tell you this story, because in a delightful way it tells us what can happen when the truth of God's presence among us is no longer a hard saying but becomes truly good news, giving joy and hope.

For the last several Sundays, in the readings from the sixth chapter of John's gospel, Jesus has been giving us a gift far greater than what the rabbi gave the old monks. He has been saying that he is the one who comes down from heaven to give life to the world. In other words, these readings have been about the incarnation or, as one author puts it, they are about the scandal of the incarnation.[36] The idea that God could take on human flesh was a scandal, a hard saying for many who heard Jesus. And so, they left him. But for those who stayed, those who continued to ponder the revelation that the Messiah is now one of you, this idea was deeply transformative. It changed them from timid disciples into powerful apostles, evangelists who would bring the good news to every part of the ancient world.

The truth of the incarnation, the idea that the divine could enter into the human, was a hard saying for those who encountered Jesus. And, in truth, it remains a hard saying for us today. It is a hard saying, because we are still somewhat ashamed of our humanity. We still find it somewhat incredible that God would want to take on our nature and live among us. For many, it is still a hard saying that God is comfortable in human skin.

In truth, God has slipped into our humanity the way a hand slips easily into a well-fit glove. Divinity is as comfortable in our humanity as your feet are in an old pair of shoes. We are in God the way a fish is in the sea; God is in us the way the sea is in a fish, giving life, buoyancy, and great delight.

The gospels are not a book of hard sayings; they are a testament of good news, for indeed that is what "gospel" means. We proclaim the gospel Sunday after Sunday, we preach it, we try to model it for this purpose—to break down our resistance to what at first seems a hard saying.

In closing, let me invite you to try a spiritual exercise intended to make the incarnation less of a hard saying.

I want you to indulge me on this for a little while. Suspend your disbelief and pretend that the Messiah is one of *you*. Pretend that Christ has secretly returned and is disguised as...Tony, or Mary, or Fred, way in the back there. For the rest of Mass and through the coffee hour, act as if every person around you might, just might be—the Messiah, Christ in disguise. This is really no different than what St. Benedict had in mind in Chapter 53 of the Rule of St. Benedict when he said, "Let all guests who arrive be received like Christ, for he is going to say, 'I came as a guest, and you received me (Matt 25:35).'"[37]

And then, if you will, continue this game tomorrow when you go to work. Approach each person with the extraordinary respect, the reverence, the awe that you would have for Christ himself.

And finally, treat *yourself* as though you might be the Messiah, Christ returned and living secretly in you. If your boss is mean to you, if you experience road rage, just smile to yourself and remember—you may be the Messiah.

If you try this, I know you will experience a tremendous uplifting of spirit, because that is the power of this truth. The truth of the incarnation has the power to lift you from your human limitations right up to the divine.

So, remember—you might be the Messiah!

Questions for Further Discussion:

1. Do you find it difficult to think of yourself or those around you as being the Messiah? Why or why not?

2. Why is the incarnation spoken of as a scandal?

55
JESUS, THE DIVINE TEACHER
Twenty-second Sunday in Ordinary Time (B)

> • Deuteronomy 4:1–2, 6–8
> • James 1:17–18, 21b–22, 27
> • Mark 7:1–8, 14–15, 21–23

It is now the season of teachers. School has started, parents are relieved and teachers are once again at the head of the classroom. Teachers deserve and receive a lot of respect. I searched my memory for a good teacher joke but could not find one. There are a thousand lawyer jokes, but not a single good teacher joke. Hardly seems fair. I think that teachers get more respect, because they have the power of the grade book. Lawyers have their law books, but teachers have their grade books.

That is what we see in today's gospel—Jesus the Divine Teacher, a very special teacher— and when we see him with the Pharisees he is carrying *his* grade book. But before we look at the grades the Pharisees received, we need to go back and consider what lesson it was that the Pharisees were being graded on. For that we need to go back a few thousand years in the history of Israel to consider an unprecedented moment in human history.

We go back to when God chose a ragtag band of wandering Semites to be a Chosen People. God entered into a special relationship of love with these people. God entered into a covenant with Israel, saying, "I will be your God and you will be my people." And to preserve that unique relationship of love, God gave the Chosen People the Commandments—rules for living that would preserve that relationship. The author of Deuteronomy captures the excitement of this moment when God, the Creator of the Universe, broke into human history. He calls the people of Israel "a great nation," "a wise and discerning people" (Deut 4:6), for what other nation has a god so close to it as Israel is to Yahweh? What nation has statutes and decrees as just as the law God gave the people of Israel?

But the Law, the Commandments, were not given as an end in themselves. They were *always* intended as a *means* to an end. They were intended as a means for preserving this incredible love relationship which God had established.

Now come forward to the time of Jesus and the Pharisees we meet in today's gospel.

In one his books the Catholic novelist Walker Percy has a character who says about another person, "He got all A's, but flunked life!" That is essentially what Jesus, the Divine Teacher, is saying to the Pharisees, "You get all A's at keeping the commandments, as you understand them, but you flunked life." The Pharisees, and many others at the time of Jesus, were focused on a complex set of rules for following the Law, but in some important ways had neglected the Covenant of *Love*. They had lost their focus on what was the essence of the Covenant—a *loving* relationship with God and all of creation. Someone said the Pharisees had moved religion from the sanctuary into the kitchen—and that is what their questioning reveals. They have the Lord of Life, the Lord of the Dance, sitting in front of them, and they wanted to talk about the rules for washing hands! A poet says about the Pharisees, "they were so busy with scrubbing 'useless pots the whole day long' that they completely 'lost the dance and song.'" They got all A's, but flunked life.

But there is something unsettling about this scene with the Pharisees. It is easy for us to nod and agree that, *Yes*, the Pharisees got it wrong. They deserved bad grades. But what nags at my conscience is that we know the lesson here is not limited to the Pharisees. The Pharisees were, after all, at the time of Jesus, respected religious people. Like us, they were not thought of as bad people.

And so we feel compelled to ask ourselves, "What grades would the Divine Teacher give us?" Do we in some way get all A's, but flunk life? Do we in our families, at work, in our church, focus narrowly on a strict observance of a multitude of rules, but fail to seek out and celebrate truly loving relationships? We don't need a preacher to point out the many ways in which we may be flunking life. And in our church, do we at times move our religious focus from the sanctuary to the kitchen? If the Eucharist is for us more about details than about the joyful celebration of God's love—in prayer, in song, maybe even dance—then our religious experience may be more pharisaic than Christian. We may be more preoccupied with scrubbing "useless pots all day long" and completely miss "the dance and song."

But there is one very reassuring thought in all this: we are being taught daily by a most unusual teacher. Not the teacher of the year or even of the century. But the Teacher of All Time and Eternity. Like the many good teachers so many of us have known, this teacher will never give up on us. This teacher is eternally patient, eternally loving. This teacher does not want us to fail. Our Divine Teacher, Jesus Christ, has shown us convincingly, through his death on the cross, that he will make the ultimate sacrifice so that we too may share in that loving relationship with God, promised to our ancestors in faith so long ago. We rejoice now in that knowledge and celebrate it in our Eucharist.

Questions for Further Discussion:

1. What does it mean to get all A's but flunk life?
2. Are we at times more Pharisaic than Christian?

56

HEALING OUR OWN DEAFNESS
Twenty-third Sunday in Ordinary Time (B)

- Isaiah 35:4–7a
- James 2:1–5
- Mark 7:31–37

One of the more memorable places my wife Mary Lou and I visited during our summer travels in France was the Lascaux Cave, located in south-central France. This cave contains probably the best prehistoric art anywhere in Europe—or in the world, for that matter. The cave was discovered in 1944 by four boys and their dog, Robot. According to the story, the dog ventured into an opening in the hillside and, when the boys went in to retrieve him, they saw something human eyes had not gazed upon in 17,000 years. On the white limestone walls were paintings of giant bulls, horses, and prehistoric reindeer. It was an amazing sight and the boys agreed among themselves to keep it their secret.

And guess how long the secret was kept? Two days!

It is tough to keep secret something so fantastic. Today's gospel is one reminder of that. Jesus heals a deaf-mute and orders everyone to keep it a secret. And what do the people do? They proclaim it all the more! Jesus does not simply ask the people to keep the miracle secret; he *orders* them to do so! Talk about disobedience! It is not just Catholics of modern times who do not listen to their religious leaders; it happened in the time of Jesus as well.

So, why the secrecy? Biblical scholars give us an answer. One of the distinctive features of the Gospel of Mark is what scholars have called the "messianic secret." Several times in Mark we find Jesus strongly urging secrecy about himself and his ministry. Thus, Jesus commands the demons to be silent about who he is (Mark 1:25, 34; 3:11–12); Jesus orders that his miracles not be publicized (Mark 1:43–44; 5:43), and Jesus commands his disciples to be quiet about him (Mark 8:30, 9:9). The reason for this secrecy, contemporary scholars tell us, is that the author of Mark's gospel did not want to present Jesus as simply a miracle worker, a bearer of supernatural power.[38] Mark wanted to emphasize the cross and resurrection as the keys to understanding Jesus. Thus, Mark clarifies after the transfiguration:

"As they were coming down the mountain, he ordered them to tell no one about what they had seen, until after the Son of Man had risen from the dead" (Mark 9:9). It was *after* the resurrection that the disciples would understand. Then the miracles would be seen in their proper perspective.

In a way, the deaf man with the speech impediment points to something in ourselves. He points to our own difficulty in hearing the message of the gospel as it is proclaimed in our own time. Each of us is in continual need of being healed of our own deafness—not the physical deafness of the man in Mark's gospel, but a more critical impediment: our faculty for hearing with the ears of our souls. We go through life struggling to hear the Word more clearly. Because if we cannot hear the Word clearly, we cannot proclaim it clearly or live it out well in our daily lives. Learning to listen in this way to what God is saying and, of equal importance, what our neighbors—family members, coworkers, church leaders—are saying, is a lifelong discipline.

Two words pertaining to hearing can help us with this discipline: the words are "absurd" and "obedience." Both words have to do with hearing and listening. The first word, *absurd,* comes from the Latin roots *ab* and *surdus* or *absurdus,* meaning literally "from deafness" or "completely deaf."[39] Something is absurd when I am deaf to its meaning. To many people in the post-Christian world, the words we will soon declare in our confession of faith, the Creed, are simply absurd. They have no meaning. And if we are honest, we have to admit that sometimes they sound a little absurd to us as well. The atheist, for presumably sincere and complex reasons, finds absurd the notion of a loving God who, out of love for you and me, would send his son into the world. Such a person is impeded from hearing the voice of God in the words we proclaim. His or her deafness is as real as that faced by Jesus in the gospel.

And what about ourselves? Do the words we recite in the Nicene Creed or the Apostles' Creed seem absurd to us? Of course they do. Why? Because they are such huge thoughts! Anyone who is not a little hard of hearing when it comes to the great truths we proclaim is not being honest with you. We are *all* impeded in our hearing of the Word of God, not because we are insincere or because we do not try, but simply because of the magnitude of the task. We go through life begging Jesus to heal our deafness a little more, to remove a little more of the impediment, to help us to listen and truly hear what God wants us to hear.

And how does the cure work? Is it done with spitting, with touching, with a loud groan–*Ephphatha?* No, it happens through *obedience,* the second word I mentioned before.

Obedience also has to do with hearing. The word "obedience" comes from the Latin roots *ob audire,* meaning to listen closely or thoroughly. Obedience does not mean something that is imposed on us against our will; it does not mean "my way or the highway." It means to listen with the heart; to cultivate such a deep stillness of heart and mind that we hear not only what is being said but also the Spirit's more subtle whisperings. Obedience means spending time with God in prayer, reflecting on the Scriptures, meditating on the Creed, until we begin to savor the words we repeat so mechanically Sunday after Sunday. Obedience is practicing *lectio divina,* the ancient practice of reading Scripture in a prayerful reflective manner, an approach any one of our Benedictine sisters could teach you. It means a *disciplined* prayer life–the Liturgy of the Hours, centering prayer, the rosary, adoration before the Blessed Sacrament. All of this is *obedience.* It is firm commitment to a life of deep listening. And gradually, over time, in subtle ways, obedience *changes* us. The life we follow, the gospel teachings we proclaim, the dogma we declare–these things no longer seem absurd. Our deafness is gradually healed. Our speech impediment is removed and we can proclaim to one another in our own words, "He has done everything well; he even makes the deaf to hear and the mute to speak" (Mark 7:37).

Questions for Further Discussion:

1. Do you experience deafness in trying to grasp the great truths we proclaim? How do you deal with it?
2. What has been your understanding of obedience?

57

BEING HEALED BY THE CROSS
Exaltation of the Holy Cross (B)

- Numbers 21:4b–9
- Philippians 2:6–11
- John 3:13–17

I am fascinated by discoveries in the natural world which shed new light on the spiritual world. Not too long ago, during a brief visit to the jungles of the Yucatan Peninsula, our guide pointed out a certain tree with unique qualities. This tree, whose name I cannot remember, is highly toxic to the touch. If brushed against, it can produce a painful rash that will last several hours. But here is the uniqueness of this tree: it harms but it also heals! The guide pointed out that the tree appears in both female and male genders. One gender carries the sting, while rubbing the bark of the other gender reduces the irritation and heals the rash.

This is not the only example of the paradox of what can harm can also heal. I have heard of snake venoms that, when processed in a certain way, become an antidote to snake bite. I suspect that there are many other such examples. It is as though Holy Wisdom has pervaded the natural world offering hidden testimony of God's love for creation.

We see a further example of this saving paradox in the first reading from Numbers where the Israelites, after grumbling about the hardships of their long journey through the wilderness, are bitten by poisonous serpents, a punishment they presume to be from God. And how are they healed? In prayer, Moses is instructed by God to "make a poisonous serpent, and set it on a pole; and everyone who is bitten shall look at it and live" (Num 21:8). Moses does just that and the people are healed by looking upon an icon of what had harmed them. The mystery of God offering healing through the same thing that caused harm is revealed in both nature and Holy Scripture.

With that as background, the meaning to be drawn from today's gospel on this feast of the Exaltation of the Holy Cross should be clear. Just as harm came to our race through a man—Adam—so now healing comes through a man—Jesus Christ—who is lifted up on the cross, like the serpent in the desert. Indeed, Jesus makes this very connection when he says, "just as Moses lifted up the serpent in the wilderness, so must the Son of Man be lifted up, that whoever believes in him may have eternal life" (John 3:14). We easily see the connection to the cross and infer correctly that it is by looking upon the crucified Christ that we can be healed from sin.

What is the *source* of all this healing? The answer comes in that short passage from John 3:16, which may be one of the best known in all the Christian scriptures: "For God so loved the world that he gave his only Son, so that everyone who believes in him may not perish but may have eternal life." This is the essence of our Christian gospel. The love which forms the dynamic life of the Trinity had to take form in creation. The mystery of the cross alluded to in this gospel really has its starting point in the mystery of the incarnation. God *gave.* It does not say that God considered creation in detached, abstract fashion; rather, it says, "God gave." The love of the Trinity is such that it calls for a total giving, a *kenosis,* a self-emptying, as the hymn in the second reading from Philippians reveals, a self-emptying by each person of the Trinity.

But why human form? Why in the form of a Jewish man from Galilee, Jesus of Nazareth? We are, of course, in the area of mystery here, but perhaps we can come closer to some insight into that mystery by remembering that our human nature, which had been harmed by original sin, was where healing *had* to take place. It was our human nature that had been created to receive the healing medicine of Christ. That healing began when Christ took on our nature through the incarnation. And when we look upon Christ lifted up on the cross, and can do so in a way that is deeply meaningful, then that same healing agent is activated in the depths of our being. Just as we are unmindful—or, in some cases, ignorant—of the latent healing powers in nature, so too we tend to forget that we now carry around in our ontological makeup a potential for healing that will restore us to the kind of persons God intended us to be from the very beginning.

What can we call that powerful antidote for our woundedness? How can we describe the hidden potential for wholeness which Christ gave us by being lifted up on the cross? There is probably no better term than *grace.* It is something freely given, something we did nothing to merit, something that is simply the product of a self-giving love of a trinitarian God. But over a lifetime we come to know its effects in our lives. We know it in quiet, meditative prayer, when the sense of distance is overcome; when God is revealed not as distant, but as close as our own breath. We know it when the experience of time becomes less burdensome; when we sense Christ, like a refreshing morning rain shower, pervading and freshening our everyday passage through time. We know it in the peace, the tranquility and joy of simply abiding in his love, his presence, in the sacraments, especially the Eucharist. And we are especially aware of that transforming energy we call grace, when we overcome our own selfishness in all its subtle and varied forms.

Many of the saints had as part of their spiritual practice a form of prayer that involved simply gazing upon the crucifix. Some of them died doing just that. It is a practice we might want to reclaim, if we do not have it. Under the influence of grace, our meditating upon the cross can release in us the grace God wills us to have. Then, like the Israelites in the wilderness, we are healed.

Questions for Further Discussion:

1. Do you see the necessity of God healing us through Jesus of Nazareth?

2. How would you describe the healing power of Christ upon the cross?

58
IT WAS THE BEST OF DAYS, IT WAS THE WORST OF DAYS
Twenty-fourth Sunday in Ordinary Time (B)

- Isaiah 50:5–9a
- James 2:14–18
- Mark 8:27–35

The title for this homily might be: "It Was the Best of Days, It Was the Worst of Days." Imagine this scene in the little town of Capernaum: Peter is coming home from a long day of following Jesus around the dusty trails of Galilee. Peter's wife is waiting for him. (We know he had a wife because his mother-in-law is mentioned in the gospels.) Peter has that look of someone who has had a bad day. With his wife's urging he tells her about his day.

Peter, anticipating Charles Dickens by eighteen centuries, says, "It was the best of days, it was the worst of days."

"How so?" says his wife, whose name we do not know.

"It started out so well," Peter says. "We were walking along on a beautiful morning, on our way to Caesarea Philippi, the sun shining, the air fresh and cool—a feeling of great excitement among us. But then Jesus turns and asks, 'Who do people say that I am?'

"Well, some in our group say, 'John the Baptist.' A few others, 'Elijah' and some said, 'one of the prophets.' But I held back. I knew those answers were not right. But then he looked right at me and he says, 'Who do *you* say that I am?' And I blurted out, 'You are the Messiah!' And I felt great because I knew I had it right."

Peter's wife looks at him and says, "So what's the problem? Why was it a *bad* day?"

Then Peter tells her the rest of the story: how Jesus began to talk about having to suffer, about dying and rising again. "So I tried to argue with him," Peter says. "Told him he couldn't be right about that. And then," Peter pauses. "Then he said something I will never forget. He called me *Satan*. He said, 'Get behind me, Satan.' And he started talking about how every disciple who wanted to follow him must deny himself, and even lose his life for the sake of Jesus and the gospel. That's why I say, 'It was the best of days, it was the worst of days.'"

Does this little fictional account of Peter's bad day sound credible? It should, because we have all been there. Each of us has walked in Peter's sandals. In fact, we walk in his sandals every day. There is not a day goes by that our Lord does not ask each of us, "Who do *you* say that I am?" Much of the time we do not even hear the question. But then there are moments of clarity, those peak experiences, when we hear the perennial question of Jesus and we, like Peter, answer, "You are the Messiah! You are my God! You are everything!"

The scene from the gospel is really like a coin: It has two sides to it. On the one side is the question from Jesus and our response. But then you turn the coin over and there is another side. It is a command: If I am Christ for you, then follow me! Do as I do! Deny yourself! Give up more and more of yourself for me! Follow me! Be my disciple! Like Peter, we can find that side of the coin hard to accept.

A coin has two sides, but it also has a middle that holds the two sides together. What holds the two sides of this gospel-coin together is trust. When we are able to say that Jesus is the Christ, it is trust in God that enables us to accept the other side of the coin. Our lives are a long process of learning to trust God enough to live as true disciples of Christ.

There is something else in this gospel we should not lose sight of. The fact that this scene was included in Mark's gospel (perhaps thirty-five years after it happened) tells us something critical. The point is this: There was no cover-up! Peter did not try to hide what must have been a very embarrassing moment for the leader of the early Church. Why no cover-up?

There was no cover-up because the early Church, under the guidance of the Holy Spirit, saw that these stories were critical for understanding the gospel. They pondered both sides of the coin. They asked themselves, just as we do, "Who do I say that Jesus is?" And they pondered: "If I say he is the Christ, how do I follow him? How do I die to self?"

But then they did something we find very difficult to do: They shared the fruit of their reflection in small communities of faith. And from those small communities came the insight into what it means to live the mystery of the cross. From that insight into truth came freedom, power, and a devotion to Jesus that spread the faith throughout the known world.

We find it difficult to do what Peter and the early Church did, because we are deeply conditioned to think and act as individuals. Individualism is the great heresy of our times. The willingness to reflect together on human experience in the light of the gospel is very difficult for us. And yet our Church, our pope, the vicar of Christ, tells us that sharing our experience in the light of the gospel is what is needed in this new millennium if faith is to flourish.

We have, of course, that opportunity right here in our parish through the small faith groups that are forming as part of the Renew program. It is an opportunity to recapture an important aspect of our faith tradition. It is an opportunity to gain greater insight into the mystery of being a disciple of Jesus. You see, we cannot avoid the mystery. It is imprinted in our lives. Everyone during his or her lifetime undergoes the transformation that Jesus is talking about. But not everyone takes the opportunity in this lifetime to reflect and find meaning in it.

From our knowledge of the gospel, we know that Peter had more bad days. But we believe this about Peter: There came a time when he had no more bad days. That was when he met the risen Christ and set out to truly follow him. We are just as human as Peter. That same hoped-for transformation awaits us.

Questions for Further Discussion:

1. Do you believe that we, like Peter, are asked the question: "Who do you say that I am?" How do you respond?

2, What is meant by the heresy of individualism? Do you see it as an obstacle to the formation of a true Christian community?

59
WHERE WOULD JESUS BE?
Twenty-fifth Sunday in Ordinary Time (B)

· Wisdom 2:12, 17–20
· James 3:16–4:3
· Mark 9:30–37

A third-grade class, presumably in a Catholic elementary school, was given the assignment of writing a letter to God. One little girl wrote the following:

Dear God:
It must be hard to love the whole world. There are only four people in my family and it's hard.

A little boy wrote:

Dear God:
Maybe Cain and Abel wouldn't have killed each other so much, if they had had their own rooms. It worked for me and my brother.

And finally, another third grade girl wrote:

Dear God:
Thank you for my baby brother.
But I prayed for a puppy.[40]

You can see why Jesus loved children. There is a freshness, an innocence, a certain wisdom and humor in what children say. The gospels are filled with examples of Jesus' affection for children. One of the few times the gospels record Jesus becoming indignant is when the disciples tried to keep children from coming to him. The gospels reveal a Jesus who has real affection for children; they portray him placing his arms around them, blessing them and healing them. Jesus was at home with children, and they with him.

I am sure you have heard the phrase, "What would Jesus do?" It is a catchy little phrase, sometimes abbreviated with the acronym "WWJD." Some use it as a reminder, when they are facing tough moral choices in this twenty-first century, to just do what Jesus would do. For instance, would Jesus drive an SUV? I sometimes think a better phrase might be, "Where would Jesus be?" WWJB! One clear answer given by the gospels is that Jesus would be with children.

Today's gospel is evidence of that. Jesus draws a small child into a dramatic scene. He offers a child as the answer to a very human question, a perennial question. The child is the *answer,* but did you catch the *question?*

The question was, "Who is the greatest?" It is a question on the minds and lips of many people: athletes, movie stars, politicians. And the answer is usually, "*I* am the greatest." But, as Mark shows in today's gospel, it was also on the lips of followers of Jesus, those who would become leaders of the early Church.

The answer Jesus gave must have puzzled his followers. Jesus placed a small child in their midst, placed his arms around the child, and said, "Here is your answer. You want to know what it means to be great in the kingdom of God? Here is your answer—receive, care for, serve this small, vulnerable child. Then, you will be the greatest."

And, of course, it is the same answer Jesus gives us today. If you want to be the greatest, care for the children.

I hope the significance of today's gospel is not lost on those of you who care for children. Jesus says that to welcome a little child is to welcome him, and, what's more, to receive the One who sent him. Not the powerful, not the wealthy, not those in positions of influence, but a small, vulnerable child is the true emissary of God. If you are caring for children in any way—teaching, counseling, healing—you have in your care an agent of God the Father. What a radical thought; what a revolutionary idea.

Let me give you some examples of how this gospel is being lived out in our parish and diocese.

Those of you who are parents, have in your care a type of Jesus, a representative of God. If you are a mother expecting a child, you are expecting a visit from Jesus himself and through him, God the Father. By bringing that child into the world, sometimes in the face of difficult circumstances and a culture which is not always supportive of life, you are demonstrating you have heard the message of today's gospel.

If you are a teacher, counselor, administrator, coach— anyone who shapes the lives of children—you are teaching, counseling, coaching, shaping Jesus. There can be no higher calling.

And even if you are not a parent, teacher, counselor or otherwise directly involved in caring for children, you may still be welcoming and caring for Jesus in the person of a child. Here is an example of that. You are all acquainted with the Benedictine sisters who, when St. Benedict's Hospital was operating, cared for Jesus in the person of the sick and dying. When the hospital closed, the Benedictine sisters continued their mission through St. Benedict's Foundation, which is now the outreach arm of Mount Benedict Monastery. And who is now being served by the Benedictines? Children. Just this past week, the Weber County Commission issued a proclamation recognizing St. Benedict's Foundation for its support of such local programs as these: A Center for Grieving Children, Boys and Girls Clubs of Weber County, the Family Counseling Services, the Family Support Center, and, most recently, the new addition to St. Joseph Catholic Elementary School. Through these programs, the Benedictines are welcoming each year hundreds of children who are Jesus himself.

Finally, let me mention the *Policies and Guidelines To Ensure a Safe Environment for Children and Minors* recently released by our diocese of Salt Lake City. A year ago, the news media brought us many reports of children and minors who had suffered abuse by a small number of priests. One of the ways our Church has responded to that scandal is by implementing a new and comprehensive plan for insuring the safety of the most vulnerable—our children and youth. These guidelines seek to accomplish that. They will affect everyone who has regular contact with children, clergy and lay leaders alike. They will help to assure that our children are treated in the way that they should be treated as emissaries of God.

I mention these examples so that you can see that the message of today's gospel is being taken seriously in our community. We may not all be parents, we may not all be teachers, and not many of us could be Benedictines, but we can live out today's gospel in many ways. We are limited only by our imagination and our will.

There is, however, still much to be done. There are still too many children who are not being treated as emissaries of God. Last year in Utah (2002), 13.1 percent of our children lived in poverty, up from 8.8 percent in 2001. That means approximately ninety-four thousand children in our state are living in a way we would not want a representative of God to be treated. Last year in Utah (2002), some ten thousand children were abused or neglected; almost fifty thousand had no health insurance.

Let me illustrate the significance of these statistics.

There is a kind of sacramental that has found its way into our eucharistic celebration. You will not find it mentioned in the Roman Missal, the official source for the celebration of Mass. It is not addressed in the General Instruction of the Roman Missal. I am referring to the blessing of the children that takes place in many parishes at the end of Mass. When these beautiful children come forward to be blessed, it is on the order of a sacramental, something that puts us in touch with the living Christ.

But what if we did not bless all of them? What if one hundred children came forward and we blessed only eighty-seven and ignored the remaining thirteen? Those thirteen would represent the children in Utah waiting to be blessed with decent living conditions, waiting to be welcomed as Jesus himself.

Where would Jesus be? He would be with the children, I am sure. And we must be with them too, continuing to give the care I described but always remembering that there is more to do. If we want to be truly great, the gospel tells us today, then we must find more ways to welcome, to serve, and to care for the children. In doing so, we will be welcoming Jesus himself and the One who sent him.

Questions for Further Discussion:

1. What are some ways that you are caring for children in your community?

2. What further needs of children are not being met?

60
GOD'S GENEROSITY
Twenty-sixth Sunday in Ordinary Time (B)

> • Numbers 11:25–29
> • James 5:1–6
> • Mark 9:38–43, 45, 47–48

When the bishop's ship stopped at a remote island for a day, he determined to use the time as profitably as possible. He strolled along the seashore and came across three fishermen mending their nets. In pidgin English they explained to him that centuries before they had been Christianized by missionaries. "We Christians!" they said proudly pointing to one another.

The bishop was impressed. Did they know the Lord's Prayer? They had never heard of it. The bishop was shocked.

"What do you say, then, when you pray?"

"We lift eyes in heaven. We pray, 'We are three, you are three, have mercy on us.'"

The bishop was appalled at the primitive, downright heretical nature of their prayer. So he spent the whole day teaching them the Lord's Prayer. The fishermen were slow learners, but they gave it all they had, and before the bishop sailed away the next day he had the satisfaction of hearing them go through the whole formula without a fault.

Months later the bishop's ship happened to pass by those islands again and the bishop, as he paced the deck saying his evening prayers, recalled with pleasure the three men on that distant island who were now able to pray, thanks to his patient efforts. While he was lost in the thought he happened to look up and notice a spot of light in the east. The light kept approaching the ship and, as the bishop gazed in wonder, he saw three figures walking on the water. The captain stopped the boat and everyone leaned over the rails to see this sight.

When they were within speaking distance, the bishop recognized his three friends, the fishermen. "Bishop," they exclaimed. "We hear your boat go past island and come hurry hurry meet you."

"What is it you want?" asked the awe-stricken bishop.

"Bishop," they said. "We so, so sorry. We forget lovely prayer. We say, 'Our Father in heaven, holy be your name, your kingdom come...' then we forget. Please tell us prayer again."

The bishop felt humbled. "Go back to your homes, my friends," he said, "and each time you pray, say, 'We are three, you are three, have mercy on us!'"[41]

The bishop in this little story discovered something about God that is right out of today's readings. He discovered that God's spirit, God's grace, God's holiness far exceeds our limited human understanding of how things should be. The bishop discovered that God is infinitely generous in pouring out grace upon creation. Once our humility enables us to realize that truth, we are left in awe and filled with hope.

In both the reading from Numbers and in the gospel, good men are shocked to learn that someone outside their inner circle has been gifted with God's grace. In the gospel, it is John who must learn that someone who is not a recognized follower of the Lord is casting out demons. And Jesus says to John, in effect, "Don't be surprised that the power of God is at work outside this little circle of followers. Whoever is not against us is for us." In the book of Numbers, it is Joshua who expresses shock and dismay that Eldad and Medad were exercising the ministry of prophet, even though they had not come to the tent with Moses to have the spirit of the Lord bestowed on them. In other words, these two had not been commissioned, they had not been ordained for this ministry. But Moses, like Jesus, and like the fictional bishop, knows that God's spirit cannot be contained. He says, "Let them be. Let them minister." Then, he expresses a wish—a *prayer* really—that captures the desire of God. He says, "Would that all the LORD's people were prophets, and that the LORD would put his spirit on them!" (Num 11:29.) Had this prayer been answered, perhaps our struggle down through the centuries with inclusion versus exclusion would not have been as great.

Throughout salvation history religious people have wrestled with whom to include and whom to exclude from God's saving plan for humankind. When God chose Israel, and called them the Chosen People, they quite naturally presumed that God's saving action was for them alone. Their exile in Babylon cast doubt on that exclusivist view of God's plan. With the appearance of Jesus, a totally new, expanded understanding of salvation was introduced: God willed all people to be saved. But even in the early Church, it was difficult for many to accept the possibility that Gentiles (those outside the Jewish fold) could receive the Holy Spirit and be part of the kingdom. St. Paul went head-to-head with St. Peter over this issue.

Our own Catholic tradition has struggled mightily with the problem of inclusion versus exclusion. It was not that long ago, many of you will remember, when it was believed that if you were not Catholic, you were probably not going to heaven. That, of course, is not the teaching of the Catholic Church.

If today we have a broadened, more inclusive understanding of salvation, it is the result of efforts by a number of Catholic theologians from the latter half of the last century—in particular, the great theologian Karl Rahner. Rahner teaches that there is an active seeking and desiring of God in every person, not just a passive capacity to receive grace.[42] Rahner calls this, "the supernatural existential." In other words, a supernatural grace given to *all*, not just those who explicitly follow Christ. Rahner used the phrase "anonymous Christians" to describe those who respond to God's universal call to salvation by self-transcendence, by going beyond themselves. This means, says Rahner, that the Church should not regard herself as the exclusive community of those who have a claim to salvation, "but rather as the historically tangible vanguard and the historically and socially constituted explicit expression of what the Church hopes is present as a hidden reality even outside the visible Church."[43] What a tremendous challenge this is for us as Catholics: to be the vanguard of how the world will someday be!

What does this mean for us here in our parish at the start of the twenty-first century? Two things. First, it should give us a heightened sense of hope and commitment. Hope, because we believe that God is unfathomably generous in bestowing grace on the world. Most immediately, it gives us hope in knowing that those dear to us—our children, perhaps—who, like the three fishermen, may have forgotten the prayers we taught them, are not excluded from God's grace. They may be praying in a more authentic way than we ever imagined, for there is a continual, hidden activity involving God and each human being, operating according to God's mysterious ways, and about which we know very little. We experience renewed hope in knowing that, in spite of the apparent bad news we receive through the media, God is at work, both within the Church and without, restoring the world, healing the wounds of war, casting out the demons of violence, and bringing about the kingdom of God.

Second, this knowledge evokes new commitment to become the tangible historical vanguard of what God is accomplishing in the world. To be the kind of Church that people will look to and say, "That is how the whole world will someday look!" Our longing, our prayer this day, is that of Moses: that all the people of the Lord will be prophets, that the Lord's spirit will be put on us all.

Questions for Further Discussion:

1. What does it mean to be the tangible historical vanguard of what we hope the world will be? How are we responding to that challenge?

2. Do you believe that hope is present as a reality outside the visible Church? Where?

61

BECOMING ONE FLESH AGAIN
Twenty-seventh Sunday in Ordinary Time (B)

- Genesis 2:18–24
- Hebrews 2:9–11
- Mark 10:2–16

The author of Genesis knew about human loneliness and longing. The author expressed these very human feelings in the story of Adam, alone in his garden with "every animal of the field and every bird of the air" (Gen 2:19). Despite their loveliness, no part of creation could satisfy Adam's loneliness, nor take away his longing for a companion.

Loneliness and longing are like threads woven through the rich tapestry of stories, songs and poetry that make up human culture. In the thirteenth century, the Sufi poet Rumi expressed human loneliness and longing in this way:

> Come to the orchard in spring.
> There is light and wine,
> And sweethearts in the pomegranate flowers.
> If you do not come, these do not matter.
> If you do come, these do not matter.[44]

For Adam, alone in his garden, all the beauty of creation did not matter; paradoxically, once given a suitable partner, a loving companion, all the beauty of creation again did not matter. Adam's loneliness was absorbed in loving another person, someone from his own flesh, someone so close to him, they were like *one* flesh.

One flesh. The words from Genesis must have been on Jesus' mind when he responded to the questions of the Pharisees, and later, those of his own disciples, about divorce. He says "the two shall become one flesh," and "what God has joined together, let no one separate" (Mark 10:7-9). We cannot fault the disciples for being perplexed by this statement, for we are still perplexed by it. The statistics on marriage and divorce are the source of our perplexity. In most parts of the country, the divorce rate hovers near 50 percent. Some say the glass is half empty; others say it is half full.

What accounts, then, for the dichotomy between Jesus' high ideal and the facts on the ground? Why are all married couples not one flesh?

The answer also appears in Genesis. It comes from Genesis, chapter three, the poetic story of the fall, that primordial event when man and woman became separated from God, from creation, and from each other. Through self-assertion, our ancestors lost the beatitude of unity with God and all creation. From then on, a return to being one flesh would be as laborious as tilling the fields; it would require the lifelong efforts of both partners, and the grace of God.

Those of us who have heard God's call to the married life—and it is only one call among many—must make our way back to the one-flesh relationship by reversing the path Adam and Eve took: we must transcend ourselves. The vocation of marriage, like all vocations, is a call to be self-sacrificing, self-giving, other-directed. When that commitment to self-transcendence is expressed in vows before a minister of the Church, we call it the sacrament of marriage. Those vows, strengthened by the grace of the sacrament, make self-transcendence possible. When consent is given and vows expressed, the married couple starts out on the long path to becoming one flesh again.

But something more happens as they walk the path of self-transcendence. Over a lifetime, the married couple return not only to unity with each other but with God. The fruit of marriage is found not only in children but in a renewed relationship with God. If the vows are broken, the journey to God is also disrupted, though certainly not ended.

Part of the delight of Rumi's poem quoted earlier is that it can be interpreted as the longing of a man for a woman, but it can also mean our longing for God. For the one who longs for God, all the light, wine and lovers among the pomegranate blossoms do not matter as long as God seems absent. Once God is present, the experience can be so all absorbing that it is as though creation does not matter. For those who have chosen the path of sacramental marriage, the gradual growth in mutual self-transcendence brings with it a rare fruit—renewed relationship with God. When that happens nothing else matters.

Perhaps this understanding of marriage as the pathway for returning to God can give us new insight into Jesus' words in the gospel today. If we are able to discover in the vocation of marriage an invitation to grow in consciousness of God through the faithful living out of our vows, then Jesus' prohibition of divorce is not just another hard saying. It is, instead, an invitation to strive always for self-transcendence. Along that path lies the way of a happy marriage and a return to the contentment of Adam.

Questions for Further Discussion:

1. Do you see marriage as a vocation? Why?
2. How do you interpret the poem by Rumi?

62
ALL THINGS ARE POSSIBLE FOR GOD
Twenty-eighth Sunday in Ordinary Time (B)

- Wisdom 7:7–11
- Hebrews 4:12–13
- Mark 10:17–30

Have you ever wondered what Jesus would be saying about all the violence lately in the Holy Land? Watching the evening news in recent years—with the bombings, the bullets, the anger and the anguish, hundreds dead—I often hear Jesus' words from the Gospel of Matthew: "Jerusalem, Jerusalem....How often have I desired to gather your children together as a hen gathers her brood under her wings, and you were not willing!" (Matt 23:37).

In today's Gospel, a young man asks Jesus what he must do to inherit eternal life. Imagine in our own time two young men, one Israeli, the other Palestinian, coming up to Jesus and asking, "What must we do to find peace?"

Jesus might remind these two men, one Jewish, the other Muslim, of their common ancestor. Both Jews and Muslims claim Abraham as their father in faith. Jews trace their heritage from Abraham through his son Isaac, while Muslims trace their heritage from the other son of Abraham, Ishmael, son of Abraham and his Egyptian maidservant, Hagar.

Then Jesus might tell the two men a story of Abraham that points the way to peace between them. The story is from Genesis; it is a story about hospitality, about welcoming the stranger and about believing that all things are possible for God.

In the eighteenth chapter of Genesis, a story is recorded of Abraham being visited by three strangers. Abraham is sitting in his tent at Mamre when he sees three men standing nearby. Even though the day was growing hot, Abraham runs to greet the strangers, bows to them, offers them water to wash their feet and a shady place to sit. Then Abraham instructs his wife Sarah, who remains in the tent, to make bread for the strangers, while he runs and selects a fine calf which is prepared for a feast. In a tradition that belongs to both Muslims and Jews, we find one of the finest examples of hospitality to the stranger.

But there is more to this story. There is a blessing that comes from welcoming a stranger. One of the men says that he will return next year at this same time and Sarah will have a son. Now both Abraham and Sarah were very old. Sarah, who is well past the age for bearing children, laughs at the stranger's prediction. Then the stranger says something that we hear echoed in today's gospel, "For mortals it is impossible, but not for God; for God all things are possible" (Mark 10:27). And of course we know what happens. Genesis, Chapter 21 says, "The LORD dealt with Sarah as he had said, and the LORD did for Sarah as he had promised" (Gen 21:1). Sarah gave birth to Isaac from whom came the people of Israel.

What lesson might the two young men learn from this story? Of more importance, what might *we* learn from it? What relevance does this story have for our own community?

We might first learn the importance of welcoming the stranger. Though they live side by side, the Palestinians and the Israelis are in many ways strangers to each other. The accounts we see are not about the children of Abraham running out in the heat of the day to offer hospitality to each other. Openness to the stranger has been replaced by fear, suspicion, and ultimately, violence. The stranger who wanders into the wrong part of Israel may receive not hospitality but mistreatment, even death. The same would be true for an Israeli in parts of Palestine. The hope for peace in the Holy Land rests on a return to the hospitality of Abraham.

And the same holds true in our own lives. We do not always welcome the strangers in our community. The immigrant from Latin America who fits a certain profile may not be welcomed by us. There is a kind of violence inflicted on strangers in our own community that may not rise to the same level as what we see in Israel but it is of the same type.

Second, the two young men, and ourselves, might learn from the story of Abraham and the three strangers that, indeed, "*All* things are possible for God." Despite the violence that at times seems hopeless, there are still peacemakers at work in the Holy Land; there are good people from all religious traditions who have *not* lost hope, who pray and work with confidence for peace, believing there is nothing too marvelous for the Lord to do. We need to pray and to act with that kind of confidence.

Finally, we as Catholic Christians draw our hope for peace among Israelis and Palestinians from the mystery of the Cross. The great Jewish writer Elie Weisel, himself a survivor of the Nazi death camps, confronted the terrible anguish of Jewish survivors who lost their faith and asked, "Where was God in the death camps?" Weisel answered that God was suffering right along with them. God was in the death camps, in the furnaces, on the gallows. As Catholic Christians, we see what is happening in Israel in the light of the Cross. In a mysterious way the suffering of Christ goes on in the world. We find hope in the Cross, believing that victory over the dark night of evil has been won, and that a new day of peace will dawn for all of God's people. If Christ has been raised from the dead, then surely all things are possible for God.

Questions for Further Discussion:

1. Do you believe that all things are possible for God? How?
2. Is there hope in knowing that Jews, Christians and Muslims all trace their spiritual ancestry to Abraham? How do we build upon that common root?

63
MARK'S BEST SELLER
Twenty-ninth Sunday in Ordinary Time (B)

> • Isaiah 53:10–11
> • Hebrews 4:14–16
> • Mark 10:35–45

On October 21, 2002, it was announced that a significant archeological find had been made in Israel. An ossuary bearing the inscription

"James, son of Joseph, brother of Jesus" had been found. An ossuary is a stone box used at the time of Jesus to hold the bones of the deceased after the body has decomposed. Hundreds of ossuaries have been found but this one was of special interest, because of the inscription linking it to Jesus.

What you may not have heard is that the ossuary was lined with newspaper. Yes, they found pages from the Jerusalem Times dated 33 AD and in one of the pages there was a story with the headline: "Jesus' Disciples Don't Get It."

Now I see you smiling and shaking your heads, but suspend your disbelief for a few moments. Imagine that what I hold in my hand is a translation of that newspaper article and it reads like this:

Jesus' Disciples Don't Get It

JERUSALEM—A follower of Jesus of Nazareth reported today that the itinerant preacher and wonderworker from Galilee had again tried to explain his "Way" to the small band of disciples who have been following him for several years. The source of the report, a man named Mark, who is rumored to be a close colleague of Peter, also known as "Rocky," reported that Jesus had tried on several occasions to teach his disciples that to be one of his followers, a person must be willing to give up everything, including life itself, if necessary.

According to Mark, the disciples James and John, sons of the prominent fisherman, Zebedee, had stirred up resentment in the group by secretly approaching the Master and asking for privileged positions once Jesus came into power. Mark, it is reported, is planning a book on the disciples of Jesus with the current working title: "The Disciples of Jesus: They Just Didn't Get It." Mark described Jesus of Nazareth as "patiently explaining once again what it means to be one of his followers." He quoted Jesus as saying, "whoever wishes to be great among you will be your servant, whoever wishes to be first among you will be the slave of all." Mark stated, "These disciples just don't get it. And perhaps they never will."

Now, the newspaper account is of course a fiction. There were no newspapers in Jerusalem at the time nor, for that matter, is there any evidence that Mark was among those following Jesus. And, incidentally, there is also a consensus now that the "James ossuary" is not authentic.

But I give you this fictional report to illustrate this point: what we sometimes regard as news is *not* news; the truly good news is not necessarily found in newspapers but in the gospel.

Had someone like Mark been "imbedded" in the group following Jesus for the purpose of writing a book, there would have been material on which to base an account. But would it have sold? Would it have been a best-seller? I think not. Had Mark actually written such a book based on the information in today's gospel, it would have been a dismal failure. Why? Because the story of James and John seeking privileged positions, and the others becoming indignant because they had not thought of it themselves, is simply not new. It is as old as humankind, a human characteristic that has always been with us and likely always will be. Such a book would have been a limited, preresurrection account, lacking the real news—the Good News—that comes to us through the gospels.

We do not need to look very far to verify my statement that the James and John power-grab is not news. We hear about it every day through the media. Indeed, our political system and government *function* on the basis of favors asked and favors given. Moreover, we know that we ourselves certainly have experienced the same motivation that James and John did. Deacons feel honored to sit one at the right and one at the left of the bishop when Mass is celebrated at the cathedral. Many priests, I suppose, dream at times of being named a monsignor, maybe even a bishop. Many good Knights of Columbus undoubtedly harbor a secret desire to be the grand knight.

James and John's yearning for privilege is simply part of our makeup as humans. And it is not necessarily bad. Just about no one in this world, unless that person be a Mother Teresa, has completely pure motives. I have heard it said that the human ego is God's workhorse. In other words, God uses our human desire for honor and recognition to accomplish God's will and to establish the kingdom of God on earth. If he wishes to be the grand knight, the first-degree knight has to *do* something. In God's eyes, it is that effort that is important, not the honor bestowed.

The fictional newspaper account does have one element of truth in it, however. Scholars agree that Mark, who probably was not with Jesus during his ministry and probably did not have a close relationship with Peter, *did* intend in his gospel to portray the disciples as slow to grasp the message of Jesus. He did this in order to make a sharp contrast with how they acted after the resurrection of Jesus. Mark was not interested in what passes for news—ordinary humans seeking positions of honor; he was keenly interested in something much more newsworthy than this. He wanted to show that the experience of the risen Lord had a transforming effect on those who followed Jesus. Mark deliberately sought to show the sharp contrast between ordinary ambition and the extraordinary motivation that would characterize James and John, and all the other disciples, after the resurrection. The good news for Mark is that the resurrection reversed human expectations: those who once sought glory for themselves would, after the resurrection, live out in their lives the words of Jesus: "the Son of Man did not come to be served but to serve" (Mark 10:45). The book Mark actually wrote became a best-seller because the good news it records applies to all generations.

The good news is as current today as it was in 33 AD. The canonization process of Mother Teresa is under way in Rome. Mother Teresa also experienced the power of the resurrection; she too encountered the risen Lord. I don't know if Mother Teresa ever desired honor and privilege for herself but we do know that her remarkable story began when she heard Jesus speak to her. She records in her letters how, on a train to Darjeeling, India, she heard the voice of Jesus calling her to become a missionary to the poor in Calcutta. That encounter began her journey to sainthood.

We are on that same journey. And as we travel, we are well advised to take with us Mark's gospel, for it will help us to be more optimistic about our human condition. Even if we sometimes behave like James and John, Mark wants us to know that the reality of the resurrection is changing us as well. Our journey involves a continual seeking of the risen Lord and a growing attentiveness to his voice. And we know that the voice we hear is authentic if it calls us to serve, not to be served. That call comes every day. We are not called to be Mother Teresa; we are called to be Mary, or Tony, or Alice or whoever. And to be that person within the circumstances God has placed us.

Questions for Further Discussion:

1. What does it mean that the human ego is God's workhorse?
2. Are you able to distinguish the good news from all the other news?

64
BEWARE OF JOB'S FRIENDS
Thirtieth Sunday in Ordinary Time (B)

- Jeremiah 31:7-9
- Hebrews 5:1-6
- Mark 10:46-52

Salvation history is a great drama, with hundreds of actors each portraying some unique aspect of God's loving mercy in our world. As we move from Hebrew tradition to Christian, these actors appear on the stage, play their part, and then exit. But there is one group of characters who seem to appear in scene after scene. I call them Job's friends. They are a chorus of voices that constrain the human spirit in its search for God. They are heard in many scenes, including today's gospel.

I call them Job's friends because their most celebrated scene takes place in the book of Job. You remember Job, I'm sure. He was the protagonist in that Old Testament scene where the question was posed: Why do the innocent suffer? Job was enjoying his domestic prosperity in the land of Uz. He is described as a blameless and upright man who feared God and avoided evil (Job 1). But then Satan reappears on the scene and, in a sidebar discussion with the Lord, proposes a test of Job's fidelity to God. "Take away everything he has," Satan proposes, "and Job will not be so pious." And God goes along with it. Job loses *everything:* oxen and asses, gone; sheep and shepherds, wiped out; camels, stolen; and, even Job's own health is taken away. But through all this misfortune, "Job did not sin with his lips" (Job 2:10).

Enter Job's friends.

The text says their names were Eliphaz, Bildad and Zophar. They came to visit Job, ostensibly "to console and comfort him" (Job 2:11). But when you hear their chorus, you soon know that they came to put their own spin on Job's experience. They came with a chorus of speeches intended to teach Job about reality and to help him become reconciled to it. Instead of hope, they preach resignation.

What counsel do they offer Job? In essence they tell him his suffering is the result of his own sinfulness, that God is somehow punishing him for some sin he has committed. *There is no hope for you, Job,* they advise. *Deal with it. Get over it.* Fortunately, Job rejects the advice of his "friends" and after a long dark night of the soul, finds peace in the conviction that God's ways are not Job's ways. God rewards Job for his faith in spite of his suffering, and restores all that he has lost.

But as I said earlier, Job's friends appear in scene after scene.

They were nearby when the three visitors announced to Abraham and Sarah that they would have a son. (Gen 18). You can almost hear Job's friends whispering, "Don't believe it, Sarah. You're too old. Think of the problems a son will bring." And Sarah's reaction? She laughed.

Job's friends mingled with the crowd of Israelites in the desert when the people grumbled against Moses and had second thoughts about the Exodus (Exod 16). You can hear them: "It was better back in Egypt. Slavery wasn't so bad. We won't make it to the Promised Land."

And you can hear the voices of Job's friends in today's gospel from Mark.

Bartimaeus was as sorely afflicted as Job. He had waited years for his misfortune to be relieved. For years he begged beside the road not just for alms but a miracle as well, for he was a man of underlying faith. We in the audience can feel the excitement building as poor Bartimaeus senses that this day might be different from all others. This might just be a good day for a miracle. The healer, Jesus of Nazareth, is in the neighborhood. This may be the moment he has been begging for. And so he cries out, "Jesus, son of David, have mercy on me" (Mark 10:47).

Enter Job's friends.

The gospel does not call them Eliphaz, Bildad and Zophar. It gives them no names. But I am sure they were there, for Mark says, "Many sternly ordered him to be quiet" (Mark 10:48). No makeup, no costume can disguise who did the rebuking. They were Job's friends. And their message was the same, echoing down through the centuries: "Accept your condition. Your blindness is the result of your own sinfulness, or perhaps that of your parents. You cannot do anything about it. Don't imagine that your condition can be changed. Surely, you deserve what you have been given in life."

Job's friends most likely were convinced that Bartimaeus' blindness, his destitution, his marginalized existence, were somehow the result of his own sin. How else explain it? The text gives us no hint of Bartimaeus being a bad person, but then neither was Job. But we know this: there is a line of thought stretching from the time of Job, through the time of Jesus, and into our modern age, which still links suffering to sinfulness, and apparent success to righteousness.

Now, the first miracle happens.

It is a moment of grace, for Bartimaeus finds the courage to ignore Job's friends. He cries out even louder, "Son of David, have pity on me." I call it a miracle, because it is a small triumph of the human spirit. The cry of Bartimaeus is the cry of every desperate person, every alcoholic, drug addict, prisoner on death row, every dropout, every depressed person, every person living what Thoreau called, "a life of quiet desperation." It is a cry for mercy from the depths of every man or woman who must struggle against not just a physical handicap, but the equally imprisoning voices of friends (and sometimes family members) who join in the refrain of Job's friends.

Most of the time when we view this scene from Mark's gospel we are fascinated with the second miracle, Jesus' healing of the man's blindness. But don't overlook the first miracle—the courage of a broken-down man who, in the face of rebuke, dared to cry out for a miracle.

Now come forward in the great drama to our own times. Each of us lives out a scene in the great drama of salvation history. Think of the times when you begged to be taken from darkness to light, perhaps from a life situation that was stifling you, a destructive relationship, a life of quiet desperation. When you were in that scene, do you remember hearing the voices of Job's friends? "You cannot live without drugs...you cannot make new friends...you cannot finish school...you don't have the talent to be a writer, a dancer, an artist...you aren't worthy to be a minister in the church...you cannot survive as a celibate priest..." and on and on.

These, my friends, are the voices of Job's friends, ordering those who call out for help to be quiet, offering words of discouragement, snatching away hopes, whispering to those in need of God that they are not worthy. They seek to convince the desperate that they deserve misery, are somehow responsible for their limitations, and that freedom is an impossible dream.

I leave you with one bit of advice about Job's friends: *Don't listen to them!*

Once you recognize Job's friends for who they are, a miracle is about to happen. When you hear them, the gospel for today teaches, you must cry out all the louder. And, the gospel promises, you will be heard. Your faith will save you.

Questions for Further Discussion:

1. Have you heard the voices of Job's friends?
2. What would you say is the source of voices of discouragement described as Job's friends?

65
WHITE GUYS CAN JUMP!
Commemoration of All the Faithful Departed (All Souls) (B)

- Wisdom 3: 1–9
- Romans 5: 5–14
- John 6:37-40

In the Cathedral of the Madeleine in Salt Lake City, Utah, there is a beautiful scene on the ceiling of the sanctuary depicting many of the holy people from the Hebrew and Christian traditions, including many saints—St. Francis, Joan of Arc, and others. On this Sunday, the Feast of All Souls, I was thinking of the many holy men and women who have gone before us but who never made it into that scene in the cathedral. If I were to design a private chapel, I would include a scene depicting the many holy persons, not recognized as saints, who have been meaningful to me in my spiritual journey. In addition to parents, many priests and religious, I would include such persons as Thomas Merton, Dorothy Day, Meister Eckhardt, Marguerite Porete, and many others. And one of the holy souls I would include is someone you have probably never heard of, a holy man I want to introduce to you today. His name is Theodore the Jumper.

I choose him for several reasons. The first reason is that he is virtually unknown. And for that reason, he is typical of all souls that we remember today—unknown to history but well known to God. Like our own relatives, whom we pray for and with today, Theodore occupied a brief moment of time on the margins of salvation history. And yet, if you get to know him, he can teach you something about the holiness of all souls. Let me tell you about Theodore the Jumper.

Theodore was a desert father who lived in the monastery of Mar Saba in the wilderness east of Bethlehem during the sixth century.[45] This monastery was founded by St. Sabas in 491 and contains a collection of ancient manuscripts. In 1986 a French scholar, while examining and photographing some of these manuscripts, made an exciting discovery. One of the manuscripts was a "palimpsest," a parchment that had been previously used but whose original writing had been scraped off so that it might be used for further writing. Using ultraviolet photography, the scholar was able to detect much older writings that, among other things, included anecdotes about earlier monks and hermits. One of those mentioned was Theodore the Jumper.

Theodore was not one of the great desert fathers and his spiritual practice may strike us today as a bit strange. But there is something edifying in Theodore's unique way of seeking holiness.

Theodore was like the other monks in the way he lived. His hut was a single room where he made baskets which he sold to support himself and the other monks. He lived a simple life of praying and weaving. But there was one thing that distinguished Theodore—his jumping. This is how the text describes his jumping:

> His manner of jumping was like this: He would set aside his robe and wear a cloth around his waist and climb a high rock near his hut. And he would squat and leap, reaching his hands to the heavens. And he would land in the same place and leap again, many times, each day, and then return to his weaving.

> Theodore put stones in pouches around his waist and discarded one with each jump. And they were not pebbles, such as any monk might use to count his prayers but of a larger size, 150 of them, and each day he would count them in and empty them out with jumping.

The text goes on to describe how at Easter Theodore would climb Mount Hermon and, on the day of the Ascension:

> [Theodore] would gird his robe around his waist and leap heavenward, arms stretched up so that the Lord might seize hold of him. But each year his feet would return to earth and he would make his way back to his hut and take up his jumping again, in hope for next year. He would say: Perhaps the Lord will have mercy on me yet, and reach down his arm to me if I leap as high as I can, and take me to himself.

The text records that some said Theodore could jump twenty, even thirty feet in the air, but no monk of Sabas had ever seen him jump higher than his head. The text gives this explanation for Theodore's jumping:

> Some explain Theodore in this manner: He thinks heaven is near above us and believes he can jump into its realm, instead of waiting for the resurrection. These deride him as the Holy Hopper. Some excuse him by saying his faith is simple and his eyes weak, and heaven seems close to him.

But Theodore had a better explanation for his unusual practice. The text records:

> When a brother asked Theodore: Why do you jump? he replied: Because I cannot sing. And in truth, the psalms in his throat are as pottery scraping.

The text concludes by recording how, when Theodore was old and his eyes clouded, he could no longer make the journey to Mount Hermon. But he would continue to try to jump, even though he could no longer leave the ground. The text concludes:

> When a brother asked him: Why do you strain to jump still, since you are no longer able? he replied: Do you not see: I am leaping nearer to heaven now than ever; the hand of God stretches ever farther down to me.

At this point, I am tempted to invite you to join me in imitating Theodore by doing some jumping. But that would not be very fitting during Mass, so let me share with you what I think we can learn from Theodore on this Feast of All Souls.

First, as I mentioned earlier, Theodore represents for me all holy men and women who have gone before us but are now largely forgotten. Obscurity is one prominent characteristic of the holy souls we remember today. Still, neither Theodore nor the ones we think of today have been forgotten by God. Jesus says in the gospel today, "Anyone who comes to me I will never drive away" (John 6:37). It is not just those we celebrated yesterday on the Feast of All Saints who are remembered by God. Just as fresh in the mind of God are those we commemorate today.

Second, Theodore is a reminder that holiness comes from doing the ordinary things of life in an extraordinary way. Theodore's spirituality is to some extent reminiscent of that of St. Thérèse of

Lisicux and Brother Lawrence of the Resurrection, St. Thérèse, in her little way, taught that every little thing we do, if done with love for God, makes us holier. The strangeness of Theodore's practice is not what is significant; what *is* significant is that he did what he did with extraordinary zeal and devotion. When we recall our own relatives and loved ones on this Feast of All Souls, we might remember the ordinary things they did in an extraordinary way.

Theodore reminds us of what we all seek in the spiritual life— freedom. Not to be free of gravity—we leave that to the astronauts— but to be free of whatever is holding us back from experiencing the fullness of God's tremendous love for us. Every time we pray, every time we reach out to God by serving our neighbor, we are striving to free ourselves from the weight of selfishness and sin that holds us back from knowing God's love. Like Theodore, our lives are a series of leaps upward to God.

Finally, if you experience joy in hearing today about Theodore the Jumper, remember that *joy* is the chief characteristic of those we honor today. They are free from the weight of care and live in the joy of Christ. It is good for us to imitate them, albeit briefly.

As we get older and approach the time when we will join the holy persons we recall today, we rejoice like Theodore the Jumper in knowing that we are nearer to heaven now than ever. And, as the journey continues, may the hand of God stretch even farther down to meet us.

Questions for Further Discussion:

1. What do you find in Theodore the Jumper that is most appealing to you?

2. Do you agree that doing ordinary things with great zeal and devotion is a key to holiness?

66

RUNNING ON THE PATH OF GOD'S COMMANDMENTS
Thirty-first Sunday in Ordinary Time (B)

- Deuteronomy 6:2-6
- Hebrews 7:23-28
- Mark 12:28b-34

Since beginning my reflection on today's gospel, I have searched for a good metaphor to help convey what it means to live out these two great commandments. I found it in, of all places, a sporting event. A few weeks ago I attended the state high school cross-country finals at Sugarhouse Park in Salt Lake City. There I found an excellent metaphor for what it means to love God with all your heart, soul, mind, and strength—and your neighbor as yourself. In case you haven't heard, the St. Joseph girls finished second in the state finals and the boys' team finished first. Very good, indeed. But when these young athletes were running at their full capacity, they probably were not thinking of themselves as a living metaphor of what it means to love God with all your heart, all your soul, all your mind, all your strength and your neighbor as yourself. So let me explain.

There is good authority for linking running with the living-out of these commandments. St. Benedict, the father of western monasticism, wrote in the prologue to his rule: "As we progress in this way of life and faith, we shall *run* on the path of God's commandments, our hearts overflowing with the inexpressible delight of love." Maybe St. Benedict was a runner, I don't know. But his imagery fits well.

So then, what can we learn from observing young people running so well in a cross-country competition? And what does it point to in our learning to run on the path of God's commandments? First, they ran as a team. That is what they said when the race was over: We ran as a team. We might then ask whether we, as Church, run as a team to fulfill these two great commandments. You see, a good runner runs best when he or she is supported by a team. Whether we are running, or walking, or crawling on our way to God, we need the support of others as we make our way along the path of God's commandments. One of the biggest obstacles to truly loving God and our neighbor is to think that we can do it alone. We cannot. We need a team. A team such as our parish provides.

But our team is not limited to local runners of the present time and place. One of the great riches of our tradition is that we have the example and continuing support of many great stars who have preceded us. We call them saints. As we run on the path of God's commandments, they are right there with us, offering encouragement. Let me highlight two examples—one a canonized saint and one likely to be declared a saint: St. Thérèse of Liseux (the Little Flower), and Dorothy Day, who dedicated her life to caring for the poor.

One of the things St. Thérèse would say to us is, "God will grant the elect as much glory as they can take." To illustrate, she used the example of the thimble and the tumbler, each of which, when filled with water, was equally full. And so it is with us. Each of us has been given a unique capacity for loving God with all our heart, soul, mind, and strength. When the race is over, we will not be compared with the Little Flower. We will not be compared with Dorothy Day. We will be asked: How much did you love? How fully did you use the capacity to love that God gave you?

Thérèse would also say to us, "Everything is grace." It is easy for us to fulfill these two great commandments when our experiences are pleasant and in times of consolation. But what about when times are difficult? Then, I suppose, we have to simply trust the wisdom of a holy person who has preceded us on the path and who learned through experience that everything is grace. Runners speak of hitting the wall, that time in the race when it seems they cannot go on. We "hit the wall" ourselves at times as we run on the path of God's commandments. When we experience failure, setback, disappointment, boredom, we need to hear the voices of those who have gone ahead of us.

Finally, St. Thérèse might repeat to us words she wrote in her book, *Story of a Soul:* "I always feel the bold confidence of becoming a great saint." The mark of great runners like Marion Jones and Michael Johnson is bold confidence. We should be no less bold in declaring that we too can become great saints. Those are words we seldom hear these days. But if the Little Flower could speak them, then why not ourselves?

And then there is Dorothy Day who, for me at least, lived out in our own times the second great commandment, "Love your neighbor as yourself." Dorothy started out on the path as a Protestant, and after suffering many personal tragedies, became a convert to Roman Catholicism. She was devoted to the liturgy, the rosary, the Eucharist, but is known mostly for her long life of caring for and defending the poor and the weak in our society. Dorothy Day began the Catholic Worker movement and even into her 80s was still protesting policies that harmed the poor. What would Dorothy Day say to us as we run on the path of God's commandments? One writer tells of going to hear Dorothy speak in the 1970s when she was in her late seventies. This person expected to hear something memorable about God, about prayer or about purpose in life. But do you know what she spoke about? Coats and blankets. She spoke about collecting coats and blankets for the needy. It's that simple. We love our neighbor, who is any person in need, by doing very practical, mundane things. Again, the St. Joseph Catholic High School students did that just this past weekend when they organized a food drive that collected more than nine tons of food for the needy of Ogden, Utah. Dorothy Day would have been pleased.

In case you are getting tired of running metaphors, take heart, the finish line is near! Let me mention just one other aspect of this metaphor, and that is the coach. No one worked harder at the race than coach Javier Chavez. He was everywhere, running alongside the runners, shouting encouragement, giving advice. We have that same kind of coach in the Church with the sacraments, the liturgy, the prayers. They are there for us.

Let me finish where I began by noting the words of another Benedictine saint, who also must have been a runner—the fourteenth-century St. Gertrud of Helfta. Following St. Benedict, she says: "Give me living faith in your heavenly precepts so that I may run the way of your commandments with heart wide open.... Make me run to pastures of eternal life...so that we, running virilely, may deserve to go happily into your kingdom."[46]

May we all run on the path of God's commandments, as one community, with bold confidence, our hearts delighting in love.

Questions for Further Discussion:

1. What does it mean to run the way of the commandments with heart wide open?

2. Who in your experience personifies the two great commandments?

67

THE RIVER OF TRUTH
Dedication of the Lateran Basilica (B)

- Ezekiel 47:1–2, 8–9, 12
- 1 Corinthians 3:9c–11, 16–17
- John 2:13–22

Ezekiel had a vision of water flowing, a stream of water flowing out of the Temple toward the east until it became a river, flowing down upon the Arabah, emptying into the sea, making it fresh. For the people of Israel living in exile at the time of this vision, a stream flowing out of the sanctuary of the Temple was a sign of hope, a sign that their exile would end, that all was not lost. They saw in this vision of flowing water that nurtured fruit trees a sign of their own restoration as the people of Israel.

Ezekiel gave no name to this river the angel had shown him. Today I want to suggest a name for it. It is a name that comes from another visionary many centuries later. In the second century of Christianity, Clement of Alexandria wrote: "There is one river of truth, but many streams fall into it on this side and that." This is the name I would give to Ezekiel's river: the River of Truth. And on this Feast of the Dedication of the Lateran Basilica, I want to explore this great river with you, follow it to its source, study its course and, in the end, suggest another name for it.

In 537 BC, Ezekiel's vision was realized, and the truth veiled by the river imagery became manifest. The first chapter of Ezra records that in the first year of the reign of Cyrus, king of Persia, "in order that the word of the LORD by the mouth of Jeremiah might be accomplished" (Ezra 1:1), the "LORD stirred up the spirit" of King Cyrus to issue a decree restoring Israel to all that the Lord had promised—the land, their own religion, the Temple. Ezekiel's prophecy had come true.

But the river of truth spoken of by Clement of Alexandria was fed by many streams falling into it on both sides. The truth about God that the remnant of Israel brought back to Jerusalem was not the same as when they were led into exile. It had been added to by new insights about God. Perhaps God was at work in people outside Israel—like Cyrus, for instance. Perhaps even pagan nations could somehow be playing a part in God's plan of redemption. And perhaps there was more truth yet to be revealed in the words of the prophets spoken in a land of exile.

Not just Ezekiel but many other prophets, like Isaiah and Jeremiah, had added new streams of thought to the River of Truth flowing out of the sanctuary. Isaiah had spoken of a savior for Israel who would be a great light in the darkness; someone spoken of as Wonderful Counselor, Mighty God, Everlasting Father, Prince of Peace. This stream of prophecy entered the river of truth, purifying it, enriching it, and offering new sources of inspiration for those who would later ponder these words.

In today's gospel we discover the source of the River of Truth. By his words and actions Jesus proclaims that he is a source of power greater than the Temple. Christ is the source of Ezekiel's river. He is the Truth of which the prophets spoke. The Temple could be destroyed—and it would be—but the Truth would remain. The gospel concludes that when his disciples remembered his words and actions "they believed the Scripture and the word that Jesus had spoken" (John 2:22). They saw that he was Truth incarnate. Christ is the source of the River of Truth.

With the advent of Christ, the River of Truth began to flow through a church. It flowed through the small house-churches for which Paul laid many foundations. And still, as Clement would say, many streams would fall into it on this side and that. It would be fed by streams of blood from the martyrs, people like Stephen, Lawrence, Agatha, Agnes, and many more. It would draw in streams of Greek thought from philosophers and scholars. Wherever this River of Truth now flowed, it began to assimilate all that was true and good, until at last it would be spoken of by its true name, first by Ignatius of Antioch and then by many others—*katho likos,* Catholic, meaning, "to gather all into the whole."

In time the River of Truth would flow not just through house-churches but through great buildings of stone and wood, basilicas and cathedrals. One of those churches would be called St. John Lateran in Rome, a gift to the pope from the Emperor Constantine in the year 311. Thereafter, for centuries, it was to be the residence of the popes and the cathedral of Rome. Today our recalling of this great church's dedication is not just the celebration of a building, but a bringing to mind of a symbol of our faith, a visible landmark as we follow the River of Truth to our day. Although I have not seen it, I am told that one of the mosaics in the basilica depicts the cross of Christ, "standing on a hill whence flow the four rivers of the gospels, from whose waters stags and sheep come to drink."[47]

My friends, today we are a part of that great River of Truth, the Catholic Church. The river whose course we have traced extends to our own little parish. It comes to us in Utah through the churches of California, New Mexico, Colorado. We trace our origins through the churches of Mexico, Spain, Europe and, eventually, the Lateran Basilica, the house-churches of Paul, until we reach our source in Christ.

But bear in mind that this river is constantly *changing*. As Herakleitos said, "No man can stand in the same river twice, because neither the man nor the river are the same." Our Church is a river of truth with streams that drop into it on all sides. At its best our Church is catholic, meaning it brings into the whole all that is true and good. To be vital, to be truly *katho likos,* our Church must always welcome the streams that flow into it, choosing the good and rejecting the misleading or false, whether the insights come from feminist theology, the democratic impulses of our American Church, liberation theology, or the theologies of the oppressed. It must welcome different cultures, and be open to new forms of expression, new ways of praising the Lord and worshiping God through music, art, and all the media. All have the potential of providing welcome additions to the great River of Truth.

You, too, must bring your truth to the Church. Through your study of Scripture, your awareness of social justice issues, your willingness to be involved, to speak out, to demand accountability, you add to the streams of thought that flow into the River of Truth. You must bring into the Church all that is good, all that is true, so that it might become even more catholic. Do not remain a side stream, do not stay a disinterested rivulet. Enter the river! Unless you add your own unique elements to this living flowing body of water, the fullness of truth will not be known.

Questions for Further Discussion:

1. Do you see yourself as part of the great River of Truth?
2. What are the streams of truth that are flowing into the Catholic Church today?

68

VOCATIONS
Thirty-second Sunday in Ordinary Time (B)

- 1 Kings 17:10–16
- Hebrews 9:24–28
- Mark 12:38–44

One of the best sources I have found for a reflection on the first read-ing today from Kings is by Adrienne von Speyr. Her little book, sim-ply titled *Elijah*,[48] is a fine reflection on this great Old Testament prophet and the poor widow who responded to Elijah's words and earned a prophet's reward. The widow of Zarephath and the poor woman in the gospel who gave her two small coins to the Temple stand like bookends supporting a wealth of insights into the meaning of humility, generosity and trust. But there is more to the reading from 1 Kings: there is also a theme of vocation, of responding in obe-dience to the call of the Lord.

"Obedience" is the word von Speyr uses to describe the poor widow in the first reading, and it is obedience that characterizes every true vocation. Von Speyr says the poor widow acts "in obedi-ence without knowing obedience" by simply going to the place where she meets Elijah. There she hears a word of the Lord spoken through Elijah that will test her obedience in a way she never could have anticipated. "Obedience without knowing obedience" is another way of describing the initial stage of a vocation, whether it be a vocation to the priesthood, diaconate, religious life, or the sin-gle or married life. Each vocation begins with a person acting in obedience to a word of the Lord not articulated but still effective. A vocation begins simply by being in the place where God wants us to be when the word of the Lord is spoken to us. For some it may be a Catholic college, a visit to a seminary, or a monastery. Or it may simply mean being in the place where God has brought us in order to live out a dedicated single life. In every case, God is mys-teriously involved in moving us to a place where we can hear the call of the Lord.

In that place, the call to say "Yes" is something that at first seems excessively burdensome. The poor widow responded to the call of Elijah in a kind of blind obedience with no hope, no reward, or guarantee for the future.[49] So, too, in any call to vocation, the demand at first can seem excessively burdensome. But if the call is from God there will be a response in almost blind obedience. If it is an authentic call, it cannot be refused because the call touches a hidden place in the person that was previously not awakened to life. In a true call to vocation it is as though God introduces a new power to say "yes" to the sacrifice to come. That is what the widow did and that is what each one of us did when the call to a particular vocation was heard.

When the call is made, a transformation of reason takes place. Von Speyr says it well:

> God always takes away calculation from the one who obeys. As soon as one lives out of God's grace, measures and scales and all human calculations fall away: reason is taken over by love. But love must be so strong in obedience that it truly wins the victory over reason; reason, as far as this is merely human, disappears in order to make place for a new reason that is an attribute or a function of love.[50]

Reason is transformed by the call of the Lord into a new life, a life of obedience that must be renewed each day. The call of Elijah began with a light task: a request for water. Then comes a more burdensome request that the woman sacrifice her few remaining scraps of food in order to care for the prophet. Though she and her son face imminent death, the woman willingly sacrifices what little she has. She responds in obedience because the Lord has awakened in her the word of God that had been latent in her consciousness until that moment. From that moment on, she will experience the miracle day after day, hour after hour.

We may see our vocation framed in the experience of the poor widow's response to the word of the Lord that came to her through Elijah. The start of our call from the Lord begins with a light request. Over time the requests become more burdensome and challenge us to respond in obedience. But when the call is authentic we respond day after day, hour after hour, because a word has been awakened in us. Gradually, we come to see the miraculous nature of that call and our response.

The reading from Kings ends with the wonderfully consoling words: "The jar of meal was not emptied, neither did the jug of oil fail, according to the word of the LORD that he spoke by Elijah" (1 Kgs 17:16). These are words to keep fresh in our memory as we live out whatever vocation we have been called to. The sacrifices we have made in responding to the word of God spoken by the person or persons who played a role in our vocation will not exhaust us. Rather, we will be miraculously replenished over a lifetime—if we are obedient. And it may be the sacrifice we make when our circumstances are as dire as those of the poor widow making her contribution to the Temple treasury that are the most meaningful. It is those sacrifices, usually made in secret, that produce the greatest miracles.

Questions for Further Discussion:

1. How would you describe your vocation? Do you believe that a call from the Lord touches a place in a person that previously was hidden?

2. In your experience, are the first requests of a vocation light, followed by more burdensome ones?

69
THE LAST HOMILY
Thirty-third Sunday in Ordinary Time (B)

- Daniel 12:1–3
- Hebrews 10:11–14, 18
- Mark 13:24–32

This is my last homily.

No, the bishop hasn't taken away my faculty for preaching. And, no, I have not had a premonition of imminent death.

None of that. Rather, I have taken up the challenge today of giving the homily I would want to leave with you, if I did, in fact, *know* it was my last. I borrowed this idea from a university in the Northeast that many years ago began a tradition of inviting each of its professors to deliver the "Last Lecture." The professor was expected to put into one lecture what he or she would want students and fellow faculty members to hear if it were, indeed, that professor's last lecture.

It seems to me a good idea for preachers in the Church as well, especially on this Sunday when the readings are about end times, about the world as we know it coming to an end. What better Sunday, then, to preach the Last Homily? So, here goes:

My dear friends, this is my last homily. And in the days, hours, even minutes, leading up to this moment, I have struggled to produce a clear statement of what I would want to leave with you as a final message. What, out of all the things that could be said, would be most essential?

I limit myself to one message, one theme, for this Last Homily, and it is this: Know that you are loved by God! Know that you are made in the image and likeness of God, that through the incarnation, the paschal mystery—the passion, death and resurrection of Christ—God is closer to you than you are to yourself. As the Muslims say, "God is closer to you than your own jugular vein." And what you experience from being that close is love.

Know that you are loved by God. It's such a simple, straightforward statement that you might wonder why it needs even to be preached on. Why isn't it enough to just say that, and be done with it? Because everyone who proclaims the good news, and preaches it, is competing with a powerful alternative narrative, a competing message. It is a message that seeks to convince you that your essential being is determined more by biology, or perhaps psychology, than by your unique relationship to God. This voice often drowns out the truth of God loving you deeply, fully, madly, with complete abandon. When the homily is over, when the Mass is ended, so this competing message goes, there is only the reality of an often cold, inhospitable world where you must find an alternative route to happiness.

That is the reality everyone who ministers in the Church has to confront. Everything we do at Mass seeks to create an atmosphere in which the truth that God loves you deeply can be experienced. By our entering into the music, by an active and conscious participation in the Mass, by the celebrant's prayerfulness, everything contributes to a deeper awareness of the real and passionate love God has for each person.

The preacher has an important role in making this possible. The one who preaches must try to break through the barriers of indifference, to awaken a memory of Love, to stir up a passionate desire for God, to somehow infiltrate this astounding truth into your consciousness and, maybe, even your subconscious—the truth that God *loves you*. Whether it be through stories, appropriate humor, a good metaphor, poetry—all of these are employed with this purpose in mind: to penetrate into your heart, to reach that still point where a part of you known only to God hears and believes this transforming truth, that you are wonderfully loved by God. God has created you out of love, sustains you in love and envisions a future for you that is pervaded by God's love. This is your human dignity, a reflection of God's glory. Accept it once and for all!

It might seem that the readings for this Sunday do not lend themselves to the theme of this last homily. Both Daniel and Mark contain words of foreboding, impending doom, destruction, end times. Where is the love of God in all *that*? I believe it is there, if we know what we are looking for.

What the authors of these letters are describing is chaos. And we are no strangers to chaos. Whether it be the Middle East, Iraq, our country, our Church, and even our personal lives, we are well acquainted with chaos. But our God is quite at home in chaos. And why? Because God manifests God's love by bringing good out of chaos. There was chaos at the dawn of creation, and from it God created all that is good. There was chaos at the time of Caesar Augustus, and into it came the Son of God. There was chaos at Calvary, and out of it came new life in Christ. There will be chaos at the end of time, and out if will come eternal blessing. We believe that God creates out of chaos and does so with unfathomable love.

So do not be afraid of the chaos, no matter on what level you encounter it. Embrace it! Embrace the chaos and experience God's love there! Trust in the creative providence of a loving God to once again bring life out of chaos. Don't be like those who want to escape the chaos by being whisked away in some kind of rapture, while the "Left Behinds" must cope as best they can. St. Thérèse of Liseux knew chaos as well as we do and yet her prayer at the end of her life was, "I want to spend my heaven doing good on earth." That's embracing the chaos! Stay in the chaos with the hope and the confidence that the God who loves you will bring about new life.

If you can find God's love in all things, in order as well as in chaos, you will have the overriding sentiment I would want you to take away from a Last Homily: joy. Not the shallow, fleeting happiness that often masquerades as joy, but a deep, abiding joy that can only be experienced by someone who has come to realize at the deepest possible level that each one of us is truly loved by God. And here is the quickest route to that real joy: accept, take in, realize, internalize, make your own, what I preach to you in this Last Homily: *You are loved by God.*

Questions for Further Discussion:

1. If you were giving a "last homily" what points would you emphasize?

2. Do you find it hard to accept the fact that you are loved by God?

70
IT TAKES TIME TO ABSORB TRUTH
Feast of Christ the King (B)

> • Daniel 7:13–14
> • Revelation 1:5–8
> • John 18:33b–37

At the end of the 2000 presidential election, it seemed as though the vote-counting in Florida would never end. If nothing else, the long ordeal at least produced some good material for the late-night comedians. I heard Jay Leno tell about a nightmare he had had. He dreamed that aliens had landed and they demanded: "Take me to your leader!" "It was a nightmare," Leno said, "because I didn't know who my leader is."

In today's gospel, Pilate has his own nightmare to deal with. It is a bad dream packed with irony. Pilate as judge is judging the judge of heaven and earth. Pilate who knows all about kings does not recognize the Alpha and the Omega of kingship. Pilate, who later demands to know, "What is truth?" is confronting the incarnation of truth.

What is the cause of Pilate's nightmare? You might say it is the illusion of facts. Pilate has a lot of facts, but facts do not guarantee the truth. The truth, we learn in today's gospel, is a different matter.

And yet we cannot fully blame Pilate. There is nothing about this man, Jesus, to suggest that he is a king. Pilate faces a man who bases his claim to kingship not on royal lineage, not on military might, but on something unheard of both then and now: kingship based on being a witness to truth. Nothing else. Pilate was addressing a king but not the kind of king that he and the other onlookers were accustomed to seeing.

There is a warning for us in Pilate's dialogue with Jesus. Two thousand years after Pilate, most of us do not fully grasp this radically different understanding of kingship that Jesus introduced into the world. Jesus is king, Jesus is sovereign for those who belong to the truth and who listen to his voice.

What is this truth and how do we come to belong to it? It is quite simply the truth about God. Jesus witnessed to the truth about God: that God loves the world; God longs to be loved by every person; God loved the world so much that God became human.

And how do we come to belong to this truth? Part of the beauty of our Catholic tradition is that the truth about God becomes more deeply rooted in us through the cycle of the liturgical year that now comes to a close with the Feast of Christ the King. You see, this truth about God is too great to be absorbed all at once. I read recently that a typical Thanksgiving Day dinner contains 3,620 calories. And to burn up all those calories takes something like thirty-seven hours of watching TV or five hours of running, depending on your preference.

Through the liturgical year we slowly digest the truth about God. We take it in, assimilate this truth, make it real in our lives. The liturgical year gives us repeated opportunities to hear that voice. During Advent we are encouraged to listen, to wait expectantly for the voice of God summoning us to a deeper awareness of the truth that God has entered human history in the form of a baby in a manger. During Lent we follow a path of prayer, penance and self-giving that prepares us to enter into the great mystery of Easter. At Pentecost we renew our belief that the Holy Spirit is active in our world. In Ordinary Time, we seek to appropriate more deeply the great truths of our religion and to find them manifested in the ordinary events of our lives. And then the liturgical year reaches its crescendo in today's feast—the Feast of Christ the King—where we celebrate a new kind of king: a king who is a witness to truth.

We have a liturgical year because truth must be sought after, rediscovered and deepened every day of our lives. The truth that we realized when we first began our journey of faith is made real at an ever-deeper level as we faithfully enter into the liturgical year. The truth about God takes possession of every aspect of our lives. This truth does not remain simply in our minds but works its way down into our hearts, into our bones, into every fiber of our being until we belong so much to the truth that we can say, as did St. Paul, "I have been crucified with Christ; and it is no longer I who live, but it is Christ who lives in me" (Gal 2:19–20). When truth has penetrated that deeply, we then become what God intended for each one of us to be: great lovers—great lovers of God and great lovers of our neighbor, whoever that person might be.

The liturgical year does that for us, if we are able to listen and to hear the voice of Jesus. Today we will celebrate with about twenty-five catechumens and candidates from our RCIA program, the rite of entry into the Catholic Church. This service of initiation marks an important event in their lives. They are asking for faith and for a fuller sharing in the life of the Church. In short, they are asking to belong to the truth. At one point in the ritual they will receive the sign of the cross on their ears and the celebrant will say, "Receive the sign of the cross on your ears, that you may hear the voice of the Lord."

This ritual act has no effect on their physical ears. No, it is intended for a much deeper level of their senses. It is intended to affect the ears of their souls, if you will. Our physical ears *do* play a part in hearing the voice of Jesus, but it is at a deeper level where we must hear his voice, if it is to have an effect in our lives.

If the voice of Jesus is to have its effect in our lives we must become great listeners and great lovers. The Carmelite poet, Jessica Powers put it this way:

> To live with the Spirit of God is to be a listener.
> It is to keep the vigil of mystery,
> earthless and still.
> One leans to catch the stirring of the Spirit,
> strange as the wind's will.....
>
> To live with the Spirit of God is to be a lover.
> It is becoming love, and like to Him
> toward whom we strain with metaphors of creatures:
> fire-sweep and water-rush and the wind's whim.
> The soul is all activity, all silence;
> and though it surges Godward to its goal.
> it holds, as moving earth holds sleeping noonday,
> the peace that is the listening of the soul.[51]

May we all become great listeners and great lovers as we celebrate our belonging to the Truth on this Feast of Christ the King. May we become witnesses to that truth.

Questions for Further Discussion:

1. What part of this past liturgical year has deepened your appreciation of the truth the most?

2. What does it mean "to live with the Spirit of God is to be a listener"?

NOTES

INTRODUCTION

1. In the ordination rite, the bishop presents the Book of the Gospels to the deacon with these words: "Receive the Gospel of Christ, whose herald you are. Believe what you read, teach what you believe, and practice what you teach."

2. William T. Ditewig, *101 Questions & Answers on Deacons* (Mahwah, NJ: Paulist Press, 2004), 82.

3. Owen F. Cummings, *Mystical Women, Mystical Body* (Portland, OR: Pastoral Press, 2000), 39.

4. Hugh Kenner, *The Pound Era* (Berkeley: University of California Press, 1971), 39.

PART ONE

Homily 1

1. Carol Houselander, *The Reed of God* (New York: Arena Lettres, 1978).

2. John O'Donnell, SJ, *Hans Urs von Balthasar* (London: Continuum), 50.

3. Ibid., 51.

4. Martin Buber, *Tales of the Hasidim: The Early Masters* (New York: Schocken Books, 1947, 1975), 97.

Homily 2

5. Abraham J. Heschel, *The Prophets,* vol. 1 (New York: Harper, 1962), 4.

6. Ibid., 10.

7. Ibid., 12.

8. Bernard McGinn, *The Mystical Thought of Meister Eckhardt* (New York: Crossroad Publishing Company, 2001), 64.

PART TWO

Homily 5

1. John Shea, *Starlight: Beholding the Christmas Miracle All Year Long* (New York: Crossroad, 1992).

2. Raymond E. Brown, SS, *The Birth of the Messiah* (New York: Doubleday, 1977, 1993), 82.

3. Ibid., 73.

Homily 7

4. National Conference of Catholic Bishops, *Go and Make Disciples: A National Plan and Strategy for Catholic Evangelization in the United States* (Washington, DC: National Conference of Catholic Bishops, 1992), 2.

5. Ibid., 3.

6. Bishop George H. Niederauer, *Precious as Silver: Imagining Your Life With God* (Notre Dame, IN: Ave Maria Press, 2004).

7. Ibid., 104.

Homily 8

8. *Random House Webster's Unabridged Dictionary,* 2nd ed., s.v. "Myth."

Homily 9

9. Brown, *The Birth of the Messiah,* 456.

10. Ibid., 457.

Homily 11

11. Brown, *The Birth of the Messiah,* 199.

12. Ibid., 197.

13. Ibid., 198, 559–62.

14. Ibid., 197.

15. Ibid., 199.

PART THREE

Homily 13

    1. William H. Sadlier, Inc., *The Liturgical Year: An In-depth Look.* See *Liturgical Year 2005: Ordinary Time,* at www.webelieveweb.com/liturgical_year.cfm?season=ordinary.

    2. Raymond E. Brown, SS. *The Gospel According to John* (New York: Doubleday, 1966), 79.

    3. Ibid.

Homily 14

    4. Muriel Rukeyser, *The Collected Poems of Muriel Rukeyser* (New York: McGraw-Hill, 1978).

Homily 15

    5. Frederick G. Holweck, "Candlemas." In *Catholic Encyclopedia: An International Work of Reference on the Constitution, Doctrine, Discipline and History of the Catholic Church* (New York: Encyclopedia Press, 1907), vol. 3, 245,46.

    6. *Stormfax Weather Almanac,* "Groundhog Day," http://www.stormfax.com/ghogday.htm.

    7. Ibid.

Homily 16

    8. Irma Zaleski, "A Very Great Gift," *Parabola* 28:1 (2003), 6.

Homily 17

    9. Mitch Albom, *Tuesdays with Morrie* (New York: Doubleday, 1997).

PART FOUR

Homily 20

    1. Thomas Merton, *The Seasons of Celebration* (New York: Farrar, Straus and Giroux, 1965).

    2. I am indebted in this reflection to Edith Scholl, OCSO, "Spontaneity," *Cistercian Studies Quarterly* 39.1 (2004), 41-47.

Homily 21

    3. Thomas Merton, *The Sign of Jonas: The Journal of Thomas Merton* (New York: Harcourt, Brace and Company, 1953), 274.

    4. Ibid., 275.

Homily 22
 5. Edward Foley, OFM Cap., *Communion in the Liturgy of the World,* audiotape of lecture to the Federation of Diocesan Liturgical Commissions, Indianapolis, IN, Oct. 18, 2002. See *Emmanuel* 109, no. 4 (July/Aug, 2003).

Homily 23
 6. Dietrich Bonhoeffer, *The Cost of Discipleship* (New York: Macmillan, 1959), 47.
 7. J. Martin Bailey and Douglas Gilbert, *The Steps of Bonhoeffer: A Pictorial Album* (New York: Macmillan, 1971), 74.
 8. Ibid.

Homily 24
 9. Brown, *The Gospel According to John,* 130n1.

Homily 26
 10. Tim Rice and Andrew Lloyd Webber, *Jesus Christ Superstar* (London: Leeds Music, 1970).
 11. Harry Kemp, "The Conquerors" in *The Home Book of Modern Verse,* Volume 2, 9th edition, selected by Barton Egbert Stevenson (New York: Holt, Rinehard & Winston, 1953), p. 3068.

PART FIVE

Homily 27
 1. Frances Young's essay is in *The Myth of God Incarnate,* ed. John Hicks. Philadelphia: Westminster Press, 1977.

PART SIX

Homily 31
 1. Brown, *The Gospel According to John,* 424n16.

Homily 32
 2. "The Easter Alleluia," from a discourse on the Psalms by St. Augustine. In *The Liturgy of the Hours,* Second Reading for the Fifth Week of Easter (Totowa, NJ: Catholic Book Publishing Co., 1976).

Homily 33
 3. *Julian of Norwich–Showings,* trans. Edmund Colledge, OSA, and James Walsh, SJ (New York: Paulist Press, 1978), 298.
 4. Gerald Manley Hopkins, "The Untitled Sonnet," in *Gerald Manley Hopkins: Poems and Prose* (London: Penguin Books, 1963), 51.

Homily 35
    5. Richard P. McBrien, *Catholicism* (San Francisco: HarperCollins, 1994), 11.
    6. Ibid., 12.
    7. St. Gregory of Nazianzus, *Oratio* 2, 71, 74, 73. In *Patrologia Graeca,* ed. J.P. Migne (Paris: 1857-1866), 35, 480-81. Quoted in *Catechism of the Catholic Church* (Washington, DC: United States Catholic Conference–Libreria Editrice Vaticana, 1994), 1589n2.

Homily 36
    8. See Jurgen Moltmann, *The Way of Jesus Christ: Christology in Messianic Dimensions* (New York: HarperCollins, 1990), 274.
    9. Ibid., 279.
    10. See Charles Cummings, OCSO, *Eco-Spirituality: Toward a Reverent Life* (NewYork/Mahwah, NJ: Paulist Press, 1991).
    11. Ibid., 105.

Homily 37
    12. John Paul II, "The Mission of the Redeemer," in *John Paul II: The Encyclicals in Everyday Language,* ed. Joseph G. Donders (Maryknoll, NY: Orbis Books, 1996), 143.
    13. ——. *Redemptoris missio,* V:42.
    14. Donders, *John Paul II: The Encyclicals in Everyday Language,* 160.
    15. Ibid., 162.
    16. Ibid., 165.
    17. Ibid., 171.
    18. Ibid., 172.

Homily 38
    19. For an excellent introduction to the story of the Everglades, see Marjory Stoneman Douglas, *The Everglades: River of Grass* (Marietta, GA: Mockingbird Books, 1947, 1999).
    20. Alfred Delp, SJ, *The Prison Meditations of Father Alfred Delp,* (New York: Herder & Herder, 1963), 138.

PART SEVEN

Homily 40
    1. Trinity Communications, *Catholic Culture: Ordinary Time.* http://www.catholicculture.net/lit/overviews/seasons/ordinary.ctm.

Homily 41

    2. I am indebted in this reflection to Deacon Owen F. Cummings for many of the insights on Eucharist developed during a retreat on *Ecclesia de Eucharistia*, given at St. Joseph Church, Ogden, Utah, June 12, 2004.

    3. *The Anchor Bible Dictionary*, 1st ed., s.v. "Blood."

    4. John Paul II, *Ecclesia de Eucharistia* (On the Eucharist in its Relationship to the Church). Given in Vatican City at St. Peter's on April 17, 2003. (Washington, DC: United States Conference of Catholic Bishops, 2003), 1.

    5. Ibid., 2.

Homily 42

    6. Pope Paul VI, in his opening address before the second session of the Second Vatican Council, September 29, 1963. Quoted by Richard P. McBrien, *Catholicism* (San Francisco: HarperCollins, 1994), p. 9.

Homily 43

    7. Henri J. M. Nouwen, Donald P. McNeill and Douglas A. Morrison, *Compassion: A Reflection on the Christian Life* (New York: Image Books, Doubleday, 1983), 62.

    8. Ibid., 64.

    9. Ibid., 65.

Homily 44

    10. Andrew Greeley, "Why Do Catholics Stay in the Church? Because of the Stories," *New York Times*, July 10, 1994.

Homily 46

    11. Heschel, *The Prophets*, 1:28.

    12. Ibid.

    13. Ibid., 27-28.

Homily 47

    14. John Baptiste de la Salle, *The Spirituality of Christian Education,* ed. Carl Koch, Jeffrey Calligan, FSC, and Jeffrey Gros, FSC (Mahwah, NJ: Paulist Press, 2004), 5.

Homily 48

    15. Congregation for Divine Worship and the Discipline of the Sacraments, *General Instructions of the Roman Missal* (GIRM) (Washington, DC: United States Conference of Catholic Bishops, 2003), Liturgy Document Series 2, Preamble: 11.

    16. Ibid., 1:18.

Homily 49

17. Cummings, *Mystical Women, Mystical Body,* 39.

18. *Catechism of the Catholic Church* (Washington, DC: United States Conference of Catholic Bishops, 1994), 1328.

19. Pronounced "HAH-duh-vike," with a guttural "h" at the end.

20. Cummings, *Mystical Women, Mystical Body,* 21.

Homily 51

21. *Catechism of the Catholic Church,* 966.

22. Second Vatican Council, *Lumen Gentium (Dogmatic Constitution on the Church),* 7.61. In *The Documents of Vatican II,* ed. Walter M. Abbott, SJ, and Joseph Gallagher (New York: America Press, 1966), 91.

23. Ibid.

24. Troparion (liturgical hymn) for the Dormition of the Theotokos (Syosset, NY: Orthodox Church in America). See also www.theolofic.com./oflweb/feasts/08-15.htm.

25. Kontakion (liturgical hymn) for the Dormition, supra.

Homily 52

26. *Lumen Gentium,* 7.61.

27. Ibid.

28. I am indebted to Our Lady of the Rockies Foundation for information provided concerning the construction of the statue and its mission. See www.ourladyoftherockies.org.

29. Roger Haight, SJ, *The Experience and Language of Grace* (New York: Paulist Press, 1979), 126.

Homily 53

30. Brown, *The Gospel According to John,* 284.

31. Ibid.

32. Gregory of Nyssa, *Oratio Catechetica 24,* as citied in John O'Donnell, SJ, *Balthasar* (London/New York: Continuum, 1991), 46n3.

33. Brown, *The Gospel According to John,* 292.

34. Ibid., 290.

Homily 54

35. M. Scott Peck, MD, *The Different Drum: Community-Making and Peace* (New York: Simon and Schuster, 1987), 13.

36. Diarmuid McGann, *Journeying Within Transcendence: The Gospel of John Through a Jungian Perspective* (New York/Mahwah: Paulist Press, 1988), 82–83.

37. David W. Cotter, ed., *The Rule of St. Benedict,* trans. from the Latin by Leonard J. Doyle (Collegeville, MN: Liturgical Press, 2001).

Homily 56
    38. *The Anchor Bible Dictionary,* s.v. "Messianic Secret."
    39. David Steindel-Rast, *A Listening Heart: The Art of Contemplative Living* (New York: Crossroads, 1983), 10.

Homily 59
    40. From Stuart Hample and Eric Marshall, comp., *Children's Letters to God: The New Collection* (New York: Workman Publishing, 1991).

Homily 60
    41. Anthony de Mello, SJ, *The Song of the Bird* (New York: Doubleday, 1982), 72-73.
    42. Karl Rahner, "Christianity and the Non-Christian Religions," *Theological Investigations* 5 (London: Darton, Longman and Todd, 1966), 121. Quoted in Haight, *The Experience and Language of Grace,* 125.
    43. Haight, 133.

Homily 61
    44. Jelaluddin Rumi, "Come to the Orchard in Spring." In Coleman Barks, ed. *The Essential Rumi* (San Francisco: HarperCollins, 1995), 37.

Homily 65
    45. George Martin, "Theodore the Jumper," *Living Prayer* (May-June 1990), 3.

Homily 66
    46. Miriam Schmitt, OSB, "Freed to Run with Expanded Heart: The Writings of Gertrud of Helfta and RB," *Cistercian Studies Quarterly* 25:3 (1990): 230.

Homily 67
    47. *Catholic Encyclopedia,* 1911 ed, vol. 9, s.v. "Lateran, St. John."

Homily 68
    48. Adrienne von Speyr, *Elijah* (San Francisco: Ignatius Press, 1990).
    49. Ibid., 28-29.
    50. Ibid., 30-31.

Homily 70
    51. Jessica Powers, "To Live with the Spirit." In *Selected Poetry of Jessica Powers,* ed. Regina Siegfried and Robert Morneau (Kansas City, MO: Sheed and Ward, 1979), 38.